HENRY & SELF

ALSO BY KATHRYN BRIDGE

::::::::::::::::::

By Snowshoe, Buckboard and Steamer
Women of the British Columbia Frontier
Royal BC Museum, 2019

Emily Carr in England
Royal BC Museum, 2014

A Passion for Mountains
The Lives of Don and Phyllis Munday
Rocky Mountain Books, 2006

HENRY & SELF

AN ENGLISH GENTLEWOMAN
at the EDGE *of* EMPIRE

KATHRYN BRIDGE

ROYAL **BC** MUSEUM

VICTORIA, CANADA

Henry & Self
An English Gentlewoman at the Edge of Empire

First edition published by Sono Nis Press. Second edition published
in 2019 by the Royal BC Museum, 675 Belleville Street, Victoria,
British Columbia, V8W 9W2, Canada. Traditional·territory of the
Lekwungen (Songhees and Xwsepsum Nations).

Cover by Lara Minja, Lime Design
Interior design and typesetting by Julie Cochrane
Index by Carol Hamill

Cover illustration: *View of Victoria, Vancouver Island*, 1860, lithograph
by H.O. Tiedemann. (BC ARCHIVES PDP1538)

LIBRARY AND ARCHIVES CANADA CATALOGUING IN PUBLICATION
Title: Henry & self : a British gentlewoman at the edge of empire / Kathryn Bridge.
Other titles: Henry and self
Names: Bridge, Kathryn Anne, 1955- author.
Description: Includes bibliographical references and index.
Identifiers: Canadiana (print) 20190074736 | Canadiana (ebook) 20190075716 |
    ISBN 9780772672612 (softcover) | ISBN 9780772673251 (Kindle) |
    ISBN 9780772673084 (EPUB) | ISBN 9780772673091 (PDF)
Subjects: LCSH: Crease, Sarah, 1826-1922. | LCSH: British Columbia-Social life
    and customs-19th century. | LCSH: British Columbia-Social conditions-19th
    century. | LCSH: Women pioneers-British Columbia-Biography. | LCSH:
    Pioneers-British Columbia-Biography. | LCSH: Women-British Columbia-
    History-19th century. | LCSH: Women-British Columbia-Biography.
Classification: LCC FC3823.1.C73 B75 2019 | DDC 971.1/03092-dc23

10 9 8 7 6 5 4 3 2 1

Printed in Canada by Friesens.

for Kevin

Sarah and Henry Crease, November 1883. Bradley & Rolafson photographers.
(BC ARCHIVES A8922)

CONTENTS

::::::::::::::::

"Sarah Lindley," by
herself, 16 June 1847.
(BC ARCHIVES PDP4847)

Preface

::::::::::::::::::

"Who was Sarah Crease?" my young daughter asked me.
"A woman who lived in England and then British
Columbia over a hundred years ago," I replied. "Do you
like her?" she asked. "I don't know," I said, "but I want
to learn more about her."

This need to learn more has kept me very busy for a number of years, and even as this book goes to press, I keep uncovering more gems: little facts that by themselves are insignificant but, when added to others, fill in gaps in the puzzle.

In short, Sarah Crease was the "beloved daughter of privileged English parents, wife of a struggling lawyer-manager-politician-judge, pioneer woman, mother of a large family, and matron of the Victoria colonial elite." She was "a complex, intriguing, adventuresome woman who also exemplified the narrowness, impertinence, and prejudice of her class, race and sex."[1] To relate this complexity was a challenge. There were so many aspects of Sarah's life that I wanted to include, and so many manuscript records and sketches that were each intriguing in themselves.

This book is intended to function on different levels. First and foremost, it is a story of a remarkable woman who lived to the great age of 96. Her story can be told only because of the wealth of archival records that have survived. But her life story is not the only story being told. Sarah was a product of her times. We can look at her life, her circumstances, her actions, her words and sketches, and learn a great deal about how a woman of her class and race viewed the world. She is a microcosm of the larger scene. For historians, this provides an important glimpse into that scene, and the opportunity to know more about nineteenth century white colonial women and their attitudes and responses to situations. Sarah was a British colonist whose views of imperialism necessitated maintaining a distance between colonizer and colonized. This position can be observed in Sarah's remarks about servants whose work ethic contrasted with hers, and in her comments about the native population. She shows a mixture of curiosity and pity (especially for the lot of the women), yet she interacts only by necessity, thus perpetuating socially imposed barriers. She also had to alter her views of class in a society where the mixed-race families of established Hudson's Bay Company (HBC) officials were the elite.[2]

It was important to me that Sarah's story be told as much as possible in her own words. I wanted to relate the story from a woman's perspective: to use the records created by Sarah, and those of her female relatives, to tell the story. This feminist desire to see the past through women's eyes is prompted by a sensitivity "to the frequency with which women's lives and beliefs have been interpreted for them by men [and] has led to a search for documents in which the historical subjects themselves describe their own experiences."[3] The life of Sarah Crease provides a wealth of such documents. The rich source of letters, sketches and diaries housed in the BC Archives permits us to hear Sarah's own voice. So, as much as possible, I have quoted directly from her own words. The story is supplemented with letters written by her sister, mother, mother-in-law and sisters-in-law. These let us see from the vantage points[4] of female family members and provide insight into Sarah's relationships.

Another priority for me was to create a biography during a time when many feminist historians are focusing not on individuals, but on women and issues of gender.[5] During the last decade or so, historians have used broad means to find out about the lives of women, most of whom never left records. Using gender as a statistical measure, they have gathered data on women from sources that include census, tax assessment rolls, court records, police files and probates.[6] For instance, we can determine how many women held property, were single parents, or were involved in crime either as victims or perpetrators, and whether they earned income, and if so, from what sources. Thanks to this kind of historical research, women's lives and circumstances can be quantified, and the impact of women in all facets of society is better understood. Gender has been added to the historical record, and feminist historians succeed in making women visible as a group.

I believe that biography provides a great companion to these statistics by giving flesh, face and personality to one who might otherwise be only quantified. The two approaches complement each other, and as one feminist historian states: "biography assists feminine scholarship in the very individualizing it permits. Many a theory only makes sense as exemplified in the life of an individual…because so much more can be known about a woman chosen for a biography, she can perhaps light up the darkness surrounding other women about whom little can be known."[7]

The title *Henry & Self* was chosen deliberately because this is the way Sarah refers to her "Self." Her diaries and journals, and her inscriptions on photographs and sketches, all use this unusual pronoun to record her presence. Rarely does she use the pronoun "I"; the major exceptions are in her correspondence with her husband and children, where she is "I" or "Mama." Rather than a belittling of identity, the title becomes a statement of her personality and preferred mode of reference. Indeed, the title suggests a woman who is conscious of her "Self" in respect to others.

"Ye old lion…," 1861. (BC ARCHIVES PDP1382)

Henry & Self also allows us to examine Sarah's relationships. Sarah's view of herself was defined by her relationships with others. This gives us another vantage point. She was variously a daughter, a sister, a wife, a mother, a grandmother, a friend, a neighbour and an elder. In each of these relationships, a different part of her emerges. Like everyone, she acted and reacted to circumstances because of the relationships she had with others. Examining these relationships[8] and her attitudes to them gives us additional insight and illustrates how these people were responsible—in myriad ways—for shaping her.

In addition to giving Sarah's life story, I also decided to present one of Sarah's written records in its entirety and to build upon it, adding context and commentary. I chose her 1880 journal, in which she wrote daily observations while on a three-month trip with her husband travelling through many areas of British Columbia. To this journal I added the letters she wrote and those she received from her children on this journey. I then annotated both letters and journals, identifying individuals mentioned, to give background and context for the observations she makes. Together, the letters and journal reveal Sarah as mother, wife and private observer.

Introduction

::::::::::::::::::

*"...your proposition of Vancouver's Island was a little
startling at first—from its great distance away—but I
am quite ready dearest to consider that as our future
home if it pleases God to direct our steps hither...."*[9]

With these words, Sarah Crease committed herself and her children to a journey that would take them, in 1859, away from family and friends in England, to a new life in a farflung outpost of the British Empire on the Pacific coast of North America. The decision would change her life forever. It must have taken great courage and great love to make such a break with a familiar and comfortable life and to gamble that such actions would allow prosperity and success for her family. But Sarah had faith in her husband, Henry Crease, and his ability to establish himself in his chosen legal profession. This faith, and her strong and supportive love, would prove crucial to Henry's success and the growth of family fortunes in a new land.

Sarah Crease, née Lindley (1826–1922), the eldest daughter of a prominent English botanist, was well-read and educated. After an extended engagement necessitated by financial circumstances, in 1853 she married a young barrister, Henry Crease (1823–1905), with whom she shared a deep religious faith, a strong sense of social propriety, a passion for art and—their letters show—a wonderfully candid, lasting love.

Married life was strained by separations made necessary by her husband's activities managing tin mines in Cornwall. She and her children lived in

London, while Henry visited on occasion from Cornwall. After only a few years, a major financial scandal erupted around his employment. The accompanying investigations forced her husband to give up his position as mine owner and manager. Although he was eventually cleared of wrongdoing, he was obliged to leave England for greener pastures overseas, a path that led first to Toronto and finally to Vancouver Island.

Sarah and the three children were separated from Henry for two years while he attempted to secure suitable employment in the colonies. His arrival in Victoria in 1858, during the gold rush, was exceptionally timely, for within weeks, the chief justice appointed him as the first barrister in the colony. He was soon busy with all manner of litigation arising amongst the miners and entrepreneurs who flooded into Victoria. His star ascended rapidly. By 1861 he was attorney general of the colony of British Columbia (resident at New Westminster). He then rose through the judicial system to the position of Supreme Court justice, eventually receiving a knighthood in 1896.

The early years in Victoria and New Westminster were extremely demanding for both Sarah and Henry. The circumstances of their past affected this new beginning. They had a large debt to pay off, a tight budget on which to house, feed and clothe a growing family, and insecurity caused by difficulties in finding affordable, suitable accommodation. The young couple faced difficult times in their first few years in the colony. For Sarah and other colonial women, the daily routines of food preparation, laundry, housework, and raising vegetables and chickens, plus the trials of pregnancy and childbirth, were exhausting. Sarah bore seven children, the eldest in 1854, and the youngest in 1872. Her second son, Henry, died as an infant.[10]

From the 1870s, once Henry's career was established, life was a little easier. It settled into a routine marked by Henry's twice-yearly absences while on circuit court. In 1875 they were able to build a substantial home, "Pentrelew." By this time Sarah was 49 years old, a matron in Victoria society. Sarah and Henry Crease were at the centre of settler social life in Victoria, which revolved around families of the upper middle class. Their lives were busy, filled not only with Henry's work, but also with many other commitments. They taught Sunday School and served on committees for the Anglican church. Art and other cultural activities were important, and the Creases often hosted or helped organize special events. Equally, they participated in fundraising for charitable works such as hospitals, the orphanage and other needy causes. Amidst these activities, the Creases raised a family of four daughters and two sons. Such a large family created ongoing responsibilities. As they grew, the children required schooling and organization of their free time. They played with schoolmates and other friends, the offspring of prominent Victoria families. Their days were filled with social visits and visitors, riding parties and picnics, dances, balls, musical evenings and other events.

All of the Crease children went to England, either to complete schooling or to learn about their English roots and stay with family. It was very important to Sarah and Henry that their children understand their social position, know their relatives and see the sights in England. It was a mark of distinction in Victoria society to have travelled abroad. Sarah and Henry were never able to return to England. Instead, they maintained ties vicariously, through the experiences of their children. In time, two of the Crease children married and produced grandchildren. Pentrelew remained the family home until 1947. After the death of the last unmarried Crease, the home and its contents were sold at auction. Pentrelew stood until 1984, when it was demolished to make way for a new building on the same site, which nestled amid a portion of the original landscaping and trees. Today, Pentrelew is perpetuated in a street name alongside the property on Fort Street.

THE RECORDS

We know much about the Creases because Sarah, and indeed all of her family, left a tremendous legacy of records documenting their lives. This large collection of diaries, correspondence, reminiscences, legal papers, paintings and photographs is housed in Victoria at the BC Archives. The Crease Family Fonds was created by four generations of the family. It was preserved and cherished by its members because they recognized its significance, not only for the family, but also because of the information it contains, which documents life and times in the colonies of Vancouver Island and British Columbia, and later in the united colony—and eventually province—of British Columbia.[11]

The collection is especially valuable because of the amount of information it contains about Sarah Crease. There are few instances when one can recreate the life and experiences of a woman in nineteenth century England and British Columbia so thoroughly and with such a wealth of detail. The records generally do not exist. In this case, however, the records abound. It is important to hear the voices of women in history. They provide a counterpoint to the traditional historical perspective, that of men, who in the course of their working lives produced the business and governmental records that have been the principal sources for historical study of the Canadian past.[12] "Without using the diaries and letters of ordinary women, the historian misses a complex female culture that leaves virtually no trace in conventional historical documents."[13] This is especially true with regard to uncovering and understanding the depth and quality of nineteenth century female relationships.[14]

In fact, within the collection are not only letters written by Sarah, but also those written to her by other women of her family, notably her mother and sister, and by several of Henry's sisters and his mother. These letters tell us much about the relationships between Sarah and her female family members, about women's concerns and interests, and about how this family functioned. Many of these letters have been quoted within this biography to provide female perspectives concerning events in Sarah's life, and to corroborate or elaborate on details not included in the male records. For her later life, other female perspectives are also available in the records created by her daughters. These shed light on the relationships between mother and daughters[15] and make interesting reading in comparison to the records of her sons and husband. In many cases, a single event or circumstance can be glimpsed from three or four different viewpoints by examining the diaries and letters of the family members. Nowhere is this more evident than in the English period of Sarah Crease's life. It is the most richly documented, primarily because of the multiple perspectives from different voices.

How and why was this collection compiled? Individually, each "wrote to keep accounts of their activities and to keep the past alive"[16] but collectively, the decision to save and retain the writings of others was a way to hold on to the memories of that person. Children kept the records of parents. Each was aware of the incompleteness or gaps in records, so pure historical documentation was not the motive. The key, I think, is in the value placed on communication, and on the individuals' need to anchor themselves in time.[17] Both Sarah and Henry's passion for recording information was inherited from their parents, who in turn received it from theirs. Both families treasured their correspondences with their children, and these letters, among many other family letters and papers, were sent out to British Columbia after the parents' deaths.[18] Thus the Crease Family Fonds also contains correspondence and business papers of the two earlier generations, which provide context for the transition from life in England to colonial life. The fact that Sarah and Henry requested these documents be sent out to British Columbia illustrates a need to retain tangible ties with their family roots and the pre-emigration phase of their lives. Again, this is an unusual circumstance. The records remaining from other colonial families do not include such a large quantity of information on the family before immigration to British Columbia.[19] Perhaps someday a further study will focus on this correspondence more fully.

Sarah was a faithful correspondent, and her letters are filled with current events and family doings. Her letters to Henry begin in 1849, near the time of their engagement, and continue, almost weekly, for several years. Subsequent years are less frequently covered until the period 1858–1859, when again the letters pick up at a regular and frequent rate. In all, almost 200 letters from Sarah to Henry have survived. Most date from the extended separations of 1849–1850 and 1858–1859.

Sadly, only a handful of Henry's letters to Sarah are extant. We know he wrote frequently to her, because she records receiving his letters at the beginning of each of hers. Why they have not survived, while most of Henry's other correspondence with family members and friends was saved, is a matter of speculation, but intriguing possibilities can be suggested.

Sarah Crease was a talented amateur artist who used her sketching abilities to expand her means of communication. She drew the scenery around her, made portraits of her friends and family, and used her art to record specific events. In this, she was not unusual for her time. A facility in sketching was considered to be a desirable achievement, especially for women in the middle classes.[20] In the days before the invention of photography, it was the only means to record visually. Sketches made on trips were often assembled in scrapbooks and used in the same way photo albums are today, to share the experiences and scenery with others and to recall the trip later.

The Crease Family Fonds contains several thousand sketches created not only by Sarah, but also by three generations of her family. Henry, too, was an avid sketcher and it was this talent that first attracted Sarah to him. The sketches are important documents because they bring people and events to life in a way that mere writing cannot. Sarah understood the old adage "a picture is worth a thousand words." She preferred to draw scenery rather than describe it, and she knew the effect of providing a visual glimpse.

Again, like the written records, the Crease family saved and treasured their sketches. As a group, these sketches have greater significance than taken individually. Their quantity and consistency in format, technique and ability illustrate that they were created with great regularity over time, and used not merely as a pastime or recreational activity. They were a means of communication. Letters contained sketches or referred to sketches. Each sketch contributes something unique to the story. Together, the written and artistic records provide unparalleled coverage of a colonial family.

HENRY AND SELF

The first section of this book is a biographical study that unfolds Sarah's life in England prior to her emigration, and then follows her to British Columbia and traces her activities and life there. A large part of the biography focuses on her time in England. It is important to know of these earlier years to appreciate Sarah Crease as a colonial newcomer. Events in England coloured her perception of life and challenged her, strengthening her character in a way that prepared her emotionally for the rigours of colonial life. Immigration to a new land did not mean that people's prior experience was invalid or insignificant. Immigrants brought their own character and perspective to the new land. They acted and reacted to situations according to their past. Knowing in detail their lives before emigration makes it possible to understand why they acted in particular ways, why they responded differently, what their strengths and weaknesses might be, and how these could be adapted to a new life.[21]

The marriage of Sarah and her husband is a story of misfortune, separation, patience, thrift, dedication and, most of all, love and great faith. Sarah and Henry Crease shared a deep and abiding love. This is clear in their letters, and also in the comments of their families. Their love survived despite a lifetime of disappointments, losses, separation and financial difficulties. It is a poignant story set in the early days of British Columbia. The art and writings of Sarah Crease bring these early days to life. She has her own perspective on life and activities around her, events that today tend to be studied as grand political occurrences devoid of personal context—such as the union of the colonies, confederation with Canada, the Cariboo gold rush and other milestones. Sarah Crease was a woman of great character whose contemporary observations about people and circumstances provides a unique insight into BC history and, in particular, a long-needed female perspective. We can learn much about nineteenth century perspectives on class and race through Sarah's comments in diaries and correspondence. What she says, how she says it and what she doesn't say concerning herself, her family, her friends, her acquaintances, daily life and special events can all be analyzed with a view to such understanding.

Interspersed throughout this biography are examples of Sarah's art. They include small, rough pen sketches originally inserted into correspondence, portraits, botanical illustrations, and pencil and watercolour landscapes. These are placed within the body of the text as visual extensions of the writing. In this way, Sarah and her family come to life. We can see the Lindley home and its gardens, visualize shipboard life, walk through Victoria in 1860 and sense the rawness of life in New Westminster. The sketches function as Sarah meant them to: as pictorial communication. Photographs are also included, primarily to show Sarah through the years, but also to document the scenery and settlements seen on the 1880 journey.

The second section of the book features Sarah Crease's journal of 1880, which she wrote on a trip accompanying her husband, then a puisne judge, on assize court circuit through the Cariboo and to Kamloops. They travelled by wagon along the Cariboo Road, constructed in the 1860s. Her journal chronicles this journey day by day and includes much information about the small wayside stops—the Mile Houses—on the Cariboo Road, and the various people she met or saw each day. As well, Sarah discusses the countryside, remarks on local events and alludes to cases presided over by

Henry. These include two of the most renowned murder cases in British Columbia, that involving the McLean brothers and Alex Hare[22] and the grisly murder of the Pool family near Lytton.

Sarah's 1880 journal, a wonderful document in itself, was written on their first journey alone together since arriving in British Columbia 20 years earlier.

The responsibilities of childbearing and rearing over more than a quarter of a century had made it impossible for Sarah to indulge in extended absences from her family. Also, the Crease family finances were always tight and frequently in arrears. It must have seemed an incredible treat finally to take a holiday, a three-month one at that, leaving the children behind, assured of their safety and health.

Sarah's 1880 journal contrasts greatly with what we know of her earlier colonial life, when she was preoccupied by daily routine. The journal is written by an established society matron on holiday. At age 54, Sarah felt secure in her social position and, as the wife of the circuit judge, expected and received deferential treatment from hotel-keepers and merchants. It was her responsibility to be sociable and to visit with the wives and families of minor government officials and prominent citizens of the small urban centres she passed through on the journey. Her daily entries record personal and candid impressions of a wide variety of people, at all levels of the social strata. These insights bring personality and life to historical individuals who played both minor and major parts in shaping the character of late nineteenth century British Columbia. Her comments also reflect a very specific attitude: that of a confident, and at times even smug, British gentlewoman. She records in detail the white society, but makes little attempt to do the same for the native or Chinese people she met and interacted with along the way. Her comments assume white superiority, and even more specifically, British-Anglican superiority. This was very typical of the day, and representative of the nineteenth century British middle class abroad. Diaries and journals kept by others exhibit similar commentary.[23]

In spite of the trip's vacation-like circumstances, many of Sarah's actions were rooted in her earlier years, when life was not so comfortable. She repairs their clothing, remarks on the costs of services and economizes where possible. She also maintains written communication with her children and family members. These letters tend to continue family dialogue regarding social events, school, daily Bible readings and other issues. In fact, except for her letters to son Lindley, in England at school, she communicates very little about the trip itself in these letters. It is as if she made a mental distinction. This trip was separate from her continuing concerns as a parent. The extant letters are included here, alongside Sarah's diary entries for the same days. They illustrate the parallel but separate sphere of her life that revolved around her children.

The trip also marked a turning point in the history of the province. Sarah watched the Royal Engineers survey the Cariboo Wagon Road in 1862. On earlier visits to Hope and Yale, she had heard the blasting on the canyon walls that had created foundations for this roadway. From the Crease home in New Westminster, "Ince Cottage," she saw the bustle of activity at the Royal Engineers' headquarters at Sapperton, just down the road. Sarah had written about and sketched all these events. The Cariboo Wagon Road was pivotal to the growth of the province. It provided the major means of communication and transportation for 20 years.

But now, in 1880, modernization in the form of a transcontinental railroad superseded it. The 400-mile route of the Wagon Road up the Fraser Canyon and beyond was about to be obliterated in many parts by the Canadian Pacific Railway, which intersected and often followed the Wagon Road for much of its route. Now, engineers with the Canadian Pacific Railway Company—like their predecessors with the Royal Engineers—sought a level route through the treacherous canyon. Construction had just begun outside Yale in the fall of 1880 with camps for crew and highly visible supply depots. Sarah's journey was really one of the last opportunities to travel the old Cariboo Road. The road had connections with Sarah's early colonial life in New Westminster, and also with Henry's work when he travelled by horse or wagon along the road to hold assize court.

The trip was also another turning point. By 1880, Sarah had ceased to sketch. Her eyesight, always weak, caused headaches and fatigue in earlier years, but as she grew older, imposed tremendous limitations. Her left eye was early on diagnosed with glaucoma, and in 1883 and 1893 she underwent operations on her right eye. This was the first journey that she did not record with sketches, instead relying on her journal to recall events and scenery. Nonetheless, her journal is an artist's journal: she records colours and scenes, and she visualizes pictures that were never painted.

Sarah titled her journal "Rough <u>Notes</u> of a trip & the first with My dear husband on Circuit to <u>Cariboo</u> and <u>Kamloops</u> & <u>NewWestr</u> During Sepr–Octr–Novr–1880." These notes were not intended as a formal record, but were instead a synopsis of each day's events. On the first part of the journey she allowed herself a single sheet of paper for each day, so the daily entries are roughly the same length. This format continued with the occasional instance when the day's activities and scenery were so interesting that she wrote another page. These observations might, in earlier years, have been translated into sketches, which Sarah always preferred as a superior means to communicate details about landscape. The latter part of the journal, the month she spent in New Westminster, was much more terse in its contents. Here Sarah recorded the daily social contacts and her walks with Henry, but little else. For her, New Westminster, despite the changes wrought since her earlier residence there, was still familiar territory, and not as fascinating or new as the trip on the Wagon Road.

In editing the 1880 journal, I have followed Sarah's written words, but have applied a consistency in punctuation to the text by interpreting her dashes as commas or periods as appropriate. Occasional misspellings caused by a slip of the pen have been corrected, but words written with incorrect but particular spelling have been maintained to preserve the original flavour of the text. Corrected surnames of individuals she met have been included in the annotations.

"Papa's plant press," drawn by Sarah to illustrate an article on drying plants in the *Gardener's Chronicle*, 13 March 1852. (BC ARCHIVES PDP5046)

Early Years

::::::::::::::

Sarah was born 30 November 1826 at Acton Green, Middlesex, near London, England, the eldest daughter of Sarah (née Freestone) and Dr. John Lindley. Sarah had an older brother, George (1824–1831), and younger siblings Nathaniel (1828–1921) and Barbara (1830–1901). The surviving children received the nicknames Totty for Sarah, Natty for Nathaniel, and Dunny for Barbara, which they retained for their lifetimes.

Dr. John Lindley (1799–1865) was a distinguished botanist and horticulturalist, fellow of the Royal Society and professor at London University. He had an impressive career.[24] In 1820 he was elected fellow of both the Linnean and Geological societies and two years later was appointed garden assistant secretary to the Horticultural Society. By the time of his marriage in 1823, Lindley had published seven major horticultural works. In 1826, he became the sole assistant secretary of the Horticultural Society, with duties in both the gardens at Chiswick and in the office at Regent Street. At this point the Lindley family moved from London to Acton, near Chiswick. In 1829, Lindley became the first professor of botany at the University of London, a position he retained for 30 years. In conjunction with his friend George Bentham, he organized a very successful series of exhibitions of flowers and fruit in the gardens at Chiswick.[25] After becoming vice-secretary of the Horticultural Society in 1841, Lindley assumed an incredible workload, which he managed until 1858 when he became honorary secretary. Lindley acted as juror of foodstuffs in the International Exhibition of 1851 and resigned from the Horticultural Society in 1862, after being persuaded to take charge of the entire colonial department of the 1862 International Exhibition. Always overworked, Lindley died in 1865 from a "softening of the brain."[26] Sarah described her father as:

> a great reader of both French and English literature and [he also] understood a little German. He was a kind father to his children—and spent much on their education although his two daughters never did justice to his liberality much to their own regret—but this was not the case with his surviving son, Nathaniel....My father was an excellent conversational host when at all interested in his guests—but he always avoided the subjects of music and religion. Music because he had no taste for it and religion because he thought little of its church officers and professions....My father was nominally a member of the Church of Eng[lan]d but made no profession of religion. He was extremely punctual in his engagements and declared he would not wait more than 3 minutes for anybody![27]

The Lindley household was immeasurably affected by Lindley's work and preoccupations. Lindley's close friends included Joseph Paxton, George Bentham, Joseph Hooker and other leading botanists of the day.[28] Sarah's friends when she was a girl included daughters of these famous men. In later years, some of these men were to prove helpful to her and her husband. Also living at the Lindley house was Sarah A. Drake (1804–1857), who was employed by John Lindley as illustrator of his horticultural publications. Miss Drake, in Sarah's words, was "the best botanical draftswoman of her day—not excepting Mrs. Withers who was unrivaled in fruit painting." "Ducky," as she was affectionately known, "was greatly beloved by my mother, sister and self."[29] She lived with the family, and in fact was almost like one of the family for many years, until her marriage in 1847.[30]

Sarah's girlhood was carefree. The family home at Turnham Green was nestled in a landscape setting worthy of a botanist of John Lindley's stature. The grounds comprised several acres, which included a semicircular carriageway in the front of the house, curving through large trees and formal gardens. Kitchen and vegetable plots faced the rear of the house, with a wide expanse of grass leading towards a less structured, wilder garden through which winding pathways led to secluded benches and secret play areas. This was Dunnyland, a special place for all the Lindley children. Beyond its fences lay 170 acres of Acton Common. It was a wonderful place for children growing up. They ran wild among the trees and shrubs, practising archery and playing all manner of imaginary games. The children were carefree and affectionate siblings, the very best of friends. The banter of childhood games, the teasing and the intimacy, remained with them as adults, ever recalling the fun and frolic of their youth.

Sarah's formal education was typical of the day. In upper-middle-class households, girls were taught domestic skills by their mother, but a governess was also employed to give girls more formal instruction. This was often interspersed with terms at a private school, either as a day pupil or as a boarder. A typical prospectus for a ladies' academy or finishing school announces: "the strictest attention is paid to [the girls'] morals, and care taken that amusement should be blended with tuition."[31] Sarah and her sister, Barbara, attended such a school. They were registered as day pupils from 1838 to 1842 at Mrs. Gee's school at Hendon, near Turnham Green. Here they were taught the usual skills for women, including reading, writing, literature, art and music. After leaving the school, the girls had a private governess, a Miss Emma Heinrich, whom Totty described as "our German & French weekly governess, at home...an interesting person and very charming when pleased."[32]

A highlight of Sarah's girlhood, one which she recalled often in later life, occurred on 28 June 1838, at the age of 11. Sarah, in company with her father (who had been invited in his capacity as advisor to the British government on the status of Kew Gardens), was present in Westminster Abbey at the coronation of Queen Victoria. Although diaries from this period are not extant, the scene made a great impression. "She often spoke of the touching youthfulness of the young Queen, her simple dignity, and also the fact that just as the Crown was placed on her head and the Peers & Peeresses lifted their coronets to theirs, a ray of sunshine struck them making a wonderful and sudden radiance."[33]

Sarah's major recreational pursuit appears to have been art. Both she and her sister were given lessons by Charles Fox (1794–1849),[34] an old friend and colleague of John Lindley. He "taught us all drawing by way of a personal favour—as he was by profession an engraver."[35] When Lindley was appointed superintendent of the Horticultural Society, Fox, because of his great interest in horticulture and his reputation as one of the best authorities on flowers, was chosen as judge and arbiter of their exhibitions. Fox also superintended the illustrations of *The Florist*.[36] He remained a close family friend until his death in 1849.

Charles Fox gave Sarah instruction in pencil and watercolour, the typical media for sketching, but also taught her copper engraving and woodblock printing. These latter two techniques were both rather unusual practices for middle-class women at this time. Generally women wished to learn only enough about sketching to maintain basic social competence, not to apply it in a more serious vein, although within the milieu of female family members of nineteenth century botanists, such skills were encouraged. Wives and daughters of John Lindley's contemporaries and predecessors were often so engaged. This was also one way in which women could participate in the study of botany[37] yet remain in their separate sphere of domestic life. For Sarah, learning these techniques enabled her to translate her own sketches into a format that could be duplicated and was suitable for reproduction in illustrated journals or other such publications.[38] Under the inspiration of Sarah Drake, Sarah's artistic interests were directed along these lines, and she became a skilled botanical illustrator and adapted her pen-and-ink sketches to woodblock or copperplate prints. In time, she and her sister assumed responsibility for the illustration of some of her father's later works, including *The Vegetable Kingdom*, 1846, and various articles in the *Gardeners' Chronicle*, which Lindley, Joseph Paxton and others had founded in 1841. Here the work of illustration was not merely a hobby. They received payment and it was viewed as a legitimate form of employment—and one that subsidized their pocket money. In this manner, the Lindley women were part of the "hidden investment" of the middle class. Botanical illustration, like other areas of women's work, was an economic enterprise that added value to family businesses or circumstances generally.[39]

> Since you left, I have made several translations from the French for the Gar[deners'] Chron[icle]. I like the work decidedly better than any other of the useful kind....I have earnt a few pounds in that way which I find most acceptable, for money seems to slip away faster than ever, I buy nothing of any account & still my purse is always empty.[40]

Sarah often submitted botanical drawings, either for her father's work or for independent publication, under a pen name, perhaps wishing to be judged on her own skill rather than on associations with her father. The use of pen names, especially in the field of writing, was not uncommon among women at this time. Although Sarah's pen name was Esther Jones, many women used male pen names, perhaps increasing the chances that their submission would be accepted in the male-oriented business world.

"MY HEART'S FONDEST LOVE"

The man who would become Sarah's husband first appears on the scene in 1848. Henry Pering Pellew Crease was born on 20 August 1823 at his grandfather's home of Ince Castle, Cornwall. His father, Captain Henry Crease, was an officer in the Royal Navy, and his mother, Mary, was the daughter of Edward Smith.[41] Henry was the eldest son and had ten siblings. He attended Mount Radford School and later Clare College, Cambridge, where he graduated in 1846. He was a "Prizeman in Divinity...an enthusiastic oarsman, and rowed his College boat 'The Lady Clare.'...After leaving Cambridge he was, with Charles Mansfield,[42] one of the first University men who devoted time to teaching in the Ragged Schools[43] then started in London."[44] In 1847 he travelled to the Continent and spent several months in Turkey and Asia Minor, then Italy and Switzerland.

The trip was undertaken because of doctor's orders, as Henry suffered from a pulmonary infection.[45] He returned to England and assisted his father in a number of legal matters, and he took up studies at Lincoln's Inn. Shortly after, he was admitted to the Honorable Society of the Middle Temple to study law. In June 1849 he was called to the degree of the Upper Bar, took his oaths and was sworn in as a barrister.

How Henry Crease met Sarah Lindley is obscured by time, but it may be that he was introduced to the family by Sarah's brother, Nathaniel, whom he met in Switzerland in

Henry Pering Pellew Crease, December 1848 by Sarah Lindley (detail).
(BC ARCHIVES PDP8710)

1847.[46] Their mutual interest in the law cemented a friendship. (Nathaniel was called to the Bar in 1850.) Henry invited Natty to his family home in Cornwall during the late spring of 1848, while on a summer break from their law studies.[47] No doubt the visit was reciprocated, because by August, correspondence reveals not only that Natty knew Henry's father and one of his brothers, but that Henry had evidently met part or all of the Lindley family, as Natty mentions "Barbara is still at Ramsgate."[48] There is no mention of Sarah. Unfortunately we are not privy to the early part of the romance.

By the early fall of 1848, Sarah and Henry both recognized their attraction for each other, although there was certainly little opportunity to act upon it. Henry was a busy man. He "read for the Bar, ate his dinners at the Middle Temple, London...resided at the famous old 'Albany' off Piccadilly...served...in the 'Special Police' who did duty in the streets of London during the Chartist Riots,[49] armed with baton and cutlass."[50] During this time he also "assisted his father in numerous lawsuits and bills in Parliament concerning the family estates in the Duchy of Cornwall."[51] Somewhere between all these activities, Henry managed to maintain contact with Sarah, although befitting the time, a young lady would not communicate directly to a young man, or vice versa. No doubt visits to the Lindley home were orchestrated by Nathaniel. Sarah and Henry shared a passion for art, and it was this bond that first attracted Sarah to him. She wrote: "you know how I have told you before, that I fell in love with your drawings, (the coloured ones in those days). I read in them a character which I was sure I could not help loving. They were free, bold, and manly, with a tenderness and refinement which quickly found a way to my heart and made one think that he who executed them had a soul which I could deeply love and honour...."[52]

Finances were in a tight way for the Crease family at this time. For several generations the Crease and Smith families acted as representatives for the Duchy of Cornwall in activities related to tin mining. The duchy controlled the underground resources yet allowed private concerns to lease land and mine tin, paying a royalty to the duchy. Henry's family worked for the duchy ensuring that these commercial concerns paid the appropriate royalties and did not mine without permission. Exploitation of the duchy's resources by unauthorized ventures was rampant, and it was a confrontational responsibility to administer. The family expended its own capital to pursue legal cases against interlopers. Reimbursement from the duchy over the years was negligible. It was an awkward situation, defending the rights of the duchy without the ability to reclaim costs. This situation began during the tenure of Henry's grandfather, and over time contributed to great losses in the family fortunes. The family, Henry's sister Julia recalled, "at one time possessed 44 manors in Cornwall and Devon but all were sold and lawsuits further impoverished the family and more over alienated all or nearly all, the County families—a result much deplored by various members of the family...."[53] Finally, Ince Castle was lost.

During 1848 and 1849 Henry, with his knowledge of the law, assisted his father in several of these legal cases. The troublesome situation with the mines reached a crisis at this time, and finally Captain Crease was left with only his small naval pension on which to support his family. For several years, Henry and his father had discussed potential emigration to another British territory, for surely such a move would open possibilities for alternate sources of income. In 1848 Captain Crease applied for the vacant position of "Lt. Governor of the Southern Islands off New Zealand."[54] Henry wrote to a close friend: "He has for years been determined to emigrate and has determined to go this summer [1848] whether he receives this other appointment or not....without such an app[ointmen]t he w[oul]d go to Canada...."[55] Despite his unfinished studies, Henry ventured: "[I am] thinking of going to colonies and taking as much of the family as I can."[56] Australia, Capetown, India and even Vancouver Island were discussed. "Did you notice a letter in the 3rd page of Thursday's Times Headed—Vancouver Island...."[57]

Between the two of them, Henry and his father sent letters of enquiry to friends and contacts within government in the hopes of securing a position. Henry wrote letters recommending his father for particular positions and citing his years managing tin mines as comparable experience. In his turn, Captain Crease enquired for details and further information on rumoured postings in India and Australia in the hopes of locating something suitable for his eldest son. Nothing materialized. It became obvious that Henry must complete his legal studies to be considered eligible or "employable" in a position suitable to his needs and expectations. As he wrote: "...my first wish is to accompany my father and the family wherever they may go—as I am the eldest and to do that I must either be <u>called</u> or <u>lose</u> all the labour, money & anxiety & time already expended on my profession wh[ich] w[oul]d be a frightful sacrifice...."[58]

During all this time, Henry visited the Lindleys. He and Sarah walked through the extensive gardens at Turnham Green, often with sketchpad and pencils. They had special, sentimental spots in Dunnyland. No doubt they lingered in its secluded corners and sat on the benches amid rambling rose-bowers, azaleas and rhododendrons. The relationship blossomed.

By early spring 1849 it was evident that the Creases would leave England for Canada. There they hoped to investigate and perhaps invest in canals and mines in the area of the Great Lakes, an area already showing promise with the discovery of rich copper veins. In fact, Cornish miners were already working on the Keweenaw Peninsula on Lake Superior.[59] "All here decidedly approve of the Canadas...," Captain Crease reported, "and I am furnishing myself with all the facts I can reach...."[60] It was also evident that Henry would be leaving his heart behind him. In April the Lindley and Crease families met for the first time. By all accounts, they liked each other immensely. Captain and Mrs. Crease first visited Turnham Green, and then the Lindleys travelled to Cornwall. On subsequent visits some of Henry's sisters visited the Lindleys, and the Lindley daughters visited the Creases and stayed for several days. Captain Crease wrote: "The girls appear quite delighted with the scenery of our Neighbourhood...everyone pleased with them. Ma says she has never met nicer girls."[61] Henry's sister Theodosia wrote to her brother: "The Misses Lindley left us I am sorry to say this mor[nin]g and very sorry were we to lose them. I have never met girls so free from affectation and so good and amiable as they are. I am truly sorry not to be able to see more of them and that we are so soon to lose sight of them [i.e., by going to Canada]. Mama and all of us gave her kisses to give to you so you know what to do ask her to give them to the owner...."[62] In fact, the families got along so well that there was some suggestion that Nathaniel and Theodosia, as well as Barbara and Anthony, showed some attraction towards each other.

Sarah knew of the Crease family's need to emigrate, and of their plans. When the final decision was made, Henry consulted his father and decided that he could not go without making a declaration to his Totty. On 27 June 1849 he asked her to marry him. His proposal of marriage was accepted on the spot! Everyone appeared delighted. Emily Crease, Henry's sister, wrote: "Your note this morning did not surprise me my dear Henry (Papa had just come in) Hurrah!! My dear Henry the only doubt in my mind about the matter has cleared up and that was Totty's own answer."[63] "...give my love to dear little Totty and tell her that all hands without a single exception are delighted to have her—and all pressing that she should join our party & proceed with us. You can hardly fancy how pleased we are—we should all be glad if Anthony & Dunny would take a liking to each other they are real good girls."[64] John Lindley was also happy. "I will drop the Dr a line. I was sure he would be pleased it is natural & reasonable that he should—no doubt Mrs L. entirely participates in this feeling....I should tell you that all here accord (& without a single dissentient) in sincere & hearty pleasure at your position with Totty. All unite in congratulations...."[65] His family might be happy, but now came the sticky part. Like all young men, Henry must convince Totty's family, more particularly her father, of his suitability, specifically with regard to his financial status.

The first step for Henry was to obtain his legal credentials. He had finished his studies but had not yet been called to the Bar. In May 1849 he was invited to be examined, and in June wrote the exams. Sarah wrote: "I hope dear Henry you will succeed in taking the necessary oaths at Winchester, Papa & Natty seem to think you will find rather more difficulty than you anticipate, but I hope they are mistaken...."[66] He was sworn in on 4 July. Sarah wrote: "I am so very glad you have been sworn, as it must now in some measure repay those at home for their patience in sparing you from them so long...."[67] Successful, Henry was now set for emigration. Within a month he left for Canada West (now Ontario) with his family. The plan was obvious. Henry meant to make his way in Canada, and with his family's investments on track and taking a turn for the better, he would get a job, perhaps a governmental position. He would then return to England and marry Sarah. Their future life might include residency in Halifax or Toronto.

"THESE MATTERS WHICH AFFECT OUR SEPARATION"

Henry was gone for 18 months. He and Sarah corresponded continually over this time. Sarah wrote an average of once a week and often, for several days running, once or twice a day. Although only Sarah's letters to Henry survive, enough can be gleaned to indicate the general content of those she received from Henry. Activities, occasions and mutual friends are discussed. Sketches are often enclosed to serve as reminders of past events or to explain or illustrate a current event. With candor and charm, the relationship unfolds. Early on Sarah writes: "Dearest Henry....I cannot sign my proper name as I dislike the name of Sarah and Lindley alone would not look very well,"[68] and so signed herself "Totty," the childhood nickname she retained all her life.

What did Sarah do during this time of separation? Well, like most women in love she thought often of her loved one and carried his "likeness" (a daguerrotype in a folding case) about with her in her pocket. "How often!!" she wrote to him, "do I think of our little walks in Dunnyland before breakfast, and of the 'Happie vallie'...."[69] One day when others had gone to church:

> I ran up stairs and thought to myself <u>what a delightful</u> morning I'll now spend!! So accordingly I emptied my pocket of all useless articles, and deposited in their stead <u>your</u> own dear likeness, some of your letters, my church prayer book, and another little book....I then hastened down again and taking a bonnet and shawl by the way, softly crept into the garden and made all possible speed for the <u>little</u> seat in Dunnyland. It was a <u>glorious</u> morning.... I looked about for a nice comfortable place to hang up your picture dear for I was determined you should be looking upon me the whole time—and after <u>many</u> unsuccessful attempts of balancing you on different twigs, and turning you up and down right and left to avoid the glare of light, wh. seemed very roguishly inclined & tried as long as it could to play all kinds of tricks with your dear old face and my feelings. I <u>at last</u> conquered all the difficulties and set you <u>quite</u> fast in a strong forked-branch, with your face turned towards me looking as dear and pleasing as anything short of reality can. I then crowned you with two roses I picked on the way.... I passed <u>four</u> hours <u>among</u> the happiest of my life.[70]

Sarah was 22 at the time of her engagement and, like most other young, middle-class women, was well-versed in the skills deemed necessary and socially acceptable, including knowledge of music, art and literature. She had a general idea of household management, but little practice with

Captain Henry Crease, RN, Henry's father.
May 1849 by Sarah Lindley.
(BC ARCHIVES PDP8532)

Mary Smith Crease, Henry's mother,
May 1849 by Sarah Lindley.
(BC ARCHIVES PDP8533)

Dunnyland sketched by Henry Crease, November 1848. Shows garden with
Sarah and Barbara, the gardener, a recuperating John Lindley in a wheelchair,
and Nathaniel Lindley. (BC ARCHIVES PDP4532)

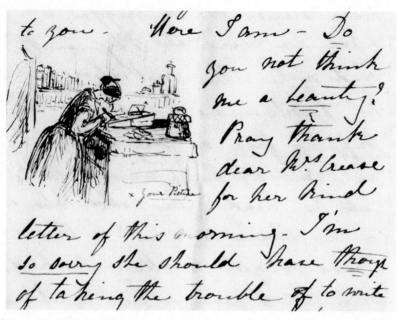

This small section of Sarah's letter to Henry shows how she incorporated small sketches alongside her writing. Sarah Lindley to Henry Crease, 5 July 1849. (BC ARCHIVES MS-2879)

specifics such as cooking or baking. Servants in the Lindley house performed these functions and other housekeeping tasks. She had a very limited experience of the world beyond the household, because in her day, a woman's place was in the house, not in the male-dominated workplaces. Only her ventures in illustrating her father's books set her apart from other women of her class. Her knowledge of commerce or comprehension of politics was limited, and tended to be idealistic or simplistic, based on information given by the male members of her family or by newspaper accounts. She was extremely sheltered by today's standards, so some of the confidences she shares with Henry in her correspondence seem naive and innocent. For women such as Sarah, the transformation to married life with all of its responsibilities must have been if not frightening, at least a great awakening to realities. In an almost unbelievable confidence to Henry on 17 October 1849 she related:

> I have for the first time in my life seen Papa perform that wonderful and mysterious operation of s-h-a-v-i-n-g!! I know all about it now! I happened

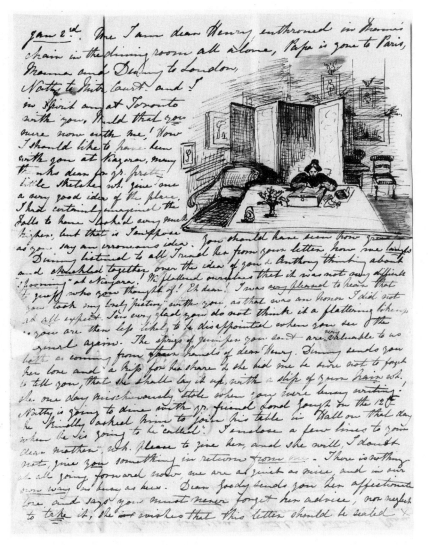

Page from Sarah's letter to Henry, 2 January 1850.
(BC ARCHIVES MS-2879)

to go into his room the other morning when he did not get up so early as usual, on account of his cold, and found him just in the very act of beginning—he bid me sit down, in that white arm chair in the corner on the right hand side—which I accordingly did—and to my great amusement saw the whole operation.[71]

And later in January 1850:

> What do you think? I made my first essay to "Run alone" last Thursday! I
> actually went to London in an omnibus by myself and found my way down
> the Burlington Arcade, Bond Street across Oxford Street down Regent Street
> into Piccadilly where to my delight I found a Kew Bridge Omnibus ready to
> jump onto, without having to hail it myself and at last got home quite safely
> without having a shadow of an adventure to relate.[72]

Things did not go as planned. Little did Sarah and Henry realize that
almost four years would pass before they would marry.[73]

Captain Crease had a large family to support. This fact, combined with
the responsibilities of managing tin mines in Cornwall during an economic
depression in the 1840s and 1850s, meant that very little, if any, income in
the form of profits could be seen. In fact, a great deal of the personal incomes
of Captain Crease and his father-in-law, Edward Smith, were directed
towards the protection of the duchy's interests: expenditures that were
necessary but generated no profits.

The difficulties with the mines and the uncertain future of any investments in Canada did not present a rosy picture. The abrupt departure of
the Crease family from Cornwall created a small scandal in that vicinity
because, although the decision to go had been made for some time, the
actual departure occurred just at the conclusion of unsuccessful legal
disputes associated with the duchy business. Captain Henry Crease was
concerned that people would think the two were linked. This episode fore-
shadowed one with his son that would occur some 10 years later.

Captain Crease took his family to Canada West in attempts to find alternative means of income. While there, he explored and eventually invested
in a number of schemes, including mining ventures and a proposal to con-
struct a canal between the Great Lakes at Sault Ste. Marie.[74] While in
Canada West, the elder Crease sons used the time not only to assist their
father, but also to establish contacts for future employment prospects.
Henry was 25 years old when he accompanied his family. His brothers,
Edward, Anthony, George, John, and Charles, ranged in age from 22 to 11
while his five sisters, Mary, Theodosia, Emily, Julia, and Louisa, were also
unmarried dependents.

Somewhere along the line, Captain Crease's investments went sour.

There was some conflict between him and his eldest son, and in December 1850 Henry returned to England ahead of his family. He gained employment as a conveyancing barrister in Birmingham, but the income was not adequate. Henry then turned to the business he knew best and worked on his own to create a mining company. He needed to earn a living sufficient to give some indication of financial security for the future, and he knew that he could not marry Sarah until this happened. The future looked gloomy for them both. Sarah wrote: "The future does indeed dear Henry appear a blank....My father who naturally is much concerned in the matter has been talking to me exceedingly kindly on the subject....The unfortunate affair which has arisen between yourself and the Capt. is I think a great perplexity to my father."[75] Throughout January 1851, Sarah continued her correspondence, but with a definite tension in her words. Finally, on 12 February:

> Oh Henry! What does this sad silence and indifference mean? Can you be so changed as to force me to believe, what I cannot bear to own even to myself! Is it possible that I have seen you for the last time—and at that time when I thought myself so happy—could you have been contemplating this unkind neglect. No, I will not believe so much as that. Oh Henry, am I never more to be of interest to you—never again to receive a kindly smile, or hear one more affectionate word. Must I begin to alienate myself from you—to become as a piece of wood or stone towards you....I will not trust myself to say any more, but remain forever Your friend, Totty.[76]

The necessity to prove financial independence was taken very seriously. At this time, women of the middle class generally had no income of their own, being dependent on their father or a male relative for support. It was understood, however, that upon marriage, a property settlement would be made. In this way, the woman would pass from dependency on her father to dependency on her husband. Although she might bring in monies to the marriage in trust from her father, she had no income of her own. The prospective husband had to prove his ability to support his wife and anticipated family in the manner to which they were accustomed. He had to prove his net worth and project accurately his abilities for the future. If he was considered financially acceptable, then a marriage settlement of the bride's perceived worth was transferred from her father to the groom. Often this money was kept in trust[77] (as it would be in the case of Sarah and Henry) and invested in an account overseen by independent trustees. The money might be drawn upon for the benefit of future children, and it was viewed as a legacy for the next generation rather than a source of expendable income or usable capital.

Although the personal situation between Sarah and Henry improved, in January 1852 things were still not settled. Sarah wrote to Henry at his lodgings in Poland Street, London:

> I wish very much dearest we could marry—every week I seem to desire it more & more and especially for your comforts' sake dearest do I wish the time could be hastened but I have such a great dread of bringing future trouble and difficulty upon you—that I could not consent to be an "incumbrance" to you (as our little Cornish-driver in Jersey called his wife) until there were sufficient means to make such an undertaking not imprudent. I should desire but a very small beginning, nothing more than what was necessary for real use and common comfort—until at least we could ascertain what the expense of housekeeping really is independently of all other accidental expenses.[78]

By June there was great strain. Henry wrote to John Lindley outlining his future prospects.

> I venture to submit for your kindest consideration a brief account of my present income and early prospects. In the hope that it may conduce to shorten the time which may elapse before gaining the great object of my life.
>
> My present income I estimate at £150 a year. I hold considerable (free) interests in 3 mines which I have every reason to suspect as to turn out valuable. But their actual market value of wh cannot be suddenly appreciated with any degree of exactness—as it may take from 9 months to 2 years before the mines cut [risk?].
>
> If sold immediately I dare say they would fetch £800. They are worth much more.
>
> As to the future. By my profession in wh I get occasional employment (this year it has been exceptionally larger than I anticipate hereafter) and particularly by connection with mining in Cornwall, I may fairly hope to ensure after 1852 a further income of not less than £100. Out of the Sault Ste Marie Canal I expect to have an interest to the amount of £2000. This is contingent upon our obt[ainin]g the Charter. This (when obtd) I should

wish to settle upon my future wife, in such matter that its enjoyment might not be affected by any untoward commercial accident happening to myself.

Other interests I have a fair prospect of obtaining from two of the most valuable mines in Cornwall (Wheal Vor Great United Mines and Great Wheal Charlotte) the leases of wh. have been promised to my brother & myself....[79]

It was not enough. John Lindley believed that the young couple should not begin their life without a guarantee of an income of £700 annually. For his part, he agreed to assist in housekeeping costs and to supply £140, expecting that Henry and his family should come up with the rest.[80] Henry was in the midst of creating a prospectus for the two mines he and brother Edward were planning to manage, and working to attract investors. He appealed to his father in Canada West. Henry's pleas show the seriousness of the situation and its effect on Sarah.

Poor dear girl it touches me sorely to see her gentle, uncomplaining patience, month after month & year after year—getting thinner & thinner & no one can tell the reason why—tho I cannot but know that hope deferred which maketh the heart sick must also have its effect upon her....[81]

The following week, almost in desperation, he wrote:

I think I should be quite justified in taking Totty (even if they refuse assent to our marriage) to try our fortune in the goldfields in Australia. There at least we can live and have a home instead of the miserable solitary life I have for years passed in lodgings.[82]

The situation was compounded by delays in communication. The Crease family was still in Canada West, and it seemed agonizingly slow for Henry to receive replies from his father. After one such delay, Henry wrote again to his father. "I hope to hear from you by return [post] to say so—or else I will be placed in such a position as will lose me dear Totty altogether of that there is no doubt…not only will there be no chance of my marrying but the Dr. will, in his disappointment…break off the engagement altogether and make two people miserable...."[83] Captain Crease, despite a severe cash flow shortage caused by unfortunate investments and the sinking of a ship (carrying his goods) in the St. Lawrence River, eventually managed to contribute a portion. The remainder was supplied by Henry and his brother Edward. Henry replied to his father:

It put me quite in a flutter at the near prospect of at last having a little nest of our own! and Totty seems the same…for she says…"Your note has put me quite in a flutter & makes my heart as light as a feather & as happy as a Queen." Now Totty will I hope get in a little better condition than she has been. Uncomplaining patient little girl! Everything convinces me that my choice has fallen on an excellent high principled girl. I am as happy as a king. How I wish you were all here to partake of it. However I think your being in Canada will work out a great end….[84]

The marriage settlement finally achieved, John Lindley agreed to buy the ironware, glass and crockery for the couple "when there is a house to receive them."[85] Sarah and Henry purchased necessities for their new life together. They met in London and shopped for blankets, china, cutlery and other items. Henry made these purchases as part of his contribution to their marriage settlement. Often they parted, Sarah with new purchases, going home by omnibus. She was quite independent in her activities, able to travel alone and meet Henry in London. She had come a long way in a few short years.

The couple planned to rent a house and considered many, determining finally that a new area of houses at the base of Notting Hill was a good location. During the autumn Sarah took the leading role in making preliminary enquiries regarding housing. She travelled from Turnham Green, met the landlords and viewed the potential houses. She wrote to Henry every few days between their meetings to keep him informed of her progress. Eventually they took a house at Number 9, St. James Square, Notting Hill: a two-storey brick house of modest size, which over the next few months they filled with furniture in preparation for their new life together. Knowing that money was tight, Sarah was very practical concerning all their purchases, dissuading Henry from purchasing more than necessary and constantly maintaining she could make do with very little. On one point, however, they appeared to be at odds. Sarah writes: "You are right darling. I must be your wife & not yr slave—but still dearest I think we might be very comfortable with only one servant having occasional help for her viz once a fortnight to keep things tidy & clean, and that would make light work for all—at least I fancy so."[86]

During this time Henry was situated just outside London working as a conveyancing barrister but was also involved with his brother Edward in completing negotiations, which began as early as 1850, to purchase three tin mines in Cornwall. Agreement was finally reached on 19 November 1852.

Crease was interested in developing a mining company to exploit the wealth underground, but he was also intimately concerned with the welfare of the miners and their families. His experiences teaching at the Ragged Schools in London during 1848 had convinced him of the merits of educating the poor and less fortunate. His plans for the Great Wheal Vor United Mines included development of miners' schools, housing and opportunities for acculturation. Sarah was in total agreement with his plans, calling them "such an excellent undertaking." She hoped to one day see "the whole thing in full operation and maybe of lending a hand myself!!"[87] On the eve of an important meeting she wrote, "I wish you may be successful in this great matter—and that both present and future generations may have cause to bless your name. I humbly pray that you may have the power of putting into execution all your noble plans for the education of the little miners."[88]

Development of the mine and the improvements for the miners involved a financial investment which was not guaranteed. Sarah knew full well the financial constraints under which she and Henry's happiness had been so long confined but, even so, resolved to back Henry in this endeavour. "I am prepared darling for any shipwreck of our little fortune so that we are not entirely drowned with it!"[89] Sarah assisted Henry in Wheal Vor business by

In this unusual self-portrait, Sarah sketched herself looking into the mirror and sketching her reflection (detail). (BC ARCHIVES PDP4812)

acting as copyist. She made duplicate copies of leases, correspondence and maps. She needed to apply her time in a useful and constructive manner, much as she had when assisting her father with his *Gardeners' Chronicle* responsibilities, by creating botanical illustrations. Now, she applied her skills and abilities on a practical level for Henry. This was to be a lifelong contribution. "You know dearest I <u>must</u> be <u>useful</u> to you for Jer. Taylor says that is one of the principal ingredients of a <u>true & worthy friendship</u>."[90]

As it turned out, Henry's preoccupation with settling the affairs at Wheal Vor delayed their marriage until the following spring. In February 1853 he moved out of his lodgings in Poland Street and into the nearly furnished house at No. 9 St. James Square. Sarah was proud of the house and the contents they had purchased together. Her thoughts are clear in this letter where she asks Henry to look:

> round the walls of the drawing room to see if there cannot be found space enough somewhere for a Book case 3 ft. 6 wide. If it could be managed I should be very pleased—for upon looking at my store of books I see I could quite fill that space and as many shelves as I have put in my sketch of an imaginary case. The <u>distances between the shelves</u> I particularly hope will be the same as those marked on the side of the sketch as they are only just sufficient to admit the books intended for them. Papa has got some beautiful cutlery for us—and this morning he gave me an order on Bailey & Co. for the ironmongery. Are we not getting on now dearest!!! It makes me so happy. What will you say dearest, if upon reckoning up at the end you find all <u>the furnishings</u> of such a sweet little house will not have cost you <u>at the outside</u> more than £350 instead of the dreadful sum of £800 as you expect!! Papa & I have been laying our heads together this morning & roughly calculating the different amounts you have paid & cannot at present anyhow make them exceed £220 reckoning £40 for the plate. I must say darling, this little discovery has made me breathe much more freely for according to your estimate I felt as if I must be the ruin of you & begin life with the character of a most <u>extravagant</u> little animal wh. you know dearest would be a stigma I should not best like especially as I hope never to deserve it.[91]

On 27 April 1853, Sarah Lindley and Henry Crease were married at Acton Church. Barbara Lindley, in a letter to Henry's mother in Toronto, described the event:

...all your friends may now come forward and congratulate you upon Henry's marriage, for yesterday at 11 o'clock that knot was tied. I suppose I can scarcely enter too much into particulars, since you all are so deeply interested in the Bridegroom, he looked remarkably well and spruce a nice frock coat buff waistcoat and grey trousers and shiny boots, his hair and whiskers fresh from Mr. Truefitts's hands, when he entered the church he looked all expectation and natural excitement...the bride's dress was white silk like the enclosed pattern a white lace scarf (like the lace dress you once showed us laid up for one of your girls) a very simple white twill bonnet and flowers not orange blossoms and honiton lace veil collar, habitshirt, sleeves and pocket handkerchief, and a bouquet of real orange flowers all the bridesmaids had bouquets, Mr. Thompson, the clergyman we attend at Brentford married them at Acton Church, they both went through the service very well, we then returned to breakfast which was made very short as Papa would allow of no speeches except just a short one from his oldest friend Dr. Wallicks to drink to the health of Mr. & Mrs. Henry Crease. Totty then put on her travelling dress which was very plain, a dark blue silk, a scarf cashmere shawl & tuscan bonnet trimmed with white & a plain tuile cap inside. She looked very nicely...there were two carriages at church & after the happy pair were carried off by a postilion & pair of white horses & old shoes in abundance thrown after them.[92]

Sarah sketched the wedding cake (see page 36), which Barbara described: "such a magnificent one it was, it stood 2 feet high with the ornaments."[93] After the ceremony, the couple travelled to the Isle of Wight, where they honeymooned at the Sandrock Hotel, walking on the beaches and exploring the headlands, sketchbooks in hand.

Married life quickly regulated itself because of Henry's responsibilities, which made it impossible for him to live full-time in London. He spent a great deal of time in Helston, near the mines, while Sarah remained in London. On 27 February 1854, 10 months after their marriage, Sarah gave birth to her first daughter, Mary Maberly, named in honour of Henry's mother and his favourite sister, who had died unexpectedly the previous year. From what can be deduced between the lines, it was a trying birth, certainly an event from which Sarah took several months to recover. After the birth, some time passed before she felt comfortable with the infant. She did not feel an immediate bonding of love with Mary, but, as in all her relationships, took some time before she felt comfortable enough with her for the love to issue forth. "It takes a <u>long time</u> for me to become really attached to either people or places but when once done they are <u>never</u> forgotten or <u>unliked</u> again."[94]

By the time Sarah was pregnant again, the prospect of another child was met with ease and a certain amount of delight. Henry was away throughout the five months preceding this birth, and so Sarah filled her letters to him with news of little Mary's antics, her charming behaviour and interaction with her grandparents. She also told Henry about her health and made frequent references to the unborn child, which they referred to as "little Fanny."

> Little Fanny continues to give <u>very</u> vigorous sign of her company. She made such a commotion within that I could not tell whether she was convulsed with pain or pleasure but something was going on which roused her little being to great kicking and tumbling. Somehow I feel a sort of affection

Sarah sketched her wedding cake. (BC ARCHIVES PDP4609)

Sarah's eldest daughters, Mary Maberly Crease, age 4, and Susan Reynolds Crease, then 2½, dated June 1858. (BC ARCHIVES F8808)

already springing up for the little unknown which I had no experience of at all with the first one—and which I hardly felt as much of—for many weeks after its birth![95]

During the spring of 1855, one-year-old Mary accompanied Henry back to Cornwall for a visit. Here father and daughter had a chance to spend time together, and for both of them, this was an opportunity to get to know each other. On this trip, armed with a pocketful of sweets, he took the time to establish this important link. As Sarah remarked: "I am so <u>very very</u> happy darling to think that you have found a warm little corner of yr. heart to spare for sweet little Mary. I was <u>sure</u> you only wanted to see a little more of her—to love her as fondly as any father need love his little daughter."[96]

Number 9, St. James Square was also inhabited during 1854 and 1855 by Charles, Henry's youngest brother, who spent his time studying and receiving tutorial assistance for civil service examinations. He wasn't a natural scholar, and he had a short attention span and retention capability. Motivation was a constant problem. Sarah did her best, assisting him daily with his conversational French, a requisite for the exams, and drilling him in factual knowledge of all manner of things. His sister, Emily, also stayed throughout the summer of 1855, principally to help Sarah with Mary, often taking her for visits to Turnham Green. It was a busy household. The usual domestic adventures emerge, including a rather unpleasant experience with a maid.

> I hope you may have succeeded darling in procuring "Cherry"—for after all we know of the other woman I could never [have] any comfort or confidence in her. They say she is a Roman Catholic! and was in the habit of taking snuff! She borrowed money of the cook before leaving and has run off with certainly 2 or 3 pounds of ours. I should not have thought I could have been so deceived as in her.[97]

The long separation during this second pregnancy must have been difficult for both parties. Although Sarah routinely writes of missing Henry and refers to the dismal comfort of a cold bed by herself, she is fully supportive of Henry's responsibilities. He was very busy with improvements at the mines. In September, after months of engineering and construction, the second new "Great Engine" at Wheal Vor was installed and ceremoniously inaugurated. "I trust the whole proceeding may prove a great blessing to all concerned, and provide sweet and honest bread to many a hungry mouth for many a long long year...."[98] This was a major undertaking and Henry really could not leave until the project was complete and fully functioning. Sarah understood this, and despite her anxiety at not having him near her during the pregnancy, would not ask him to leave the mines. During her eighth month, her mother wrote to Henry chastising him for being absent from Sarah's side. Sarah apologized for her mother's interference and reassured her husband:

> I would on no account have you neglect your public duties, or hasten over any important business—to be with me a little sooner. Even if I expected my confinement tomorrow darling I would not wish it—for thank God, who has provided us the means of so many comforts I have every thing around me, including kind friends in both servants and relations calculated to minister to every want attending such a time.[99]

Despite tight purse strings and an absent husband, Sarah was happy in marriage. In August, sitting at the desk in her sister's room at Acton Green, she wrote to Henry.

I am now in Dunny's little room—and as I breathe the sweet air and look on to the green and peaceful garden, it seems to suggest to me nothing but thoughts of love and happiness with the only wish that my own dear Love were by my side to enjoy them too. I am sure that if we were together here at this present moment we should feel as lover-like as possible and were it not for the change in my figure—for a moment, could forget that we are an old married couple. But I would not if I could darling really change the present for the past. On no account would I go back to the old days—for in a real and sober happiness they are not to be compared with these.[100]

On 18 November 1855, a second daughter, Susan Reynolds, was born.

But what was it like for Sarah during these years? As we know, Crease's financial situation for several years had been close to the edge. His previous business difficulties were explained to the satisfaction of Sarah and her family as being largely the result of circumstances beyond his control or unfortunate and unforeseen calamities arising from independent causes. He was now attempting to diversify his sources of income. He could not rely wholly upon the law for opportunities. The income derived from legal work in itself was insufficient to support a family, and he had no personal income to fall back on. Developing the Cornish tin mines was a long-term project designed to provide security and income for future years. For the short term, Sarah expected finances to be tight. She was in complete agreement with her husband in these endeavours, and she trusted Henry's abilities and his business acumen. Sarah willingly resolved to make things as easy for Henry as she possibly could, and she did not complain of the necessary absences when Henry worked in Cornwall at the mine site and she and the children remained in London. During some years, Henry was absent for more than six out of twelve months, and had only fleeting trips to London, where he might stay overnight with Sarah. These absences must

This is an example of the fine pen-and-ink sketches Sarah produced to illustrate her father's botanical publications. (BC ARCHIVES PDP8063)

have been difficult for both of them. Henry was physically separated from his wife and young family and, as both a husband and father, must have felt cast adrift from his intimate life. He was away so often in young Mary's life that neither of them knew each other or felt comfortable together. This awkwardness was to him one of the great sorrows of the situation.[101]

Sarah too felt the absence of the children's father keenly. Although she was near her parents and sister in Turnham Green, and her brother worked at a London office, she lived an independent existence at Notting Hill. The household included a servant, who assisted with the children and various household tasks. Several young women in succession filled this capacity over the five years, so the household was less than settled. Relationships between mistress and servant remained just that, mistress and servant, nothing more, despite the intimacy of daily contact and familiarity. Sarah relied on these young women, but limited their relationships to conform with the greater social framework of the class system.[102] The servants assisted with child care, releasing Sarah from round-the-clock motherhood. This gave her precious free time to visit with friends, or, especially while pregnant, to rest and reserve her strength. Henry's extended absences made it necessary for her to keep alive to both Mary and Susy the knowledge of their father. She established rituals whereby the children kissed "dear father's likeness" before going to bed, and she introduced him in conversation about daily routines and events. Her letters to him often included smeared lip marks traced in pen: the loving kisses of Mary to her father.

It was particularly difficult for Sarah during her second pregnancy, as Henry was away for most of the second and third trimesters. His absence at this time of her life coincided with a critical development in the tin mines, which he and his brother were expanding with the construction of a new engine upon which the economic future of the project depended. Henry's presence at the mine site and his meetings with shareholders required his absence, throughout which Sarah remained steadfast. Her letters admit her loneliness for him, but never does she request his return or question his absence. She is fully aware of the importance of his work. He was working hard to solidify their future, to establish a successful enterprise that would be the economic means of supporting him and his family. It was also more than that. Sarah and Henry's aspirations for the tin mines were based on the premise that worker exploitation was morally unjust. They supported schemes designed to improve the lot of the average worker. In 1855 Henry contributed to the Notting Hill British Day Schools, an educational enterprise begun four years earlier.[103] Sarah too supported the "Plan for the Relief of Female Slop-Workers by the Establishment of a Self-Supporting Workshop." The committee was led by noted reformer the Earl of Shaftsbury and included Charles Mansfield.[104] The plan had a stated objective: "to supersede the class of Sweaters and Middlemen, who now intercept, in great measure, the remuneration of those wretched Females by bringing the Workers into direct relation with the employers." This task was made possible by establishing a day nursery and a sale shop and creating a needle-women's working association.[105]

Henry embarked on their own scheme of economic and social reform in microcosm at the mines. The schools, the cultural activities and other seemingly non-profit enterprises he developed at this time were indicative of the visions they shared. Henry wished to prove that he could both establish a

Descending a mine shaft was not a common experience for middle-class Victorian women. Sarah describes the process in this clipping from a letter to her parents, ca. 1853–1856.
(BC ARCHIVES PDP1390)

This rough sketch of the house in Antron, Cornwall, was clipped out of a letter and pasted into a scrapbook. Sarah Crease, ca. 1856–1857. (BC ARCHIVES PDP4838)

sound financial venture and improve the lot of workers. It was a belief ripe for the times.[106]

In 1856 Sarah and the children moved to Antron, Cornwall, close by the mines, where they could finally live with Henry as a family. Sarah and Henry, along with Julia Crease, took drawing lessons in Falmouth and spent several afternoons on sketching excursions. They both inspected the schools, and in February 1857 "presided over a Lecture on Geology at Our Schools."[107] In August Natty with Sarah's parents arrived on a 10-day visit; in early November, Emily Crease visited; and on 21 November, Dunny arrived. Two days following, third daughter Barbara was born. Despite being together as a family, it was not a happy time, for economic conditions precipitated Henry's personal and financial failure in Cornwall.

"THIS SEASON OF TRIAL & HUMILIATION"

The events of his downfall moved swiftly. During the fall of 1857 it was obvious to some of Henry's friends that serious problems were looming, yet he did not admit them to anyone. Complaints of extravagances and irregularities came to the attention of some directors of the London board of the company, culminating in charges of fraud and mismanagement. On 26 November there was an enquiry at the mine. In December a committee of investigation was struck, and Henry was asked to resign as director. On the advice of his friends, Henry, after a fleeting few hours with Sarah, left by boat for Normandy to escape angry shareholders.

Henry left Sarah to deal with the bailiff and creditors. Luckily her sister was staying with them and could assist in this frightening time. Some of Henry's friends and business partners also helped ease the situation. One friend authorized Sarah to refer creditors to him and also advanced Sarah the money for the journey to her parents' home, "and did all in his power to protect us, asked us to go to his house till we could return to our friends, in fact did everything he could."[108] All the while, Sarah and Dunny were fearful for Henry's safety. "It was an immense relief to us to know you were all safe, until then night & day we were haunted with fears, thank God however you got across the water...."[109] Sarah and Dunny hurriedly packed up the family's belongings and arranged shipment to Turnham Green. Sarah, perhaps to avoid embarrassment, kept out of sight as much as possible. They travelled by cart to Falmouth and then on to Plymouth and Southampton, where they boarded the train for London. Sarah and baby Barbara stayed behind the curtains in the ladies' compartment while Dunny managed tickets, luggage and the two eldest children.

A day or so earlier Dunny and a friend had removed all Henry's personal correspondence, diaries and pre-1857 business papers from the mining office. Dunny, in her desire to ensure that documents reflecting criticism of Henry or his business doings not fall into the hands of his enemies, burned many letters and other business records. This she confessed to Henry in letters written several weeks later, when she was haunted by remorse, realizing that in her haste to protect Henry, she may have caused more damage by ensuring his inability to produce documents, which though disparaging in tone, might have been evidence crucial to his rebuttal. "The destruction of those horrid letters haunts me," she wrote.[110]

Exactly what went wrong is uncertain. The financial crash of 1857 contributed greatly, forcing companies to re-examine business practices. Henry's object in developing the mines had always been to promote the interest of the mines and the people working in them, their families and communities, as witnessed by early prospectus descriptions.[111] As he wrote in his defence:

> I therefore did many things which I should not have done had rigid economy been my principle of action. The establishment of the School for the Miners' Children, Horticultural Shows, Donations to objects dear to the working Miner…Commodious Washing Places for the men coming up from under ground, and…similar expenses, were therefore charged to the mine. It was of far greater importance for a large undertaking like Great Wheal Vor, to be carried on in a liberal manner than that the mines should have been made unpopular by parsimony in the expenditure. This…in the face of an extraordinary emigration, and the desperate work we were at times engaged in… when the men's lives were not safe for five minutes together; for it was only thus we could hope to attract and keep the best men that could be procured, instead of filling the mine with boys.[112]

Antagonistic suppliers and competitors were determined to undermine Henry's enterprise, which represented a threat to the established way. Skilled labour was at a premium because of mass migration from Cornwall to gold strikes in Australia, California and, shortly, British Columbia. These all united to create a difficult situation. Dissension among London investors, culminating in charges of financial misappropriation by Crease, was the last straw. A legal suit was brought against Crease,[113] and though it failed, it was enough to force him to withdraw from the mines and divest himself personally of his own finances. Under the advice of his brother-in-law Nathaniel Lindley, Henry gave power of attorney to a trusted advisor and left Cornwall until things cooled down. He travelled to Le Havre in Normandy, where he established himself, using a fictitious name at the post office to receive mail. He was far enough away from creditors, but close enough to return to London quickly when necessary. Unable to return until the affair was settled, Henry remained in Le Havre until April 1858, when, following advice from many friends, he quickly and quietly returned to England to say goodbye to Sarah, and then left on the *Daedelus*, bound for Canada West and Toronto.

How much did Sarah understand of Henry's situation? Henry's flight into temporary exile and her forced and surreptitious removal from her new home were the culmination of several months' uncertainty and tension.

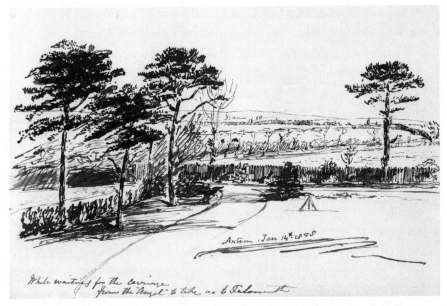

Anterm. Jan 14th 1858

While waiting for the carriage from the "Angel" to take us to Falmouth

Sarah still had the inclination to document her surroundings even on her flight from Cornwall after Henry's disgrace. (BC ARCHIVES PDP4619)

Did Henry confide his problems with cash flow, the anger of creditors, or the distrust and divisiveness of the directors, many of whom disapproved of expenses that did not reflect increased profit? The record is not clear, but we assume Henry kept most of it to himself. Sarah, living with him near the mines, amid the miners and their families, dealing with local merchants and storekeepers, must have picked up some indications of turmoil. Surely, Henry's behaviour at home would show signs of tension. What would she do in the situation; what could she do? Her life was linked financially to Henry's.

Sarah herself was occupied during the fall of 1857, coping with two small children and the last trimester of pregnancy. Imminent childbirth and recovery afterward must have complicated the stressful situation, but a wife's place was to support her husband and this Sarah did. Years earlier, while waiting so long for Henry to earn the financial security necessary for John Lindley's approval for his daughter's marriage, Sarah learned patience of a sort that many others could never master. The long, painful wait before marriage taught her that nothing in life comes easily or, once achieved, should ever be taken for granted. Sarah, and indeed all members of her family, held Henry in high regard. His moral standards, his Christian beliefs and his sincere willingness to find his way in life were widely respected. Sarah knew when she married Henry that she would never be rich. She understood that for a barrister with no personal income to support him, a simple lifestyle could be maintained with thrift, but unless other opportunities presented themselves, it would be a life that could border on genteel poverty. Add to this the reality of a wife and children to support, and the outlook was bleak. This did not matter to her, as she believed in Henry and God. She believed that virtue would be its own reward; that hard work, coupled with righteous thoughts and deeds, led to happiness of the soul. She expected life to be a struggle, as it in some way prepared her and Henry for greater glory in another life. What she could not foresee were the number of times their faith and love would be tried by circumstances, often beyond their control. The painful wait for marriage anticipated the more painful situation she found herself in during 1858. The crisis at the mines, Henry's resignation, the committee of investigation and its report and aftermath, the forced exile of Henry—all tested her beliefs in God and her husband.

Did Sarah believe Henry free of guilt in the charges levelled against him? The letters that survive show no animosity or doubt.[114] According to her sister, Sarah was unaware of the charges levelled by the committee of investigation and the extent of Henry's troubles. "Totty knows nothing of this [the committee's charges] for Papa does not wish to discuss the matter with her, or distress her in any way."[115] But surely she must have been disappointed, not just in the loss of future financial security, but in Henry's judgement. Although he was eventually cleared of wrongdoing, at the time, the perception of conflict of interest in his business dealings was there, if not direct conflict. Henry and his brother owned interests in other mining ventures adjacent to Great Wheal Vor, which led to misunderstandings amongst his business acquaintances. He should have been more business-like in his dealings and made a more obvious and clear separation of his private financial affairs (including the expenditures on progressive amenities for the miners) from his affairs conducted as manager of Great Wheal Vor mines. This he did not do, which left him open to criticism and suspicion

Simply titled *The Home*, 1858, this charcoal-and-watercolour sketch shows the Lindley home, with sweeping pathway, cold frames against the house and Sarah walking with a parasol. Seated to the right is sister Barbara (Dunny), amidst the trees behind are Nathaniel (Natty) and his fiancée, Sarah (Sally) Teale. Sarah Crease, artist. (BC ARCHIVES PDP4513)

among a board of directors split in its support. In the end, it was sloppy business practice and Owenite idealism, not fraud or deceit, that caused his downfall. His sister-in-law, Dunny, said it best: "do not ever again touch speculations, believe me you are of too sanguine a temperament ever to make them profitable, besides laying yourself open to temptations that would try even a saint."[116] Again, Dunny no doubt echoed Sarah's thoughts when she wrote: "…although I believe most of the accusations to be false still I cannot but suppose some of them to have a foundation."[117] This belief that Henry was innocent of the larger charges, but perhaps guilty of minor indiscretions, is echoed between the lines in later correspondence.

Dunny told Henry: "She seems to bear her trouble wonderfully, she is peculiarly constituted I think to bear up against that which could quite overwhelm others."[118] Later she wrote: "Totty is looking pretty well. I am constantly weeding out the grey hairs, her forehead wants a Husband's hand to iron out the wrinkles, which are trying hard to become permanent. She is a good little Puss, is so cheerful when with us, whatever she may be when by herself. Just now she is working very hard for Papa who finds her invaluable, for she can do just what he wants."[119] The summer of 1858 wore on, and Henry still was not settled. Barbara wrote: "It is sad for you poor old fellow all by yourself, but it is very hard upon poor Totty, to be married & separated from her Hubby...."[120]

It is difficult to recreate this period, because no letters exist between Sarah and Henry. Luckily, many of Barbara's letters to Henry provide clues about Sarah's feelings, but the exact sequence of events following Henry's flight is not well-documented. Gaps in correspondence occurred several times during their lives, always in times of personal trauma. One explanation is that the letters were purposely destroyed. In 1856 Sarah wrote: "I will burn one of yr letters recd this morning darling as I would not more than yourself run the risk of any other eye than mine reading those things which are so precious to me, but which none should see or know of...."[121] The next day, "how _much much_ I love you darling and how over powered with love & gratitude I feel for yr. most precious & most beautiful letters. While resting on the sofa for a short time today—I took one after the other out of my pocket and read them all over again. I could hardly bear to part with _one_ of them but I thought I _must_ do so, or you would never trust me again—so with my own hand committed two or three to the cruel flames— and felt all the while as if they were dividing me from my love...."[122] Why did they deliberately destroy particular correspondence? We can never know for sure. Were the contents too intimate, or perhaps compromising to an outside reader? If Sarah followed Henry's request to destroy letters, why then did Henry not burn hers? Almost 200 of Sarah's letters to him written between 1849 and 1858 exist, yet not a single letter from Henry to Sarah remains. Was he that sentimental and unwilling to part with them? There can be no clear explanation for the mysterious gaps in diaries and correspondence that occur in an otherwise extremely full written record.[123]

Sarah's position throughout this affair was embarrassing and extremely upsetting. All her and Henry's hopes and dreams appeared to be lost. Their investments were tied up in shares of a mine that was not fully producing, and dividends had not yet been declared. The charges against Henry's honour flew in the face of everything they stood for, and despite her family's support and belief in him, the charges affected public perception and were

Back living with her parents after Henry's exile, Sarah kept busy reading, writing letters and continuing her illustrative work for the *Gardeners' Chronicle*. She is shown here in the library with an open box of Henry's letters on the table, 1858. Sarah Crease, artist (detail). (BC ARCHIVES PDP3129)

morally judgemental. Tainted by scandal, the dream of financial security gone, what could be worse? Only continued separation. Henry's work in Cornwall was meant to ensure their future togetherness. That had all changed. Henry had to physically remove himself from his family while the charges brought against him were answered. He could only maintain contact by mail. Then, suddenly, he was advised to depart for Toronto in hopes of leaving the situation behind him and of making an immediate fresh start. What did Sarah have to say in all this? The records are not conclusive, but it appears as though she had very little to say. Henry had to leave to distance his family from his financial situation. There was no guarantee he would see them again.

Indeed, as Henry left England, watching the familiar shoreline in the distance, he mused upon his situation and Sarah:

> They have been to <u>me</u> 5 happy years with her—altho a great portion of the time has in the other relations of life been a period of great & harassing responsibility. I wonder what the future has in store for me...And what is that little girl—doing & thinking of now—that gave herself up to me for life— thinking of me I'll be bound....Totty. What gentle thoughts & memories <u>that</u> name conjures up—What was she doing, then I wondered once more for the 10,000th time—I felt she was thinking of me—then and there I

prayed—I "prayed with my <u>heart</u> tho I shut up my eyes"—that she might always have Gods Holy Spirit in her <u>heart</u> and then all she <u>did</u> & thought & said w[oul]d <u>surely surely</u> have good & <u>trusting</u> thoughts of him who was so thinking of her—prayed too that it might be given to her to believe in his general honor & integrity & truth—that tho' they sh[oul]d never meet again—he might have in the hour of sorrow & struggling for <u>her</u> & her <u>little</u> ones—the consolation of one day hearing & knowing that it was not his mother that bore him <u>alone</u>—who never once in her heart doubted or distrusted him—when all beside fell, some entirely, some only <u>partially</u> from him....[124]

In a rare commentary, Henry speculated on his marital situation. The clues in this passage indicate that even prior to his downfall, he sensed disappointment, or perhaps unhappiness, on Sarah's part:

...was Totty happy there [at Antron], and what <u>could</u> have made her take a dislike to leave her old home & come & live with me—Many things I thought of as the reason—perhaps I was too <u>warm</u> or <u>selfish</u> or there was some <u>jarring thing</u> I was ignorant of too rudely touched—or something wanting I c[oul]d not supply. Perhaps my ways were so different or she was ashamed of her husbands position—It could not be his birth, descent & education or his avowed principles—something I felt there was—which reflection has since confirmed. Then came the thought—was it still existing— if so the enforced separation was providential—and all the ill that fell upon me—welcome, most welcome—wanting respect—love is but a shadow of itself....[125]

GREENER PASTURES

In 1858 Henry Crease began the unenviable task of starting all over. He was in debt, his name was under a cloud of suspicion and there was no obvious means in sight to bring an end to the situation. The great economic crash of that year had created a dearth of opportunities. Business everywhere was suffering. Short of taking up whatever conveyancing business he could find (which would bring in little income, surely not enough to support a wife and three children), Henry had to look elsewhere. Again the possibilities of Canada loomed large. Surely nothing could be worse than remaining in England with the loss of face, the spectre of creditors and the knowledge that he was incapable of providing for his family. There really was no choice. Sarah's parents agreed to take in their daughter and grandchildren. Nathaniel Lindley agreed to act on Henry's behalf with regard to the situation at Wheal Vor, and as an advisor with power of attorney who would act for Henry in all his financial affairs.

Sarah and the children's return to live with her parents marks a remarkable yet typical situation for women at this time. She grew up dependent on parents, in particular her father, for financial support. Upon her marriage, her father, like many others, had established a trust fund for her and her children. Perhaps in hindsight, John Lindley was wise to establish a trust fund for Sarah. Given Henry's financial uncertainty prior to the marriage, such a trust was a cautious and very practical idea. Henry's financial downfall only a few years later proved his wisdom. In Sarah's case, certain stringent conditions governed the use of the trust. The principal was to be maintained in investments and only drawn upon for uses agreed upon by the trustees who administered the fund. It was not set up to provide short-term relief from financial difficulties, but rather was intended for the future use of Sarah and her children. Thus, when Henry fell into troubles, they were deemed *his* troubles. Throughout her marriage, Sarah was very cognizant of the thin financial tightrope upon which they balanced. She made economies where she could to keep Henry's expenses down. Even with Henry away so much of the time, Sarah had to apply directly to him to pay local and minor bills such as the butcher's and grocer's. Henry would then send a draft or cheque to cover the bill. Sarah did not even have pocket money of her own.

Sarah moving back in with her parents put a crimp in the Lindley budget. Dr. Lindley did not have a pension or a large retirement income. In fact, he had spent the early part of his life paying off debt incurred by his own father.[126] The addition of Sarah and three young children to his household greatly increased his expenses. Sarah must have experienced humiliation as well as gratitude.

These early financial difficulties and embarrassments, with the consequent extended separations, had a powerful effect on Sarah and coloured her perceptions. Circumstances in later life and her reactions to them all have a grounding back in the events of these early married years. She never forgot the pain of separation caused by uncertainty in finances. Nor did she

Sisters Mary, Susan and baby
Barbara Crease in the dining
room at the Lindley home,
ca. 1858. Detail from a larger
sketch. Sarah Crease, artist.
(BC ARCHIVES PDP4587)

forget the anger, confusion and humiliation that accompanied reversals of
fortune. The embarrassment of credit refusal, sending wedding gifts to be
auctioned, escaping creditors by night, and prolonged dependence upon
family and friends were situations she never wanted repeated.

Henry left on 6 April 1858 for Toronto, where he hoped that this time
he would be successful. He would be the man at the right place at the right
time. He would secure a governmental position, or civil appointment, and
once set up, would send for Sarah and the girls to join him. These things
were not to be.

Henry quickly re-established contact with the influential friends he had
cultivated eight years earlier and spent time studying local mining, law and
politics in hopes of securing a position. First thoughts were of something
connected with the developing railroads or mining. The vacant position of
secretary to the Law Commission was also a favoured possibility. Sarah
wrote: "Papa wishes you to become a Govt surveyor of Land for the purpose
of making new roads, railroads, canals or such like. He says if once so employed by Govt and they find the work <u>well done</u> it gives one a claim upon
them wh. they will always recognise." Sarah herself believed:

you are <u>best able to judge</u> and I shall feel perfectly satisfied with whatever occupation you may find circumstances are indicating you to choose. If it is the Law I trust your health & spirits will be equal to the task if it is anything else, I equally hope you will meet with a due reward for yr. labor. Be it what it may I trust it will have God's blessing with it and if it should please Him to give you some employment that will suit both <u>body</u> & <u>mind</u> and enable us to <u>live</u> to<u>gether</u> as a little family—I shall be <u>very very</u> thankful. By living together, I mean not take you away from us for any long periods of time for I am but a <u>woman</u>, darling, and feel all the weakness of my sex.[127]

She then goes on to report on the children. "…and now for a few words about the dear children—they are quite well darling and progressing in intellect every day. Mary is rather thin. Susy as sturdy as ever and dear Baby a fat, soft, happy little soul. Mary & Susy are both very fond of her and dance their dolls about in front of her wh. makes her laugh very heartily…."[128]

Henry sent his father-in-law three letters from influential people in Toronto.[129] "They show the opinion entertained of him in Canada—one of these is from Mr [P. M.] Vankoughnet, late Minister [of Agriculture] in the Canadian Government—and the second is from Judge Haggerty—the third from the Rector of the Cathedral at Toronto."[130] He sent duplicates to his father and to Sarah. Despite his best efforts, a position was not forthcoming. The political climate favoured homegrown talents, and in many cases, local men received preferential treatment for appointments. Despite his connections, the commercial outlook held little opportunity for a man of his experience.

Mr. Vankoughnet's letter to Henry exclaimed: "I feel great regret at not having been able to secure for you any eligible appointment under the Government…. Anything which I can do personally or officially to serve you shall be done but an official certificate from the 'Minister of Agriculture' in Canada would not help you much in England." The rest of the letter, however, is pivotal and, in retrospect, extremely prophetic:

…it has occurred to me that you might with very good chances of success push your fortunes in the new country to which so many eyes are now turned. Why not seek a home in New Caledonia the El Dorado of which so many dreamed in ages past but which you and I can see as a reality? Were I free from the ties of family, property and politics I would not hesitate to commence life anew in a British Colony on the shores of the Pacific. The romance of the thing has every attraction;—but the realities it presents to enterprise energy and industry are no less enticing—There can be no doubt that a very large population will gather there at once—that Civilization Law & order will prevail, that all the complex machinery of artificial life will be rapidly set in motion—and those who are among the first arrivals will have the best chances. Now it seems to me that you are just the man for such a place—your five years residence in Canada has given you the requisite knowledge of life in a new Country. Your visits to the Upper Lakes and to the Mining Regions on Lake Superior have taught you to rough it on the water, & in the Bush & I might add the Rocks—your business habits, as well as a professional man as in working the large concern with which you were connected in Cornwall adapt you for almost any position in life—and in the new Country there will be abundant choice—Why may you not be Sol[icito]r. Gen. or Attorney General? You have good interest at home, and might I should think get a Govt. situation there, if you desire it.[131]

Taken with the idea, Henry immediately wrote to Sarah, who replied:

Acton Green
August 12th 1858

My dearest Hubby

Yours of the 23 24 25 of July reached me on the 10th. Many thanks for it darling and for every atom of Love contained in them.

Your proposition of Vancouvers' Island was a little startling at first—from its great distance away—but I am quite ready dearest to consider that as our future home if it pleases God to direct our steps thither. Many thanks for the Newspapers which have given me the opportunity of reading what has been published respecting the Colony. Papa says it is a much finer *climate* than Canada and one which I think would suit me better—the extremes of heat and cold not being so great. My dear father so fell in with your idea of the advantages of the place that before we had said a word to each other respecting it, he wrote to Lord Salisbury for a useful letter to Sir Edw. Lytton, by which he expects at least to get a favorable hearing—there will hardly be time for an answer before this mail leaves—so I fear I shall not be able to tell you the result this week. My father wishes to defer writing to Mr Featherstonehaugh until he finds his assistance is necessary—for the same reason in writing to the mother. I said nothing about Mr Ed. Geach's influence—for if able to save it, it may hereafter be of service to themselves if however my father cannot manage it alone, no time will be lost in bringing every power to bear. Just now every body is away from London so you must not be disappointed darling if matters are not concluded as quickly as you might expect. I have been eagerly searching for what information I can find respecting the country. I have as yet found nothing about the island itself but in Douglas's journal in the years 1825 & 6 of his botanical wanderings along the river Columbia from Fort Vancouver, he mentions many beautiful shrubs, trees & flowers which we cultivate in our gardens and are so familiar with that to see them again in so distant a country, would be something like meeting the face of an old friend. He gives also a good account of the kind & inoffensive ways of the native tribes. Frost, he also notes did not commence until the 15th of December. I am glad to see by one of the papers you sent, that the idea of making a railroad from Lake Superior to the new settlement, comes under the consideration of the journalist. I hope it will be taken up by the Canadian government for doubtless if there were direct connection between the two Colonies it would be of vast importance to Canada and soon put her on a par with the Mother country as far as commerce is concerned. Papa's idea is that it would be a capital thing if you could be associated in exploring the line of communication being employed under government—which would give you a claim to their further provision for you. I have no voice in the matter dearest for I know not <u>what</u> to wish for, except to <u>be with you</u>, have our little ones with us and the means where with to exist.

I have been interrupted here my darling Hubby by the receipt of your letter of the 29th enclosing copies of Mr Vankoughnet's, Mr Grassette's and Judge Haggarty's letters—all of which are very kind and to the point but those of the two latter I like best (G's & H's). The same post brought a kind letter from Lord Salisbury to my father giving one to Sir Edw Lytton but added that the appointments which he sought were he <u>feared</u> all preoccupied—however we shall see. My father seems heart & soul in the matter— and is I think not a little pleased that <u>you</u> should have <u>proposed</u> what he in <u>his own mind</u> thought of for you, but did not know whether you would like it. He has great confidence in Lord Salisbury's power and willingness to oblige—and says if anything is to be had he will no doubt be able to get it and if not <u>now</u> yet when anything turns up. I have however (notwithstanding the scruples mentioned in the first part of my letter) enclosed a few lines with your letter to the Capt. telling him what my father is doing and asking him to get Mr Edw. Geach to use his influence <u>now</u> in getting you the appointment you desire. It was better worded darling than I have expressed it here—but the purpose was the same. I commend the whole affair dearest Love into the hands of our God and feel comforted....

Do not think my own dearest Hubby that I am getting or wishing to value less your dear precious love—on the contrary—the more my heart expands towards Him who is the author of all our happiness—the greater is my tender love and attachment towards my dear lord and master—towards whom my heart yearns and longs to be near him—but we are not yet divine dearest, neither of us. If you were darling, you would judge me a little differently to what yr letters express to me that you do—you would not brake [sic] a bruised reed—and you would know that I am not a free agent in these matters which affect our separation. My prayer and desire is, (God willing) that as soon as an appointment is procured I and the little ones should join you at once, and enter our adopted country together. This dearest is my truest wish. We could join you at Toronto or elsewhere and proceed together. I fear there will be opposition to this plan—but—provided you desire it, it is what I should most certainly wish to do—and what is more, God helping me, will do.

1/2 past 10 pm. I feel so relieved, my darling Hubby in having so freely opened my mind to you and so inwardly happy and quietly elated do I feel at the possibility of seeing you before very long—that I cannot sleep without expressing it to you. How earnestly do I hope that our present painful separation will soon be no more—when we do meet again darling. God grant nothing but death may again divide us. I have a presentiment dearest Hubby, that an appointment will be found you and that I shall ere very long find myself with our three little treasures ensconced in the cabin of a fine large Steamer ploughing her way across the wide Atlantic, until at last we all four find ourselves in the warm embrace of a dear, devoted, Hubby & father— but I must not build my castles too quickly—or they may all tumble down— but in the mean time darling you may like to know once more how willing and ready I am to join in any [?] which shall best secure our speedy union and lasting happiness. Should Emily have no better prospects in view, how would you like her to join us? provided she were quite willing to do so. I should like it much. For her own sake however I wish her a happy home of her own in which ever country she may prefer. I should have said England, but knowing her partiality for Canada perhaps she might choose that.

Your account dearest Love of the prevailing habit of drunkeness is indeed awful, and would in itself alone I should say be quite sufficient to make the poor women miserable and unhappy. How can it be otherwise, darling for those who have <u>any</u> thoughts about the future or <u>love</u> for those who so forget their high origin and demean themselves below the brute beasts and set at naught the holy will of God. It is <u>sad sad</u> that a young Colony looking for prosperity and happiness, should take such <u>direct steps</u> for bringing a <u>curse</u> upon it instead of a blessing. Should Canada therefore never be our home it will be a great reason for never regretting it—but <u>why</u> should <u>all new settlements</u> dearest have the same propensity? It surely is an evil to be most vigilantly guarded against for what may not <u>arise of it</u> and to what may it not <u>lead</u>?

…Your Box is by this time I hope fairly launched on the wide seas but I have not yet heard from Mssrs Carman & Pearson by <u>what</u> ship it is gone. I trust it will reach you safely and that its contents will please you and help to beguile the time until you shall have your little wifie and bairnies there all pulling at your beard together!!! How will you like that, my beauty!….

The dear little children are quite well and flourishing. Mary sends you a little note written with her own hand but guided by mine in all except the kisses which are quite genuine—the words are also the same. I must now go to bed my darling Hubby. "Holy Angels guard <u>your</u> bed. Heavenly blessings without number—gently falling on <u>thy</u> head!"

Ever & for ever <u>Your own</u> lovingly attached & devoted little wife.

[P.S.] Aug. 13th. I have nothing more to add this morning dearest love beyond the assurance of my <u>fondest love</u> and <u>attachment</u>. You cannot I think want to hear <u>that</u> again! Do you dearie? Is it <u>still</u> music in your ears? I <u>trust</u> it is. My poor heart would be sadly seared if it were not so. Oh you must love me my darling and help me to bear the ills of life as I <u>hope to help you</u>. Warm & tender love is so <u>great</u> a sweetner to daily troubles and trials that I cannot give <u>my</u> consent to your becoming more <u>indifferent</u> towards me although to know that yr bodily & mental sufferings are less is a cause for thankfulness so long as this our separation <u>must</u> endure but I think I see the <u>day breaking</u>. I feel a change is coming that the day is close at hand when I shall say adieu forever to all dear ones here and leave the shores of old England for the arms of my <u>own true Love</u>—my "<u>dear old lion</u>" my <u>darling Hubby</u>. <u>God</u> be <u>with us</u> dearest, <u>where ere</u> we go. This is all I ask….[132]

The advice Henry received was unanimous. With his background in the mining industry and his law credentials, New Caledonia (soon to be called British Columbia) was the place to go. The first great influx of gold seekers flooded into Fort Victoria in the summer of 1858 following reports of gold discoveries along the Fraser River earlier that spring. The population of the fort ballooned from several hundred to 10,000 some few months later. Results from the gold diggings were relayed via San Francisco to Toronto and England.

Vancouver Island was established as a colony of Great Britain in 1849, having earlier been a part of the vast fur-trading preserve of the HBC west of the Rockies. In 1858 the mainland became a separate colony, British Columbia. James Douglas, former HBC chief factor and governor of Vancouver Island, also served as governor of British Columbia. In this way, legal jurisdiction of the goldfields came under British control. In September 1858, no further civil appointments had yet been made.

Henry's family cast its social net wide. Old friends, friends of friends, government officials and others were approached and solicited for assistance in securing Henry a position. The Marquis of Salisbury interested himself in Henry's plight. John Lindley approached Sir Edward Bulwer Lytton, secretary of state for the colonies.

My hope is, that you may be able to place in some situation under government in British Colombia [sic] my son in law Mr. Henry Crease concerning whom you will find a statement in a separate memorandum enclosed herewith. Much as I desire to receive such a mark of favor at your hands, I should not make the request did I not entertain the most confident belief that such an appointment would be conducive to the public service. Mr Crease's qualifications being as I believe peculiarly valuable in a colony like British Colombia, a strong constitution, a robust frame, a resolute temper, a practical knowledge of Indian life & the difficulties to be encountered in the N. American bush and the skill in the control of large bodies of miners, being united in his person to the manners and education of a gentleman and the professional knowledge of a member of the English Bar....his object is not merely to obtain employment, but eventually to settle with his family in the Colony, and that he would be ready to accept any appointment for which he is qualified and which is not unbecoming a gentleman.

For myself, as a man not wholly unknown in science and whose services have been freely placed at the command of government upon occasions of considerable importance, I should hope that this application will be regarded by you as one to which you may properly extend your favorable consideration.[133]

Henry himself wrote to Edward Ellice, George Simpson and Dr. John Rae[134] of the HBC at Red River, thinking that perhaps the influence of the company in the matter of civil appointments might be valuable. In London, Totty contacted Mr. White, a Member of Parliament who "knows A. G. Dallas intimately y[ounge]r. son in law of Govr. Douglas of Vancouvers Isld," and who unfortunately could not assist. Dr. Hooker offered them a loan of £200, which was declined with many thanks, with a request instead for "introductions to B. Columbia of persons having party influence at home." Anyone and everyone was contacted. Many of the letters of introduction included the information that "It is believed that a number of Cornish Miners will join Mr Crease when established in British Columbia and he is ready at a moment to proceed there from Toronto where he now is."[135] It must have been a discouraging blow for Henry to receive the news in Totty's letter.

> Aug 18th My own darling Hubby. I am quite désolé at the unexpected blow received today upon our hopes of an Appointment in Columbia. Sir Edw. Lytton writes that he regrets very much not having a single one to give away, all being previously filled up. I feel this disappointment darling very keenly for I was not prepared for it—and had hoped that the clouds were beginning to clear up—but now it seems to me they are thicker than ever—and so impenetrable that my heart is almost ready to sink my darling. But how will you feel dearest when you receive this. It would be such an unspeakable comfort if we could feel convinced beyond a doubt as to the right course to pursue that, I think, would enable us to concentrate all our energies upon the one main object and make some progress in it. My father says he has no parliamentary influence and he fears can do nothing more than what he has done. He never asked anything of any govt before and this is not very encouraging. He has been talking the matter over this eveg. and he says if he were by your elbow he should certainly advise you to be quite independent of Government favor. It is at the best of very questionable advantage and what is more—you are never free never your own master. His words are my darling tell Henry to depend upon himself. It is far more satisfactory—far better pay—if I were he I should find my way across to the new settlement and with my law set up for myself—there is to be plenty of simple legal cases and if he only manages well he may take a high position and soon make people of necessity go to him instead of his going to them. I can offer dearest no opinion of my own on the subject—all I desire darling is to be able to live

together again, that is as plain as certain—as that I am now writing to my dearest love my darling Hubby.[136]

Finally, following the advice of a family friend, Henry decided to leave at once for British Columbia so that he would be in a position to accept any appointment that might arise. Totty wrote, attempting to keep up his spirits. "There is no more news about B. Columbia & the Hudsons Bay Compy.— everything in that direction appears at a dead lock—although I don't be- lieve it is—workings are going on underground wh make no noise at pres- ent and until the thing is done we may hear nothing of it."[137] Henry penned in his letter book: "Failing B. Columbia there remain Australia, N. Zealand, China, India & Hope."[138] Indeed, Henry's spirits were low. Writing to his father, he confessed worry over Sarah's ability to adjust to rough circum- stances of life in the colonies. "I much fear Totty's adaptation to any Colony—if I succeed and can offer all sorts of comforts, it wd smooth mat- ters wonderfully." This worry progresses to absolute despair. "I have given up the idea of seeing them [Totty and the children] again—and so may as well go off at once to where the best chances are—and remit all I can get back to England to support them and paying debts & get a home for the girls [his sisters], one or 2 of whom perhaps, when things get a little settled would not object to come out to me to keep house."[139]

On 1 November,[140] Henry left Toronto for New York, and two days later he boarded the *Arago*, bound for Victoria. He arrived at Esquimalt Harbour in early December, and lost no time in developing friendships with other men of a similar age and social position resident in the colony. In fact, he spent his first Christmas with Semlin Franklin, a prominent merchant and his family, and was invited by James Douglas to his home for New Year's Day.[141] These early contacts in many cases developed into lifelong friend- ships, which extended to Sarah upon her arrival, and overseas to family in England.

Henry's first and most important conquest was James Douglas. At the earliest opportunity, armed with his credentials and testimonial introduc- tions, he had paid a formal call on the governor, a customary practice among newcomers of Crease's social standing and pretensions. He was primed with information about Douglas provided by Totty, who sent him copies of despatches published in the *Times* in London, which notified him of Douglas's botanical interests (to which Henry could converse most freely, having been exposed to high-level botanical discussions among Sarah's family for years!) and snippets regarding Douglas's family connections and acquaintances held in common. He approached Douglas and appears to have struck a resonant chord. They took a liking to each other. Crease built up a high regard for Douglas and his efforts to shape the new colonies. Douglas, for his part, respected Crease's legal knowledge and appreciated his opinions and viewpoints on a variety of matters.

Communication by mail in those days took several weeks. By February 1859, Sarah still had no news of Henry since his arrival in Victoria. Her letter of 1 February reflects the anxiety and concern she felt in not knowing his movements or circumstances. The sense of physical and emotional loneliness brought on by prolonged separation (it was now 10 months since Henry had left his family and England) was compounded by the ever-present worries of their financial position.

Acton Green
Feby 1st 1859

My <u>dear darling</u> Hubby

Morning noon and night and every hour besides are you in my thoughts and fondly cherished in my heart of hearts. Every night as I lay my head on my pillow, do I <u>wonder</u> where you may be laying yours—and I humbly and earnestly long for the days—when each others arms shall be our sweetest pillows. <u>Fondly</u> darling Hubby do I think of the happiness we <u>have</u> enjoyed and feel thankful that the remembrance of it is still so fresh and comforting. Your dear letters are so precious to me and the burthen of them of such vital interest that the anticipation of them almost unnerves me and makes me all unstrung and out of time. If I should not hear from you by this mail, I shall try to console myself with the idea, that you thought it best to hear and look about a little before writing down, & sending home your hopes & <u>fears</u> respecting the new country. Of the latter I trust there are not many although we must expect a shady side to every picture on earth, and my own expectations are much moderated since reading that little book on Brit. Columbia, and am glad it has done so for there's not much wisdom in dwelling on the pleasures of air bubbles. My trust darling Hubby is in the High and Mighty One who inhabiteth Eternity—and my <u>great</u> comfort is in <u>His Power</u>. To <u>His</u> Care I commend you, my precious Hubby, every night & morning, and

Salish plank houses (in the foreground) of the Songhees Reserve make a contrast with the non-native Victoria across the harbour. This view looks east towards the James Bay Bridge linking the Fort and town with "the Birdcages" and James Douglas's house. St. Joseph's Hospital and St. Ann's Academy are barely visible in the centre beyond the bridge. (BC ARCHIVES A-2699)

Looking north from "the Birdcages" towards Wharf Street and the Point Ellice Bridge, 1859 (detail). Note ships at anchor at the foot of today's Fort Street. Lt. Richard Roche photo. (BC ARCHIVES G-4031)

earnestly and fervently do I pray that His Grace may ever prevent and follow you. That He may comfort and encourage you by a <u>constant assurance of His presence</u> and <u>loving watchfulness</u> and that <u>His</u> riches may be <u>yours</u> both now and forever....

Now darling that I have let off a little of that which thank God is still and I trust ever will be uppermost in my mind, I must look in my diary and see what has happened since I wrote for the mail on the 17th of last month. First I as noted down. Tues. 18th Dunny and self took Mary & Susey to a little party at Dr. Hooker's—and much they enjoyed it and returned laden with pretty things from a Xmas tree, which Mrs Hooker had bestowed much time and trouble upon ornamenting. There were but two other children besides theirs and ours—so that the kindness shewn to ours I felt doubly meant. Sir William Hooker came in to see the tree. wh. when lighted was beautiful— and he made many kind & pleasing remarks upon little Mary & Susy whom he had not seen before. Willey and Charley were their little beaux for the eveg. You would have been amused to have seen Willy's loving attentions to Susy—who was rather annoyed than pleased by them. And their roll in the curtains was also great fun. Dr. H. enquired very kindly for you, and thought you had done well to reach San Francisco so soon. Emily and I generally manage to pass several hours together in the course of the week—either she comes here, or I go to her. We both enjoy the meeting. She calls me a little bit of home and I call her a <u>little bit</u> of you. Granpapa has had two new teeth put in, which makes him look quite blooming. I do not understand or like to enquire into his mining affairs, but I understand (from Emily of wh. please take no notice) that he considers the compy. (Whl Vor I presume) have treated him fairly and done what it could for him. Now this is the case perhaps dearest you may know better than I. At all events I trust it is as good as they would represent—but I have so poor an opinion of their principles altogether that I would rather have heard he had <u>nothing whatever</u> to do with them.

How often have I thought of the truth of your German proverb—who touches pitch, I forget the original words I believe they are still sanguine of great undeveloped riches in Whl V. but <u>here</u> the cry is, it will all end in a bag of smoke although I will not <u>admit</u> that such would be the case under proper management. However I would rather that all I loved were <u>quite clear</u> of it, as all such large and dangerous subjects....Natty has been busy in our affairs lately—getting in the Mortgage money and putting it in the Funds, now that Edward is available and will cooperate with him. <u>All</u> our money is now in the

Funds £1100—odd—excepting £40 in a Bankers deposit account wh money is the surplus of the N. Hill furniture money and is in the names of Natty and myself being all that is available for an emergency—and out of which we propose (should your letters confirm our views) sending you shortly, a box of law books with a wig and gown—for in consequence of a letter in the "Times" from their correspondent we hope and believe that the money cannot be better applied. I anxiously await darling your first letter from Victoria after an interview with the Governor, before which nothing will be done.

Your notes of the passage from N. York I value exceedingly darling, most especially knowing the difficulties under which they were written. I traced the writing in ink, before letting it out of my hands—and read it aloud twice here before giving it to Emily who forwarded it to Plymth. from whence I have recd. it safely....

Poor Papa is gone to Town to day to put himself in the dentist's hands and have 4 teeth extracted preparatory to a whole set of new ones, the expense of wh. will be rather more than he likes. Since I wrote last he has had an interview with Lord Salisbury. When he urged him in person to use his influence with Sir B. Lytton in some practical form so as to procure an appointment for you in B. Columbia—Lord Salisbury promised he would go to Sir Edw. Lytton the next day and do his best—which I doubt not he has done although we have heard nothing since.

Natty and Sally spent a few days here last week—both have colds—especially Sally who is I think far from strong—and still much debilitated by the meazles [sic]. She is getting quite out of heart at the prospect of no little Nat. but we try to cheer and encourage her hope as much as possible. I have lately had two or three spells at my old songs and have each time felt the better for it. There is so much that is happy & pleasant connected with them that I almost forget the present in dreams of the past. My voice is stronger and clearer now than it was all last year so that I have a little more satisfaction in using it especially as fondly & (may be too flatteringly) indulge the hope of its one day rejoicing the heart of my precious—darling Hubby. Dunny declares I must come for a run in the garden before it is dark so my darling

Heres a ⬭ kiss and now away.[142]

On 18 December Chief Justice David Cameron, who was Governor Douglas's brother-in-law, appointed Henry as the first barrister qualified to practise on Vancouver Island. Henry quickly attracted clients and worked on cases involving conveyancing and litigation. He kept himself as busy as he could bear, doubling as his own clerk. It helped pass the time, and the monies earned were diligently saved and applied towards a home for Sarah and the girls. Soon it was clear to him that here, in this new colony, was an abundance of work and opportunity for men of his background and social standing. The key was making those crucial first contacts among early settlers and HBC officials.

By February 1859 Henry had made a good beginning, was in great demand and had a steady business. It was time for Sarah to join him. The first task was to arrange shipment of basic household necessities. Such items were not always to be found in Victoria's limited mercantile establishments, and, if available, they were exorbitantly expensive. It was much more economical for Sarah to crate their own furniture, linen, kitchenware and household goods, and to send them by ship ahead of her. The next step was to find other, socially similar individuals travelling to the Pacific coast with whom Sarah and the children could travel. A companion would ensure adequate propriety and, on a purely practical level, make it easier for a mother to deal with three young children and luggage on a long journey. One of the first choices for a potential travelling companion was the newly appointed Bishop of Vancouver Island, George Hills. Hills was ordained in January 1859 and indicated his intent to depart soon after for the colony. This was not to be, for extensive fundraising campaigns and negotiations with patron Angela Burdett-Coutts (who was to supply a church) delayed his departure until the following November. Sarah could not and would not wait that long.

In the meantime, Sarah packed. Her next letter to Henry tells of the preparations.

Acton Green
April 1st [1859]

My darling Hubby

I am coming! I am coming! When the Rose begins to blow!—What do you think of <u>that</u> darling. I can't wait for Mr Booker, altho' he is such a very good fellow! But I shall (D V.) come with the Bishop or some of his party, I expect, but I must not speak positively, as nothing yet is finally arranged. The money for the passage is however found and there is the first great difficulty over. Uncle Edwd has given me a good help towards getting it. He has cashed a Bond of the Hort. Socy for £100—and made me a present of £50 besides—so I think he has acted like a good old Uncle. I have been packing away, all this week darling—and to day completed the last of seven boxes, which on Monday are to go on Board the "Gomelza" which is to carry them round the Horn, and deliver them I trust all safe and sound into your care. If they don't sink to the bottom. I don't expect they'll burst—for all are strongly bound with iron—and with the exception of the largest & the smallest all are tinned inside—all of which Darling has cost no end of money. I don't think the Bishop sails before sometime in July but even then I shall very likely be with you dearest to see the arrival of the cases. At all events I will enclose you a memorandum of the contents, that you may have an idea of what is coming.

A New Copper Boiler–Baby's Bath–old Pentagon table–Toys–Blankets Muslin curtains from N. Hill, a few silver spoons & forks–Plated candle sticks and cruet stand–Green wine glasses &…(old fashion but very good) Brushes, Baskets, Counterpanes–Box of tapes & cottons–ditto, old treasures belonging to a dear old H.P.P.C.

B 2 Featherbeds–1 bolster–2 pillows–Guitar in case. Blankets–a few books– spices. & Box of light articles of dress–Fur Muff &&.

C Soap–starch–blue–few candles–Blankets–roll of carpet–toilet glass–a few books–& brown teapot.

D Body linen–Bed linen–Quilts–dresses &…1 pr boots.

E 1 Bolster–2 pillows–1 blanket. Soap for hands. Child's boots & shoes. Great fam[il]y Bible–Prints–few books, Riding habit & other clothes.

F Infants & children's clothes–some house linen–& some sketch books.

G 1 doz. old Port–5 bot. Champagne–2 bot Gin–sauces

So you see darling with such a good stock in hand—we shall want but very little more—to be quite comfortable—and for fear you should get too much—I will just enumerate all that I think necessary.

2 Bedsteads–for self & children

1 Table & 1/2 doz. chairs,

2 Washing basins–& jugs &…a few plates & dishes–a few cups & saucers

1 gridiron–1 frying pan–2 saucepans

2 wash tubs–2 small ditto (for plates & dishes &…) and 2 or 3 common basins of difft sizes—for puddings &…

I say nothing about the fireplace for I know not what may be the common thing—something of an oven. Dutch or American—would be very valuable—and a <u>kettle</u>. I quite forgot that.

If we can start with these comforts I shall be very thankful and God helping me—darling—I will do my <u>best</u> to extract all the good I can out of them—for the benefit of the whole community. I have got through the fatigue of packing wonderfully—but I fear you would be <u>shocked</u> were I to tell you, how Goody has primed me, with beer, wine, & brandy to keep me going! The work is however <u>done</u>—and not badly—and after a little more sleep I feel I shall be <u>none</u> the <u>worse</u> for it. Our little treasures are quite well—and have taken a lively interest in the packing business. Next Tues. DV, Susy and I start for Norwich and Carlton—leaving Mary behind to go with Grandpapa Crease to Plymouth—the old gentleman seems however in no hurry to return—so I have my doubts if little Mary will go at all. She shall do so however if it be possible—but my funds are already at the lowest ebb— & the passage money being so heavy £200 I shall not be able to bring with me any more household things—or I fear make any more purchases beyond what is perfectly necessary for the voyage for self & chicks. Many thanks to you my <u>darling</u> Hubby for the essence of sweetness contained in the three lines enclosed in Papa's letter. They were very very precious to me—and gave me a thrill all over—you dear old rogue—so here I send a deep loving kiss ⬭ to make you do the same![143]

Fortunately, Henry's reply to one of Sarah's earlier letters has survived. For all the many letters written by Sarah that are extant, not one earlier than this one survives from Henry. As well, this is the only surviving letter from Henry at this early time in Victoria and it provides interesting details of colonial life.

Government St. Victoria
12 April 1859
My sweet Wifie

Your letter of the 1st is now before me. I got into the P Off [ice] & helped to sort the letters or I wd not have had it till tomorrow. And my let[ter] would have had no reply. <u>There</u> wd. have been a <u>pretty</u> kettle of fish! I see darling you are expecting regular letters but I can you…promise them sweet one. It pains me very much to say so—as it is—you may imagine that doing all the copying of verbose Legal documents—drafting & settling them in the first place on all sorts of obtuse and unheard of questions that could only arise out of such a Colony as this.—going even to points of Imperial Jurisdiction & law of nations wh. I hardly heard the name of before keep one pretty busy tho' the <u>dollars</u> come in slowly—at least compared to what I wish.

It's quite disheartening. I make 5 or 600 dollars one week, and the next they are all gone. Tho with a decent library as I have now 85 books without counting my jolly & useful little <u>Cabinet Lawyer</u>! (<u>tell Dy</u>!) or those I am now going to acknowledge.

And this subject deserves separate & special mention—

I was met at Esquimalt—whither I had gone in a boat to pay a call at the Marine Barracks—by the Report that a huge box was waiting for me and there was no cart strong enough to dare the roads bet[ween] this & Esquimalt. It was my first day out since my recovery—so I could not go to see it. Indeed I was drinking in the balmy air & lovely scenery—soft tho' so rocky & wild. (Its' awful rocky & woody everywhere) that tho bursting with curiosity & heart beating with the thoughts that my <u>dearie's</u> handiwork might be there (your old Lion is the same <u>warm old lover as ever</u>!)—I wd. not quit the water—where I feel so much at home & comparatively happy.

I slept at the McKenzies at Craigflower (after Colville's place—Mr C was a warm friend of Mr. McKenzies)—who with the girls Mrs Mac & all his circle have been kindness itself &…having you there & the little ones when you arrive and the next morning opened it. In my haste I ripped off the cover put it back against the wall but unfortunately it fell back and one of the long rusty nails went nearly right thro' my hand.—left luckily—But oh what a glorious sight was there! I capered about the room, till Burnaby who allows great latitude to the effect of a parcel from home was perfectly amazed at my antics. How I <u>wd</u> have <u>hugged</u> you dearie had you been there—<u>you little Mrs Winnin' ways</u>!!!! Not a single thing in it which did not seem to me <u>the most</u> necessary & useful of all, till the <u>next</u> was in my fingers.

As I am known <u>now</u> to every one in the Colony, my box made quite a sensation—and has been since the object of general & affect, inquiries. A Box from Eng<u>land</u>—

How shall I thank you ah for the mementos It contained? I handled them all with moistured eye, darling. They seemed to bring the <u>packing them up</u> so vividly before me. Goody duly spectacled busy with her valuable contribution. The Dr. racking his brains to rob himself to serve my darling pet's 'hubby'—Natty earnest & anxious to put every useful book he could think of into the chest. Then Sally—fishing up <u>her</u> pleasant gifts dear little Dunny packing in hers—the dear little ones—with open eyes wondering what so large a package could mean perhaps thinking their old dad could not be so far away after all. Emily sending a glass wh. I much wanted—as our Antron one was broken on its way—and many more thoughts—all helped to swell the heart of the Absent One darling, but none more than the feeling that the little darling of all was there presiding over the packing & rejoicing that so many useful things would cheer up a loving old Hubby—and tie one more link in the Chain of Love which ties our Hearts in one—<u>across a World</u>!

Col Moody sent word to me today that he had written to the Colonial Office very strongly in my favor as a Barrister here (unsolicited by me)—and had sent in a Report to the Governor (Douglas) (who called <u>twice in person</u> to see me during my illness <u>now past & altogether gone</u>—a thing he was never known to do before, requesting I might be made a sort of <u>Judge</u> for B. Columbia with a residence in <u>Lytton</u> at the Forks of Thompson's River & Fraser—[remainder of letter not extant].[144]

Extrapolating from this letter we can only guess that it is typical of the letters Henry sent to Sarah. He describes the colony in detail, its environs, the inhabitants and their activities. Several distant acquaintances were resident, making it possible for Sarah to associate names with families in England. The land was somehow less distant when it was inhabited by people who had some relationship to those in her own social sphere. This, combined with Henry's descriptions and drawings, helped to flesh out the colony. It was some time before she managed to confirm the details of her voyage to join Henry, but in the months preceding her departure from England, she sent out trunks and various containers full of items they would eventually need.

On 5 September 1859, after a tearful goodbye to family, Sarah with daughters Mary, Susan, and Barbara, in addition to a maidservant, boarded the *Athelstan* at Gravesend.[145] During the five-month voyage Sarah found enough to do and, needless to say, the six shirts she had planned to sew were not completely finished. Her letters to Henry's sister Emily and his mother give some of the details and are nice companions to the pen-and-ink sketches she executed of the children and crew members. She also wrote "home" to various family members.

Sarah completed a number of ink-and-wash drawings showing seascapes while on the *Athelstan* bound for Vancouver's Island. (BC ARCHIVES PDP3072)

Calm and balmy weather in September 1859 allowed outdoor activities. Sarah got along well with the other passengers, with the exception of one man, who asked Mary and Barbara if they wanted their dolly to visit their aunt and promptly threw it overboard! (BC ARCHIVES PDP4539)

7 October 1859, On board the "Athelstan"

My dear Emily…The Capt has just come in to say he expects we shall see some of the Cape de Verd islands tomorrow morning. I have been looking at the map with him & see we are now in the climate of yr. friends the O'Connors at Gambia… Here we are a month's voyage from England and I am thankful to say in a fine state of preservation—our worst time is I hope now over & since that we have had a delightful cruise—for the first week or 10 days after we left the Downs the dear children suffered more than I expected—and my servant being utterly useless I was obliged to exert myself until at last I was thinking I should be obliged to give up when all of a sudden the wind changed and we all revived to my great relief. Our fellow passengers could not behave with greater kindness and propriety had we picked them out of all our friends—they are all 3 gentleman of birth and behave as such. Poor Capt FitzStubbs to whom we all took too strong a prejudice in no way deserves it—he is a most good natured easy going merry fellow—full of jokes and childish tricks—indeed a great part of his time is spent in playing with & teasing the children especially Baby who is now quite at home with him and gives him as many kisses as he asks for...our Captain...is quite as kind & thoughtful as we expected also the Steward who does all he can to fatten the children and his good feeding is beginning to tell upon them— The days pass very quickly but I find it impossible to accomplish in the way of needle work any thing like what I anticipated. The general state of things is most inducive to an easy idle life—at least I feel I have not strength for any thing more—and fortunately more is not required. I hear dear Mary her lessons every day except writing and spend the rest in nursing Baby on my lap while reading or writing, playing chess or cribbage or the Concertina which I am learning in company with Capt. Lennard & his friend—and make about equal progress with them—Mr Walker the Barrister is a very quiet intelligent man—and in many respects reminds me much of dear Natty....[146]

My dear Grandma, we are now almost hourly expecting to fall in with a ship homeward bound wh. will carry our letters so I am writing before hand to have a few lines ready for you...I enclose a hasty copy of a sketch I made one day & wh. the Captain begged from me. I send it as giving a better idea of our party than any words would express. You & dear Grandpa will I am sure be glad to hear that my fellow passengers are as kind and gentlemanly in their behaviour to me as if they were our own guests at home...the heat is not so intense as I expected—but it gives us much headache and makes us very languid and sleepy. Yesterday we saw a couple of sharks but no hook being prepared neither were caught—indeed no fish has been taken yet although many efforts have been made.

On Sunday last (9th) we had a famous squall of rain with thunder & lightning wh. lasted about an hour—we were all delighted at the chance of having fresh water so when we of the woman kind were shut down close below—all hands on deck set to, to catch the water—and succeeded in saving above 1000 gallons. It was fine fun to all employed as we could testify by the jokes and peels of laughter we could hear over head. . . . our fastest rate of sailing at present has been between 8 & 9 knots an hour—but just now it is hardly two. We were becalmed off the Canaries nearly a week. I have many anxious thoughts about you all & wish I could know that matters were going well with you. God bless, protect & guide you....[147]

If Sarah appeared happy with her fellow passengers, they were equally delighted with her and the children. Her mother wrote: "Capt. Crease has seen the Capt who brought your letters, and all the gentlemen of your ship think themselves very fortunate in finding you so amiable, ladylike and agreeable and as for the children they are to them a constant source of amusement."[148]

The voyage ended on 23 February 1860 when the *Athelstan* arrived in Esquimalt Harbour and unloaded its precious cargo. What a reunion it must have been for everyone concerned. For Henry, it was the end of a long, anxious exile. How hard it must have been for him to leave his family behind against his inclination to have them with him during those difficult times. He no doubt reflected on the words of Dunny, who earlier had told him: "It would be far better to have a little place ready to receive her & make her comfortable at once, than by taking her & the children with you, seeing them all in want of that wh. it was not in your power to give them."[149]

Dunny's advice to him showed much wisdom, and to his credit he accepted it as the best plan for their future. She later encouraged both him and Sarah by saying: "it is a Stern master that holds you apart & says, not yet, wait a little while & then you shall meet again, never I hope to be parted more."[150]

Susy feeding at 1. P.M.
a wooden frame, to keep the dishes from running off –

Sarah also recorded shipboard life in sketches and letters. (BC ARCHIVES PDP4758)

Plate 1. Engagement photo of Henry Crease, June 1849 (detail). From original daguerrotype by Beard, London.
(BC ARCHIVES A-8923)

Plate 2. Engagement photo of Sarah Lindley (detail). From original daguerrotype by Claudet, London.
(BC ARCHIVES F-0494)

Plate 3. "My mother, Sarah Freestone Lindley," 7 April 1848 by Sarah Lindley.
(BC ARCHIVES PDP1380)

Plate 4. "My father, John Lindley," January 1848 by Sarah Lindley.
(BC ARCHIVES PDP4831)

Plate 5. The Lindley home and grounds, Acton Green, Middlesex, 1861.
Attributed to Barbara Lindley. (BC ARCHIVES PDP4568)

Turnham Green
Dec 27th 1849.

Behold us! dear Henry as you would have found us
on the evening of the 25th (Xmas day) had you been
a little bird and looked in upon us. Do not
criticise my rough sketch too severely, but if it should
recal to memory bye gone days and create some
kindly emotions for those at Turnham Green, the
whole desire of my heart will have been attained.
I must tell you we were a very merry party, for I do
not think you would guess it, from the sober faces
above. Our visitors to dinner were the Bishop (for the 1st time)
our old friend Mr Curtis (who asked Edward to remember him very kindly
to you when he wrote next) your brother Edward. Mr Teil, and
our cousin Anthony Freestone. In the evening three of the

Plate 6. Page from Sarah's letter to Henry, 27 December 1849. (BC ARCHIVES MS-2879)

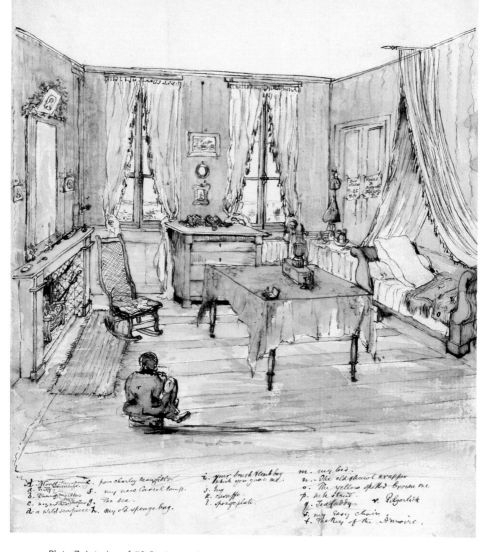

Plate 7. Interior of #9 St. James Square, Notting Hill, 1853. This is Sarah and Henry's first home after their marriage. Sarah has identified certain items in the sketch with the letters **A** through **T**. (BC ARCHIVES PDP4610)

A likeness of Henry "the companion of my wanderings"

B framed likeness "of Dunny"

C framed likeness "of my mother"

D "a wild seapiece"

E "poor Charley Mansfield"

F "my new Carcel lamp"

G "The Sea"

H "My old sponge bag"

I "Your brush & comb bag which you gave me"

J "jug"

K "Caragle"

L "Sponge plate"

M "My bed"

N "The old shawl wrapper"

O "the yellow spotted brown one"

P "Ink stand"

Q "Tea Caddy"

R "Pilgarlick"

S "My easy chair"

T "The key of the Armoire"

Plate 8. *James Bay*, 10 October 1860, looking south over James Bay to the "birdcages," the first legislative buildings. The white house on the far shore is that of James Douglas, then governor, and his family. The parsonage of the Rev. Edward Cridge is on the left while "Kanaka Row" houses of Sandwich Islanders (Hawaiians) are in the foregound. (BC ARCHIVES PDP2897)

Plate 9. *Bridge leading to Red Gover[nmen]t Buildings from the top of which this view is taken*, October 1860. (BC ARCHIVES PDP2898)

Plate 10. Panorama view of the Fort and town of Victoria taken from the "birdcages." James Bay Bridge (now site of today's causeway) leads north towards the Fort seen on the left, September 1859. The water on the right is today filled in and the site of the Empress Hotel. Lt. Richard Roche, photographer. (BC ARCHIVES A-2850, A-2852)

Plate 11. This engraving from R.C. Mayne, *Four Years in British Columbia and Vancouver Island*, is based on Sarah's sketch of 1860 (illustrated on previous page).

Plate 12. Henry Crease, ca. 1861.
Charles Gentile photograph.
(BC ARCHIVES G-590)

Plate 13. Sarah Crease, June 1863.
George Farden, photo on leather
(pannotype). (BC ARCHIVES G-2520)

Plate 14. *Interior of the old Hudson's Bay Company Fort*, 25 September 1860. This watercolour (like the others Sarah sent to her father that year) includes extensive notes and identification on the reverse. (BC ARCHIVES PDP2892)

Plate 15. *Fort Street*, September 1860, is a pastoral featuring a bullock cart and dirt road. Sarah identifies on the reverse: The Methodist Chapel, the old HBC stockade and "old tumble down HBC barns." In the centre is a white house she describes as "our first house in Victoria an old wooden one built by the H.B.C." (BC ARCHIVES PDP2891)

A Colonial Life

::::::::::::::::::

The boom town of Victoria had few houses suitable for families, as most of its energies were directed towards individual immigrants and itinerants. Henry took Sarah and the children to a small set of rooms he had rented. He had worked long and hard to provide this accommodation, and had managed to furnish it very simply to cover their basic needs. The household goods Sarah sent ahead of her were wisely utilized. Sarah's mother approved of Henry's arrangements, but nevertheless still cautioned Sarah to be ever mindful of their financial situation. She wrote: "I find your good Husband has a nice little house for you and things in it, all paid for, take care dear child and make any shift rather than get into debt."[151] Many years later, daughter Susan recalled these rooms:

> The children's and nurse's room was reached by a ladder. Needless to say the door of this had to be locked everytime Mother or nurse entered or left it. There were patches of tin adorning the lower part of the walls whose use was soon made apparent by scratchings and rubbings behind them. The appearance of a big rat one day sent the nurse in hot pursuit of a cat and the 3 children into a bath standing ready for use, from which they dared not step while they and the rat had the room to themselves.[152]

From this place they soon moved to a cottage on Fort Street. Within a few months, the nurse left them to be married.

It must have been an awesome task for Sarah to assume housekeeping responsibilities in such a setting, even though she had previous experience in London and Antron. Nevertheless, it was her new life, and she accepted

Sarah Crease, ca. 1867. (BC ARCHIVES A-1217)

all the challenges that came her way. The Crease family remained in these quarters until the autumn, when they were offered a more economical situation. This came in the form of an invitation from Benjamin William Pearse, then assistant surveyor for the colony, with whom Henry had struck up a great friendship, based in part on their similar background, as Pearse was born in Devon.[153] He was a bachelor, yet lived in a massive stone house that he had just built for himself. "Fernwood" was much too large for just him alone; would the Creases share it with him? It was ideal. They moved in on 15 October and remained for 18 months, during which Sarah sent back to England several small ink sketches depicting the scenery around the house and panoramas showing the view overlooking the Strait of Juan de Fuca, seen from atop "Rockland" hill, behind Fernwood. *The view from our Dining Room Window at Fernwood* (not illustrated) and *View from our bedroom window at Fernwood Victoria Vancouver's Is.* were enclosed in letters home. They were sketched at the bottom or ends of pages, and later were clipped out and inserted in family scrapbooks amid other artworks and photographs. These works are rough sketches with no pretense of aesthetic merit. They were purely a means of transferring information. Clipped portions of correspondence surrounding the sketches indicate their direct relationship to the text. For Sarah they functioned purely as an alternative means to communicate; for example, *View from our bedroom...* is complete with annotations and identification of geographic features. The site amid rocks and bushes overlooks a lowland area leading to the ocean. The view is a panoramic sweep from Chatham and Discovery Islands across Mount Baker to San Juan Island. Sarah captured this view again in a watercolour *Which was taken from B. W. Pearse Esq. Drawing Room Window at Fernwood, 19 November, 1860* (not illustrated). It contains similar components and illustrates the same breathtaking view.[154]

Between September and November 1860 Sarah painted a series of 12 watercolour drawings depicting various scenes around Victoria, including views of the old HBC fort (finally dismantled in 1862), street scenes showing the growth of wood frame commercial buildings, views of the harbour and Indian villages. She sent these drawings back to John Lindley in England. Lindley was a commissioner of the 1862 International Exposition to be held in Hyde Park, London. He displayed these drawings in the "British Columbian department of Canada" section along with other local products

"A wretched attempt at giving you an idea of the view from our Dining Room window," October 1861. (BC ARCHIVES PDP1406)

Sarah sketched the magnificent views looking over Oak Bay towards Mount Baker. (BC ARCHIVES PDP4737)

such as foodstuffs and mineral specimens. They were labelled as "the work of a colonial amateur" with no acknowledgement of the artist. Sarah recorded: "My father's sole object in displaying these poor sketches to the public, was simply for the interest of those who had dear friends or relations in Victoria B.C. and for those who might be thinking of going to that Colony themselves."[155]

Not only are the 12 watercolours pleasant scenes of Victoria in 1860, they also have wider historical importance. On the reverse of each sketch, Sarah wrote detailed information about the significant components of each scene. In this way she combined written and visual means of communication to transmit as much information as possible. The sketches themselves document human aspects of the colony. The bustle and activity of 1860 Victoria was captured in three works: *Fort Street, Yates Street* and *Government Street*. Both brick and wooden buildings were shown, along with a clutter of traffic on boardwalks or in the street. The commercial prosperity of Victoria comes out most clearly. Further written references on the reverse of the sketches indicate specific businesses, activities and associations. "Our first house in Victoria an old wooden one built by the H.B.C." and "The 'Colonial' & 'French Hotel' Restaurants, Henry's Chambers are just beyond the 'French,'" are but a small sampling of the written notes she included in order to make the sketches function to their full potential as sources of information on the colony. In contrast to these "colonial scenes," Sarah also executed views illustrating the previous regime of the HBC. *Interior of the old Hudson's Bay Company Fort* and *S. W. Bastion of the old Fort with 12 nine-pounder guns* record the original Fort Victoria that by 1860 was obsolete. As noted on the latter, "The old stockade facing the picture are now all pulled down (Jan. 1861) & open the harbor to the full view of Fort St." She recorded the transition of Victoria and its growing population as the seat of colonial government in *Bridge leading to Red Gover[nmen]t Buildings from the top of which this view is taken, James Bay,* and in *Victoria Harbour & James Bay from the Church Hill*. These set the colonial settlement in the wider context of the surrounding landscape.

A third category of subjects centred not on the white presence in the colony but on the Indigenous population. These sketches place the infant white colony in perspective by providing objective information about the size, situation and composition of the Indigenous settlement, and subjectively reveal clues as to the attitudes and perspectives of the artist. Sarah's *Indian Village opp. the Town* (not illustrated) isolates the reserve from its relationship to the town across the harbour. This reflects the prevailing attitude of her day, one that caused the Songhees reserve to be moved in the first place from a site even closer to the town (consequently covered over in 1859 by the "birdcages," the first government buildings). To someone unfamiliar with the physical geography of Victoria, there are no clues to anchor the village in place in relationship to the white settlement. Sarah does, however, attempt to describe the unfamiliar architectural type in understandable terms and adds notations such as "built of <u>rough</u> planks of wood & small trunks of trees" and includes a floor plan. Similarly, *Tsartlip Indian Huts outside the Governor's Garden* presents a close-up view of the Tsartlip people and their habits and housing. Although details of landscape and setting provide context, again the scene is isolated, with no glimpse of the governor's garden and house, or any white presence. It was clear that for Sarah, as for most settlers, human habitation in the colony was very much "us and them." This attitude was typical of British colonials, who believed the rhetoric of imperialism that portrayed the British as civilized and Christian in heathen, dark and uncivilized lands.[156] Sarah did not relate well individually with the Indigenous population, but she was nevertheless curious about their habits, customs and appearance.[157]

Initially, the Creases were on an extremely tight budget. As a barrister, Henry relied primarily on commissions from private individuals. He was not a member of the colonial government or a political appointee, so did not have a fixed salary. He had to seek out his clientele and, to maximize income, could not afford clerical assistance. Sarah helped him out in this regard, as she had in the past, by making book copies of all his legal correspondence, keeping his letterbook and doing accounts. The pressures of domestic responsibility made it impossible for her to do it all, and the first few years of Henry's practice were particularly exhausting. Diligence and initiative eventually paid off, for in October 1861 Crease was appointed attorney general of the mainland colony of British Columbia. The family remained at Fernwood until he was settled in New Westminster and had a house built for them, which they promptly named "Ince Cottage" after

A view of Ince Cottage and the Fraser River beyond. Designed by architect John Wright, the cottage had a sitting room, two bedrooms, a kitchen, a storeroom and a servant's room. Various outbuildings include a fowl house, root house, woodshed and chicken yard. The cottage is surrounded by vegetable gardens, fruit trees, raspberries, gooseberries, currants and strawberries. Flowerbeds and shade trees were soon planted. Richard Maynard photo. (BC ARCHIVES A-8317)

New Westminster on the Fraser River, ca. 1862–1864. Government House is on the left. F.G. Claudet photo (detail). (BC ARCHIVES A-3328)

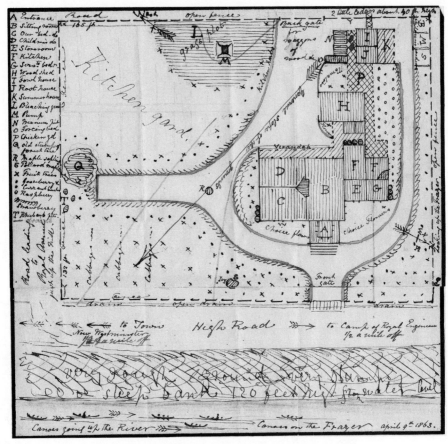

Plan of Ince Cottage and gardens by Sarah Crease, 1863.
(BC ARCHIVES CM/C815)

Henry's home, Ince Castle in Cornwall. The house was located on Sapperton Road, a half-mile outside New Westminster and midway between the settlement and the Royal Engineers camp.

In 1862 the whole Crease family moved to New Westminster. The journey there, by the steamer *Caledonia*, was even more eventful than usual. It "took three days because the paddlewheel became disabled and the rudder dropped out. It was only when a passenger managed to rig a substitute with the aid of iron curtain rods (being taken to the new home) that the steamer was able to proceed."[158] Slowly the steamer made its way across the strait and up the mouth of the Fraser. Sarah took advantage of the slow movement of the vessel and made three rough sketches depicting the vast, unsettled forests along the Fraser River below New Westminster. She sent these to her father, enclosed with letters. They are snapshot views, completed on the spot and with no attempt at refinement. But despite the fact that they were roughly executed, being little more than line drawings, the sketches capture the isolation of the young settlement. They are of an identical size, horizontal in format, and are divided roughly into two sections. The lower half represents the river, and the upper half the broad panoramic sweep of shoreline as it was visible from the water. In each sketch the rough, treed and mountainous terrain is evident. Two views are devoid of human activity yet, when combined with the third sketch in the series, are placed in perspective. The third sketch, *Our first glimpse of New Westminster*, 11 May 1862, combines the elements of river and shoreline with the human scale. In the foreground is a canoe, while the middle ground contains the "first glimpse" of a jumble of frame buildings constructed on a hillside up from the water's edge. It really must have seemed small and insignificant set in the dramatic setting of nonstop forests and looming coastal mountains.

It is interesting to compare these first impressions with the more finished sketches Sarah completed in New Westminster four months later. One of these sketches, titled *The Frazer, New Westminster B.C.*, has all the same components as the earlier ones, yet it is given human scale with the inclusion of people in the foreground, steamers on the river and settlement in the middleground area. It was created at leisure and carefully delineated with an attention to detail and composition. Subjectively, it transmits a very different feeling, and a change in Sarah's attitude and viewpoint. The wildness and isolation are gone, replaced by tranquillity and harmony. The people in the foreground are seated overlooking the river and the passing ships. A picturesque grouping of wind-torn tree trunks and birds flying over the river completes the impression. After several months' residence, Sarah appears to be more comfortable and at ease with the environment. She next undertook a series of sketches that would provide detailed information about her new home to loved ones in England. These sketches were meant to reassure her family that despite its isolation, New Westminster was manageable. Two further sketches showed the Crease home in its rough setting: *E. End of Ince Cottage, New Westminster, B.C.*, and *Ince Cottage, N.W., View of Pine Stumps on banks of the Frazer as taken from bridge over first Ravine.* In

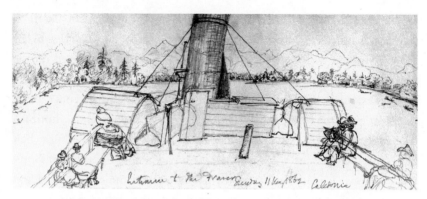

Henry Crease sketched this view on board the steamer *Caledonia* as the Creases approached their new home in New Westminster. (BC ARCHIVES PDP1413)

Our first glimpse of New Westminster, 11 May 1862. Sarah's quick sketch while on board the steamer shows how small the settlement looked amid forest and mountains. (BC ARCHIVES PDP1414)

both instances Sarah paid particular attention to her depiction of Ince Cottage. It includes as much detail regarding construction, layout and size as could be conveyed. A floor plan and layout of the gardens provided further details. It was important for her that she show as accurately as possible her new life, and that both she and Henry had succeeded in making a home from the wilderness. In both sketches the residence, although nicely detailed, represents somewhat less than one-fifth of the entire sketch. The remainder of the sketch puts the cottage in context—that is, its actual setting. Property lines are indicated by fences, and the rough "colonial" setting is revealed by vast fields of tree stumps. Sarah shows the important activities

Hills Bar, just down river from Yale, was probably the richest claim on the Fraser during the gold rush of 1858. (BC ARCHIVES HP62584)

of claiming and clearing new lands. Comparison with a contemporary photograph of Ince Cottage shows how accurately she drew the scene.

The family's move to New Westminster in 1862 did little to ease their financial situation. Expenses of moving, building Ince Cottage, and raising a family constituted a large draw on the limited salary of a colonial official. To add to the anxiety, creditors in England, claiming unresolved bills, approached family members in hope of satisfaction. In 1863, Barbara Lindley wrote that "the creditors say [they] had been very patient with Mr Crease but they never expected to have been treated by him as they had, but if he would pay them £125 and £15 within the next 6 months, they would not proceed against him."[159]

The family continued to grow. Two children were born to Sarah while in New Westminster: a fourth daughter, Josephine, on 7 August 1864, and a son, Lindley, on 13 March 1867, when Sarah was 40. An additional pregnancy in 1865 was not carried to full term.

Daily life in the colonies was demanding. Sarah adapted, and was more successful in doing so than Henry thought her capable of when he wrote in

This pencil sketch, completed four months after Sarah's arrival in New Westminster, depicts a tranquil river view, much different from her first impressions.
(BC ARCHIVES HP62582)

In September 1868 Sarah sketched a number of scenes in the Fraser Valley, Hope and Yale. (BC ARCHIVES HP62581)

This view from the "End of Ince Cottage" looks towards the house of neighbour Arthur Bushby. September 1862. (BC ARCHIVES PDP4559)

Ince Cottage is seen on the top left, overlooking the newly cleared forest. (BC ARCHIVES PDP4560)

Barbara, Mary and Susan Crease while at New Westminster, 1865.
Charles Gentile photo. (BC ARCHIVES A-8336)

1858: "I much fear Totty's adaptation to any Colony."[160] The situation of housing was one challenge, but the responsibilities of childbearing and child-rearing were even more demanding. Despite several miscarriages, between 1864 and 1872 Sarah gave birth to four children while she tended the three others born before leaving England. Preparation for childbirth rested solely on the mother to be. Gone was her support network of family. Instead, she had to rely on nearby settler women. Nurses were scarce, and the busy and irregular schedule of the local doctor made it impossible to be assured that someone would be in attendance at the time of birth. She also had to be mentally prepared for the possibility that this support system might break down at the last minute because of unforeseen circumstances such as inclement weather, illness or accident. New relationships among fellow female colonists

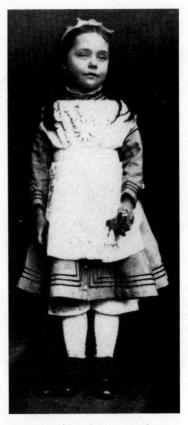

Josephine Crease, age 6.
(BC ARCHIVES HP22993)

were crucial. The anxiety of being so far away from home and family at this important time was not eased by experience in birthing. Having three children already, Sarah knew what to expect, but the solitariness of her situation worried her. As her mother wrote, "I am very anxious for your safety, my dearest Totty....are you likely to get sufficient attendance during your confinement? I wish I could send you a nice nurse, but is no use wishing you are to[o] far, far off, I can be of no use...."[161] As it turned out, her mother's fears were confirmed, and Sarah's first birth in the colonies was unattended. Henry recorded: "At 9 am wife safely delivered of a girl after 1/2 hr labor. I only being present. Nurse (Mrs Keary) came shortly after Mr. [Doctor] McNaughton Jones."[162]

In the colonies, despite the lack of available help, large families were

Susan, Josephine and Mary Crease with their father, Henry Crease, when at New Westminster, 1867. (BC ARCHIVES A-8314)

common. Responsibilities for raising a family effectively curtailed much of the women's "free time." No diaries exist for Sarah from 1860 to 1868, and she wrote sparingly until 1863, indicating the domination of family duties over leisure. The few clues about her non-household activities are terse notes recorded by her husband in his daily diary that list the occasional visit made and regular Sunday church attendances.

Although unaccustomed to doing without, Sarah had some experience in making do with very little. Her upbringing had been comfortable, but had always stressed the virtues of self-reliance and thrift. This attitude served her well upon marriage to Henry and, in light of their financial difficulties in England, it became a practical necessity. This experience was invaluable in her new life in the colonies. Although not unfamiliar with fashion and current trends, she followed the instruction and training given by her mother and made do with less frivolous items in household furnishings, food and fashion, favouring items that, although current, would be serviceable and worthy of investment. Reducing daily expenses and foregoing unnecessary ones was a major way in which Sarah could assist Henry. Purchases of new clothes for herself or material to make dresses for her daughters were foregone. In 1869, following the death of their mother, Barbara sent out a trunk full of linen, clothes and jewelry, both as a means of sharing the legacy and to help Sarah with the expenses of buying clothing for a growing family.[163]

In addition to bearing and raising children, women were generally responsible for running the household. The absence of many customary amenities required a major adjustment on the part of middle-class women abroad. Sarah Crease found it "rough to live in, and lacking every mechanical contrivance that tends to be labour saving."[164] A myriad of duties related to the physical maintenance of the house and furnishings; the cleaning and upkeep of personal items such as clothing, linen and bedding; and the acquisition, processing, storage and preparation of food. Many of these activities were seasonal. Winter was a time of indoor work such as mending, sewing and refurbishing. Spring traditionally brought a turning out of the house and its effects, scrubbing down the winter's accumulation of dirt and grime, taking advantage of the balmy weather to air bedding and linen. Spring through summer were times of intense activity relating to production and gathering of garden produce. Crops and vegetables planted in the spring were tended through the summer, and finally harvested. Berry and fruit picking and vegetable gathering led in turn to canning and preserving. Autumn brought fall crops, stockpiling of foodstuffs and preparations for winter.

Sarah mentioned these activities in her letters and daily diaries, and featured some in her sketches. A diagram that accompanied a letter home illustrated the division of the land surrounding Ince Cottage, with space labelled for the various vegetable and berry patches and fruit crops.

The lack of servants had a big effect upon the children, who, as soon as they were able, shouldered a portion of household duties. Eldest daughter Mary was eight when they moved to New Westminster, and two years later had become indispensable to Sarah. She assisted with the younger children and took on certain housekeeping responsibilities. The perennial problem of obtaining servants had a major impact on Mary, as Sarah notes: "want of servants. Can only spare Mary to go to school."[165] Sarah's three eldest girls were of great assistance in raising the younger children. The girls were 10, 9 and 7 in 1864 when Josephine was born. They were experienced helpmates for Sarah with babies Lindley (born in 1867), Harry (born in 1869) and Arthur (born in 1872). Such responsibilities, however, affected their education, as is clear in Sarah's letter to Henry's sister in 1869:

> Mary has attended the school [Angela College] for a few months, but has not yet returned after the holidays, everything being so unsettled, and baby so delicate & myself not strong enough to do without her help at home…it is with me a constant subject of regret that they [Mary, Susan and Barbara] are not learning all that girls of their age should be learning…from the constant pressure of domestic drudgery….[166]

Domestic responsibilities were at times eased by hiring servants or domestics, although budgets only permitted one or two at a time. Sarah's letters home to her sister and mother frequently mention the comings and goings of servants and the problems associated with employing good help, which was obviously a constant concern. A few months before the birth of Josephine in August 1864, Sarah wrote, "Soon to be without a servant. Ellen leaves in a few days—Should like to have a man and his wife for permanent servants."[167] A month later: "Parted with Ellen and glad at last to get rid of her. Indian boy only now—but a <u>dear</u> one. Self not very well. Obliged to stay in bed—Dear Henry and Mary so kind in managing the housekeeping for me."[168] The following month: "Recd a woman servt Matilda Mahoney from Victoria a few days before confinement."[169] A notation in her letter-book explained that from August 1864 to January 1865 there were many omissions "from want of time to enter them—cause little baby in arms—and no servant."[170]

Problems with servants continued throughout the next year, due primarily to the employment of a Miss Blanche Compigne, referred to the Creases by friends in Victoria.[171] Her conduct was the subject of scandal. In March 1865 Sarah wrote her sister-in-law a "long acct of Miss Compigne and the great coolness of those who sent her to us—her lover Mr. Brown quickly given her the slip."[172] In May, after having a miscarriage at five months of pregnancy, Sarah wrote her sister enclosing "a letter from Miss Compigne to her Mama. [I am] trying to get her a good husband in our neighbour Mr. McCrea."[173] In June "Miss Compigne has left us today for Mrs. Goods—The time had fully come for her to leave."[174] "Miss Compigne married <u>to-day</u> Walter Moberly Esq. just made Asst to Surveyor General at £500 per annum."[175] From August 1865 until the following March, the Creases employed a "Big Irish woman"[176] named Sarah. In May 1866, with Henry away on circuit, Sarah wrote:

> Dearest Hubby, We have all been longing to let you know what a charming Chinaman we have got. I don't know <u>when</u> we have had things so comfortable as since he came. He is clean, orderly & industrious, bakes & cooks to our hearts content—and (what we most feared about) washes the clothes <u>quite as well</u> as Sarah at her best. So dearest—on <u>this score</u>—we have all been in an incessant state of rejoicing to have got rid of our <u>great</u> aversion! [Sarah the Irish servant] and to have in her place such a <u>real</u> treasure! Although this will only reach you at Yale, yet I think it will make the journey down the pleasanter, to know how <u>comfortable we</u> have been! <u>God</u>, I'm sure sends <u>such</u> Chinamen, as all <u>good things</u> come from <u>Him</u>, & I'm sure we daily thank Him for His gift.[177]

Sarah's whole attitude towards servants—her treatment of them, high expectations and uncompromising standards—is typical of her white middle-class counterparts. The Creases first employed available white women, then through necessity turned to young Indigenous boys and women, then later, as Chinese immigration increased, relied on Chinese men. Servants continued to come and go with great regularity. Some were dismissed because of unsuitability—viewed as an inability to understand what was required, or an unwillingness to do it—and others left of their own volition.[178]

The scarcity of servants and problems associated with them was not unique to the colony or to colonial life, but was made more critical because often the servant in question was the only employee and responsible for a large role in ensuring the smoothness of domestic life. If the servant left, the wife had to take over, shouldering a double portion of physical labour, whereas for most families in England, the loss of a servant would represent a temporary inconvenience, and the duties could be shared by the remaining servants until a replacement could be secured.

Leisure was regulated not only by the duties of business and the home, but also by the seasons, which determined the type and amount of home responsibilities. Relaxation, social activities, and diary-keeping and letter-writing occurred primarily when the demands of domestic chores and responsibilities were fewer. Almost no personal records and little correspondence issued from Sarah during the summer. Copious letters in the fall described the events over the previous few months, and calendar annotations of the past year were compiled in December or January.[179]

Henry's diaries provide a sense of the social side for this period. He wrote brief entries such as seeing "the old & new year in at Trutch's House on Fairfield farm," dining at the home of Peter O'Reilly and his family, "Evg at Gov. Seymours," and attending a "Grand Ball at Gov Kennedy's Victoria V.I. (Castle Cary)."[180] Outdoor activities included outings to houses of friends in Victoria: "Left with little Mary for VVI [Victoria, Vancouver Island] in a visit to the Alstons," and family picnics "up the arm [of the Gorge] with the Pearses t[a]xing but pleasant," or at the seaside. "In afternoon walked with wife & the 3 children to Gonzales Hill. Tea & hot cross buns—in the sands of Foul Bay at the foot of the hill—with fire." New Westminster outings included a four-day trip to Yale, attendance at the opening of the Alexandra Suspension Bridge, "boating and trip to Burrard's

Inlet" and "picnics to the head of Pitt Lake & up the Coquitlam."[181] Sarah refers to "visitors and gay doings."[182] These pleasures were simple and not dependent upon monetary expenditures. Even in 1878, economizing continued. Sarah writes to her son at boarding school and tells him how they celebrated Henry's birthday: "We did him all the honor we could without spending money, & he took me with him for a nice quiet country drive— which I enjoyed much. We drank his health at dinner...."[183]

The other preoccupations of Sarah and other immigrant women were social acceptance and the nurturing of friendships. Most women left behind family and friends, so establishing new female networks in the new country became extremely important, not just to counter homesickness but to provide support among each other, to take the place of lost intimacy with sisters, mother and family.[184] The socially imposed barriers between white women and Indigenous women limited the female companionship of settlers to other settlers. The small number of white women in the area therefore created great loneliness.[185] During the 1860s the ratio of white women to men was as low as 1 to 100, improving extremely slowly by the end of the decade. Given this reality, women did not have the luxury of choosing friendships, but only the necessity of cultivating them. Settler society in the new colony was very different from that at home. Mary Crease warned her daughter-in-law of this based upon her personal experience in Canada West. "It is perfectly surprising how you get accustomed to a Colonial life—everybody is the same—not the same feelings to guide you as in England—perfectly different."[186]

Like most newcomers, Sarah also attempted to form social connections in hopes of furthering the position of herself and her husband. Establishing an economic and financial footing for the family might be dependent upon making and maintaining contacts to promote connections in the fields of business and government. Although one's initial social status was based on one's standing in England, relationships developed and grew on the basis of performance and conduct in the colony. Sarah and Henry Crease were there because the colony offered chances for opportunity and advancement. They arrived in the colony with an inherent social standing created primarily by Henry's profession and to a lesser degree by Sarah's position as the daughter of a gentleman. When he arrived, Henry had letters of recommendation from influential men, which went a long way in establishing credibility and favour. He developed friendships with earlier immigrants such as colonial surveyor Benjamin Pearse, registrar general Arthur Bushby, and former schoolfellows Chief Justice Matthew Baillie Begbie, contractors Joseph and John Trutch, and public servant Edward Graham Alston. Such social and personal contacts had to be formed and nurtured to ensure chances for further recognition. In short, the "old boys' network" was alive and well. The Creases mixed principally with those of their own type: British emigrants of professional or governmental background. The wives and families of these men were, by extension, Sarah's preferred acquaintances, although her longest-standing friends remained those she cultivated in her years at New Westminster. She undoubtedly felt an affinity with these women, who were similar in age to her, raising young families amid colonial conditions. Agnes Bushby, many years her neighbour in New Westminster, and Mary Moody, wife of Royal Engineer Richard Moody, became Sarah's intimates, and their close contact continued by letter despite geographical separation.[187]

As staunch members of the Church of England, Sarah and Henry developed close friendships with various clergymen and their families. While in New Westminster they attended Holy Trinity Church, and in Victoria, they were members of the Christ Church and St. John's congregations. They attended church regularly (often twice a day in Victoria) and faithfully devoted themselves to scripture readings, personal prayer and reflection. The depth of their convictions is manifest in their correspondence to each other and to others. Bible verses, general religious discussions, advice for appropriate readings, and suggestions for spiritual comfort in times of stress and sorrow occur throughout their daily journals and diaries. In later years Sarah was active in church affairs, including fundraising and charitable work.

Sarah became extremely rigid in her religious beliefs. There is no known reason, as little in her early life suggests such a path. Although her mother had strong religious leanings, her father never professed any interest, and he stayed at home while the others attended church, a situation Sarah viewed as natural and normal as a young adult. By the 1860s she had become increasingly intolerant of other religions, had specific opinions regarding the importance of the Church of England, and referred disparagingly to

Methodists and Roman Catholics. This pronounced orthodoxy perhaps developed under Henry's influence but does not appear to have been unusual for the times. It was not uncommon for nineteenth century English Protestant middle-class people to hold narrow and often rigid religious views. With the increase in scientific examinations of nature and the world knowledge gained through colonial experiences, "a fervid Christian faith, now being challenged by intellectuals, was being clutched at and then held in a bigoted and highly emotional fashion. Suffering was inevitable, they felt in this sad, bad world, but true belief in Christian redemption together with heart felt devotion and constant prayer, could save every soul."[188]

Sarah's orthodoxy became public when she and Henry sided with Bishop George Hills in his dispute in the 1870s with Dean Edward Cridge. The dispute concerned the use of "ritualism" in church services and eventually ended in a civil court case that split the Anglican community in two; Cridge established his own Reformed Episcopal Church, taking with him roughly half the congregation of Christ Church. Sarah's religious principles even led her to write privately to her father just months before his death in 1866, when he was mentally confused and failing. Her letter, well-intentioned as it might have been, was scathing in its condemnation of Lindley's lack of religious conviction.[189]

VICTORIA'S ELITE

In 1866 the colony of Vancouver Island was annexed to British Columbia. For Sarah and Henry, the most singular catastrophe was the decision to locate the colony's capital in Victoria. It just did not seem fair. They had established a home, invested locally and believed they were finally on track. Now it was all for naught. Even brother Nathaniel in England realized the significance of this decision when he wrote: "The inconvenience and loss which your change of residence must involve is keenly felt by us all."[190] Not only had they built a home and were then in the midst of planning substantial renovations to it, but also Henry had invested heavily in land in New Westminster and Lulu Island. These investments, made in the names of their children, included a large stretch of land along the Fraser River.[191] Nathaniel offered financial assistance at the time.

Having some money to send Henry I have awaited myself dear of the opportunity of sending you £50 so which I am sure will be welcome just now— for the changes consequent on the removal of the capital will I fear be a sad blow to you all I trust that whatever happens Henry will not lose his appointment—unless he gets a better—He must do all he can in that way— not get disheartened or disgusted & leave the colony & start fresh where he has no connections and no position....[192]

As it turned out, both Henry's position and salary were reaffirmed, a situation that ensured that the "days of arrears of pay and no pay are gone forever."[193] However, the financial losses in land and property when New Westminster ceased to be the capital were not recovered for many years. With this forced removal to Victoria, again the Creases searched for suitable accommodation for their growing family. It was not an easy task. On 4 December 1868 they moved into "Woodlands," the home of James Bissett, an HBC employee on leave in England. "Have at last taken a house, smaller than our present one. Can just squeeze into it & hope not to remain long. Must wait patiently for a chance of buying land for a homestead. Prices all gone up so."[194] They remained almost two years, until October 1870, when they rented the "Gibbs house," a residence in James Bay. During this period two more children were born: Henry Hooker on 30 April 1869, who died the following year in June, and Arthur Douglas on 1 March 1872, when Sarah was 45. The family was now complete.

In the spring of 1871 the Creases "Bought [the] House of E. G. Alston esq. & land of Sir J. Douglas out of Trust Monies."[195] Alston, an old friend from England, was leaving the colony. He allowed Sarah and Henry to purchase not only the house but also its furniture. That autumn renovations to enlarge the house began, but in December, just before completion, the house burned to the ground, target of an arsonist. There was no insurance. It was a disaster of great magnitude, and the family had to endure the discomfort and inconvenience of a far-too-small rented house even longer than they ever imagined. In response, Sarah and Henry sent the eldest girls on extended visits with family friends. These visits were often undertaken not just for the obvious means of reducing numbers in a cramped residence, but as a means of offering the girls' services as helpmates to young mothers. To the girls, no doubt, it was a welcome relief from the close quarters of their own family, freedom from parental interference, and the opportunity to stretch their wings.

The following spring, negotiations began with John Wright, architect of Ince Cottage, for the construction of a completely new house on the same property. "Pentrelew" was completed in 1875. It was one of the finest and most substantial country houses in Victoria.

In 1870, when Henry Crease was 47, he was appointed puisne judge, responsible for conducting criminal trials throughout British Columbia. These trials, known as assize courts, were authorized by the government and held on a fairly regular fall and spring schedule. Criminal court matters occurring within the year were tried at either the spring or fall assize. Crease went on circuit, holding court in various settlements along the way. He was familiar with these long journeys. His first one had been in 1859, when, acting as defence attorney, he accompanied Judge Matthew Baillie Begbie on the assize route through the Cariboo. Later, as attorney general, he had also travelled to outlying settlements. The circuits, sometimes in the Cassiar region, sometimes to the Kootenays and Cariboo, lasted several months. Consequently, Henry was absent from home for long periods.

Sarah, in her capacity as the wife of a member of the Legislative Assembly, then an attorney general, then a judge, moved in a wide circle of society that embraced clergy, various governmental officials, businessmen and their wives. After the Creases had lived both in New Westminster and Victoria, this circle of acquaintances spread geographically as well. Sarah maintained ties with the women she first met in New Westminster, whose husbands, like Henry, rose through the ranks to become powerful and influential members of the government. Colonial and early provincial society retained this tight nucleus of families who had grown in stature because the men attained pivotal political positions. Families like the Pembertons, Pearses, O'Reillys and Trutches were in the same position. These connections, the friendships carefully maintained from those early years in New Westminster, the social acquaintanceships among the wives and families of Henry's colleagues, all contributed to a busy social life for both Sarah and Henry, and for their children.

Sarah went to greath lengths to involve her family in the social scene. One such example is a picnic she undertook in July 1870, while Henry was away on circuit. It was the last one of the season before Mary, Susan and Barbara returned to school in August.

> All Monday was occupied in giving invitations and making arrangements for our last seaside picnic, which proved to be rather an extensive one, between 50 & 60 children with some of their parents. I will simply mention the families—from some of wh. we had 5 or 6—Douglas, Helmcken, Munro, Carr, McDonald, Charles, Nagle, Ker, Jenns, Mrs Fellows & Miss Dela-comb, Mrs Nicholles & Ward. Emily brought in her party Mrs Trutch & Miss Zoe Musgrave. The Cridges, Ashes and Holmes with Florry King we asked but did not come....They all seemed to enjoy themselves so much as we could expect on such a hot day as it proved to be. All went off well, no one was hurt & no crockery broken. We had a long day from 11 am to 10 pm. The heat and fatigue was rather too much for me but I am nearly right again now.... Dear Mary cooked all the provisions, and as our drinks were of a very mild nature I do not think the expense can be ruinous.[196]

The decade of the 1870s was one Sarah spent in juggling the needs of teenage girls and babies. The emotional demands of puberty and adolescence were difficult to handle with a house full of toddlers and their own special needs. It must have been exhausting to manage everything. Henry had his duties away from the house and family, but Sarah did not have such an escape. Surely the emotion expressed by their friends Alexander David Pringle, the Anglican minister at Hope, and his wife, Marie Louisa, must be one echoed by Sarah:

> [The boy] is cutting his teeth which is an awful infliction on us....for the drudgery and never ceasing petty annoyances of 4 such little ones, sometimes is almost more than we know how to bear. If the physical labour were ten times as much, it would be more acceptable, provided it were constant & limited, but I cannot tell you the trial of incessant calls to do the work of nursery maids & housemaids, to both of us, from the time when we commence the day by washing & dressing the bairns till we put them to bed at night.[197]

Sarah acknowledged that for the time she was powerless to extract herself from the domestic situation. In response to Emily Crease's concern that she have a break and perhaps come to England for a visit, Sarah replied: "I should greatly enjoy such a change with my dear husband and eldest girls, but that is never likely to be, for I have quite given up all hope of ever seeing London again myself. My second little family quite precludes any idea of being able to leave them for such a journey, if there were no impediment in the way of means, which of course is as great as the other."[198]

During these years Sarah's letters and diary notations are filled with comments about the health of each family member. In March 1871 she records that everyone is ill. "Mary had neuralgia, Susy a bad throat & cough, Babs a bad foot with erysipelas & headache, Henry with rheumatism" (his first episode). The sicknesses lingered into June; unsatisfied with the medical care, they changed doctors.[199] Childhood illnesses passed from one to another. Susy exhibited symptoms of scarlet fever while on a visit with friends in Esquimalt, and thus remained quarantined there for two months, from December 1875 to February 1876. That November Mary developed a frightful cough and was dangerously ill with measles. The following month, on 9 December, Barbara came down with measles, followed by Josephine on the 11th and Lindley on the 24th. At Christmas, Sarah and Henry ate alone; everyone else was upstairs sick. Susan was finally out of quarantine on 9 February 1876 and sent to friends rather than return to a sick household, for by the 23rd, Mary was diagnosed with diptheria. March 3rd, Sarah notes "our darling child dangerously ill. Medical treatment ice morphine inject. Soda water, champagne beef tea & egg injections."[200] Four days later she began to sweat, and the fever broke. By the 29th she was recovered, but as Susan noted: "has cut off all her hair."[201]

FAMILY LIFE

As the girls matured, inevitably the issues of independence and romance emerged. Upon completion of school, Mary Crease, the eldest, wanted to be useful, and was allowed to teach at the Anglican school, but her sisters were not given this option. They were the daughters of Judge Crease and therefore, however tight money might be, were not allowed to accept positions for remuneration. Posts such as governess were offered on occasion, but had to be refused. Instead, they were allowed to attend friends of the family in times of illness, or assist with tending infants on a temporary

(BC ARCHIVES F-8827)

(BC ARCHIVES F-8825)

(BC ARCHIVES F-7378)

(BC ARCHIVES F-8826)

In the summer of 1878 the Creases visited Victoria photographer S. A. Spencer.
Clockwise from top right: Sarah, Mary, Susan, Arthur.

basis. The short and often cryptic comments in the diaries of Susan Crease, and reading between the lines in correspondence, indicate an almost desperate need to break away from the autocratic demands of the parents.[202]

As a matron in society Sarah held tight control over her children. She and Henry actively discouraged associations with those they felt of inferior social and economic status, particularly when the girls became of marriageable age. Suitors were not encouraged among the majority of the social set in which the girls revolved. Young men and officers in the Royal Navy ships stationed at Esquimalt were in constant demand in Victoria for dances and parties, but despite their popularity were not preferred as sons-in-law because of the potentially long separations of months and years necessitated by their naval careers. Well-born young men with little or untried financial means were also discouraged. Separation and financial insecurity were not acceptable to parents who had spent much of their adult lives affected by these circumstances.

One can see why Sarah became so rigid with her daughters, given her own circumstances in life. She vowed that they would not have to endure the same financial hardship and embarrassments that she had in her marriage. The Creases' early financial problems affected their prosperity in the colonies because they could not leave them all behind. The indebtedness lasted a long time and was compounded by changing circumstances in their situation, which put them two steps back every time they made one step forward. It altered Sarah for life and made it difficult for her to give her daughters the freedom to conduct their own lives or make their own decisions or, perhaps, their own mistakes.

Mary, as the eldest, had always been Sarah's chief support with the other children. Because of this, she was not able to enjoy the same freedom of childhood that her younger siblings would experience. Her schooling, although adequate, had been continually interrupted because of domestic responsibilities and moves from Island to mainland and back. Perhaps it was a need on Sarah and Henry's part to redress this situation, compounded by the practical reality of building a new house, and the consequent upheaval and cramped quarters of the rented house that prompted their decision to send Mary abroad. In 1872, at 18, she travelled to England to visit her relatives. Sarah wanted Mary to keep in touch with both the Crease

A view of Pentrelew from Rockland Avenue, looking across the back
garden to the house. (BC ARCHIVES G-6087)

and Lindley families. Although she longed to see England again, Sarah acknowledged that it was more important for their children to have a sense of
their roots and to maintain connections with family. Another reason for
sending Mary abroad was that a British background and first-hand knowledge of England was considered an advantage in Victoria society: "no one
else who is now in or who comes to Victoria or B.C. will be able to crow at
you for not having 'been to England.'"[203] Consequently, Mary took private
drawing classes in London, and also Latin, music and dancing lessons.[204]
She stayed with Sarah's sister, Barbara, and Barbara's husband, Edmund
Thompson, a clergyman, and also with her uncle, Nathaniel, and his wife,
Sally. These two had a young and lively family, much to the initial dismay
of Mary, who had hoped to escape young children on this time away.[205]
Mary attended her first ball in London, dressed in a ballgown purchased
especially for her by uncle John Crease.[206] She visited Turnham Green and
saw the old home and neighbours.[207]

Sarah's letterbook records many letters written between mother and
daughter. One of Sarah's first admonished Mary for writing to her friends

with news first, rather than her parents, thus making it quite clear that part of Mary's responsibilities involved reporting back by regular post. Mary's trip was conceptualized at 12 months, but as the reality of building Pentrelew progressed so slowly, the trip was extended, much to the delight of her aunt Barbara and uncle Nathaniel, who were loath to see her go. Mary was away for just over three years and she returned home not a girl, but a young woman who had already had at least one romantic yearning (towards a young curate, resident at her aunt's home).[208] The years away from parental control had given her a taste of new possibilities.

In 1876 Mary met James M. Richardson, a young officer on HMS *Amethyst*, which was stationed at Esquimalt for several months. He was one of many admirers, but paid special attention, visiting many times over several months. Finally, a few days after a dinner and dance at Pentrelew, Susan records: "Mr Richardson came up in the morning & stayed all day, slept the night. Things are coming to a crisis betw[een] him & Mary."[209] Richardson "had a long talk" with Sarah and Henry, who were adamant that there could be no engagement until he was financially stable. Therefore there was no public acknowledgement of a relationship. Susan noted: "he is to marry Mary some day I suppose but they are not to be regularly engaged yet as he cannot support a wife."[210] On 7 November Richardson and the *Ameythst* sailed for Valparaiso. "Heigh Ho!!" noted Sarah, who was relieved at his departure and confident that his absence would have the necessary effect on Mary. It obviously did, for several months later Mary wrote to break off the relationship.[211]

Mary continued to be in popular demand with the young men of Victoria, and family diaries are filled with notations about who visited, paid attention, walked her home and flirted. Mary seemed to fall in and out of love on a regular basis. Sometimes unrequited, as her sister noted: "James Douglas [Junior] came with Martha. Mary could hardly bear the meeting—she cannot get over her love for him—horrid man that he is!"[212]

Susan, just a year younger than Mary, appears to have been very much in Mary's shadow. She did not have the advantage of three years abroad away from the provincial scene and parental control, nor the exposure to English society and cultivation of social graces. She was also the middle child of the three eldest girls. Younger sister Barbara, although socially active, was often in delicate health, and as a result was pampered more than Susan. In Susan's mind, Mary was always the lucky one at love, and she the one never so lucky. Her diaries are passionately filled, listing the social comings and goings, the suitors, the rivalry and the frustrations of unrequited love and the need to be in love. "Poor me!" she writes. "Shall I ever meet anyone I like so much who will care for me I wonder! I do love him. I cannot help it—but must try & not let him know that."[213] Her writings show the frustration of her situation, and her views about her mother's inability to understand or even care. This view, common among adolescent girls, continues when she is a grown woman and is no doubt based on a certain reality. Reading the correspondence of both Sarah and Henry to Susan and Josephine from 1889 to 1890, when they were in England studying art, one would think the parents were instructing teenagers rather than women of 35 and 26. Sarah writes: "of course, you and Susie will take particular notice of the correct way of setting a table and everything connected with it and all sorts of other little things, experience of good taste your observant young eyes are sure to notice."[214]

Daughter Barbara seems to have been sickly on and off for years, suffering from recurrences of St. Vitus Dance (now known as Sydenham's Chorea), an after-effect of rheumatic fever, which she probably suffered in 1860 when "Poor little Babs nearly dying, Dr. Trible attended."[215] The symptoms were insidious, involving first a restlessness and irritability, followed by irregular, uncontrollable, jerky or twitching movements of the head, face and fingers, and slurred speech. She was able to recognize the early symptoms, and in 1877 her sister recorded: "Barbara first mentioned her fears of a return of St. Vitus Dance. I feel rather anxious & have advised her to tell Mama—if she does not, I shall." The following day, Sarah took Barbara to the doctor. "Our fears were not unnecessary," Susan writes after Barbara returns with a prescription and is again in bed.[216] In 1880 and 1881 Barbara was well enough to take extended vacations with friends, travelling to Yale, and later by steamer with her friends the Croisdailes, along the eastern coast of Vancouver Island and north to Metlakatla. In 1883, however, she was ill most of the year, but rallied in May for a month-long trip "up country" with her mother and father. At this time also, she became engaged to Henry Ridley, of Yale, a longtime family friend. The symptoms and weakness progressed, and on 24 September she and her parents left on the steamer *Dakota* bound for San Francisco and specialist doctors. Also in San Francisco at this time, Sarah underwent surgery for severe glaucoma. Susan was informed of this fact on 19 October: "First heard of darling Mother's having lost the sight of one eye—Had piece cut out of the other."[217] After 18 days' recovery, Sarah was finally able to visit Barbara in the hospital: "once again looked upon dearest Babs in St Mary's Hospital. Speech better, but strength, less."[218] Two weeks later, Mary arrived and she was shocked at her sister's weakened and skeletal condition. Eight days later, very peacefully, Barbara died. Her body was brought to Victoria and laid to rest in Ross Bay Cemetery. The loss sent her father to bed for a month, and was a terrible tragedy for the whole family. Susan's first reaction was "poor child & poor dear Mother!!"[219] The news had to be broken to Lindley by letter, as he was still at school in England.

> You know how very ill poor Babs has been; but at a distance its impossible to realize it. I did not till I saw her about a week ago—she was so altered from extreme emaciation, even her features were different...and the doctors seemed to be able to do nothing for her, could not discover the cause of her illness and were unable to treat it...We can't feel sorry for her that she is out of reach of all pain and trouble now, but for our loss we can't help being sorrowful...she died so quietly and peacefully.[220]

By the 1880s Sarah and Henry Crease were established members of Victoria's social elite. Through hard work and diligence, they now had an impressive home and gardens, were able to send their children to school in England, and had greater leisure time because the family was growing up. But beneath the surface were complicated undercurrents and tension. Money was and always would be a problem. The salary of a colonial and later provincial official was not exhorbitant. The expenses of a large family, with its expectations for education and advancement coupled with the need to fulfill social obligations through entertainment and philanthropy, made saving near impossible. The family was very conscious of expenses, and comments about costs incurred and the necessity for thrift are frequent in all their records. It may have been a subject that preoccupied the women more than the men. Susan wrote that "Mama talked to me the other day about our debts. Mary is going to give nearly all her allowance for the next 6 months. B[arbara] all but 25 dollars & I all but 10 as I have still 28 in the Bank. Dear Papa, is not to know anything about it. Mary is frantic to do something to earn money. I can only save & will do that as much as I can."[221]

Examining the mother-daughter relationships, tension of another kind is apparent. It becomes clear that despite an intense love, Sarah's relationships with her daughters showed a need to control their outward actions, with perhaps little acknowledgement or understanding of the daughters' needs to make their own decisions. As the girls became women and time marched on, suitors, especially young naval officers, continued to be discouraged, and opportunities diminished. In 1883 Susan noted: "George [Wake] came to dinner & I sang to him after—spoke again of our love & the hopelessness of the cause."[222] Neither parent seemed to be aware that the time for protection of their daughters from possible misfortune in love was over, and that the women needed to live their own lives.

In 1883, just before her death, Barbara Crease became engaged to Henry Ridley. The engagement was surely allowed as a concession to a daughter who did not have long to live.[223] Susan had no such opportunities, and remained unmarried, although at age 41 had a passionate yet platonic friendship with then–Lieutenant Governor Henri-Gustave Joly de Lotbinière, who, at 77, was a lonely widower.[224]

Mary was the only Crease daughter to wed, and she did so, at the age of 32, against the wishes of her parents. She married Frederick George Walker, whom she had known for three years. Although Mary and her sisters remained close (they acted as bridesmaids at the wedding), the estrangement between Sarah and Henry and their eldest daughter was not easily overcome. Like her father, Walker was an Englishman trained in the legal profession. Unfortunately, also like her father, he had a business failure and left his family.[225] Mary and her three children had to move into Pentrelew with her parents, as she had no independent means. History did indeed repeat itself.

In contrast, Sarah's relationships with her sons show little of the same restraints. They were encouraged to excel at school, and when they came of an age when the schooling in Victoria was no longer sufficient, they were sent off to England, as was customary at the time, so as not to miss out on

Josephine and Lindley Crease, 1878. S. A. Spencer photo.
(BC ARCHIVES HP24200)

a proper educational grounding that would prepare them for a professional adult life. Lindley was just 10 years old when he left for four years, and his departure was emotional and heartbreaking. Lindley was Henry's particular pet, and Lindley, in turn, doted on his father. The decision to send him away at such a young age must have been soon regretted. Sarah noted in her diary that for several weeks following, Henry was very low and despondent.

Perhaps because of this impact on the parents, Arthur was sent to England older, at 14. Midway through Arthur's years in England, Susan and Josephine arrived for a two-year stay. He was not quite as isolated as Lindley had been.

Only Mary, the oldest, and Arthur, the youngest of the children, married. Barbara, had she lived, might have married, but Lindley, despite two engagements, remained a bachelor. Susan, Josephine and Lindley remained at home throughout their adult lives. Most of their friends did marry, and the Crease daughters remained close to these friends, visiting and entertaining as before, and at times acting as godparents to the next generation of children. Susan searched for a mate throughout much of her adolescence and adult life; Josephine, nine years her junior, had the advantage of time to recognize the futility of such angst, after watching Mary's problems and Susan's emotional rebellion. She had her art as a passion, and focused her energy on lessons, sketching parties and, latterly, to the organization of the city's art scene.[226]

The marriage rate was much higher among other young women in Victoria at the time. In 1881 the average age for women at marriage was 20 years.[227] Surely the overly protective attitude of Sarah and Henry, coupled with extremely high, and perhaps unrealistic, expectations for their daughters, contributed to the situation, but another explanation was the reality of finances. The Creases had little actual wealth. They maintained social status because of Henry's position, but there was never any financial advantage or dowry to be brought into a marriage. This contrasts greatly with many of Sarah and Henry's peers in Victoria's social elite, where actual wealth was coupled with social position.[228] Without wealth to offer their children, all Sarah and Henry could do was require economic security from prospective suitors. This narrowed possibilities considerably.

SARAH AND HENRY

In 1880, when Sarah accompanied Henry on his circuit to the Cariboo, the eldest were no longer children, but young women: Mary, 26; Susan, 25; Barbara, 23; and Josephine, 16. Sons Lindley and Arthur were 13 and 8, respectively. Mary, Susan and Barbara were busy, active in their own social

On the lawn at Pentrelew, October 1890. Left to right: Henry, Lindley, Sarah, Josephine and Susan. (BC ARCHIVES F-6880)

circles that were composed of the sons and daughters of colonial settlers like themselves. They were popular, and their diaries attest to a constant stream of visits and visitors, tennis parties, sketching expeditions, church and other social activities. Josephine, at 16, was just completing her school studies, while Lindley was in England attending public school. Young Arthur, at 8, remained at home with his sisters, attending the private Boy's Collegiate School.

Sarah and Henry were gone for three months. The daily journal Sarah kept while on the trip is reproduced in full in this volume, as are letters she wrote to Lindley in England and her children in Victoria. Her journal indicates that she wrote many more letters to her family members in England, but these have not survived. Letters to Sarah from her children are also included in the following reproduction of Sarah's journal to give both sides of the discourse: parent to child, and child to parent. Together the letters

Henry & Self, ca. 1900. (BC ARCHIVES F-8823)

provide us with a glimpse of Sarah's family responsibilities and ongoing concerns while on her trip. In later years, Sarah and Henry travelled together on circuit on several other occasions, but the journeys were much shorter than the 1880 one, chiefly because the completion of the railroad in 1885 made travel much more efficient and less arduous.

Unfortunately, Sarah did not make sketches while on the 1880 trip. She tells Lindley that she did not feel the need to do so, but this is only partly true. At age 53, she was having problems with her eyes, which would lead shortly after to trips to eye specialists in San Francisco and a series of operations for glaucoma. In 1883 Josephine recorded: "Mothers R. Eye operated on for Glacoma [sic] in S.F."[229] In 1887 Sarah's diary notes: "Dr. O. M. Jones examd my eye. No stronger lenses to be had." In 1893 she again travelled to San Francisco for an operation on her right eye. "The left eye too far gone."[230] Eye problems had plagued her most of her life, and often caused headaches and fatigue. Consequently, her artistic output is quite remarkable. She produced a tremendous volume of sketches with great regularity over the years, beginning with the hundreds of fine pen-and-ink botanical illustrations and continuing through the illustrated letters and sketches completed on various journeys and holidays, and finally, the sketches she produced in British Columbia. In contrast to these hundreds of works, there are but a handful produced after 1877. With failing eyesight, uneven attempts would have frustrated and embarrassed her, so she just curtailed the activity.

She did maintain her interest in art. Diary notations by her family indicated that she was present on many sketching afternoons, attended art exhibitions, and knew both amateur and professional artists. She encouraged her children in a love of art. All became talented artists. Susan and Josephine even attended art classes at King's College, London. Josephine, in particular, continued to sketch right up until her seventies. In 1909 she was a founding member of the Island Arts and Crafts Society, and she served on its executive for over 30 years.

The 1890s were hectic and busy times for the Crease family. The decade began with a complete break in family routine. Susan and Josephine travelled to England, thus leaving Sarah and Henry alone at Pentrelew for the first time. In October 1889 they rented the home to a family for a six-month period and headed south to California. In April 1890 Henry applied for and received a leave of absence for an additional six months. The trip was planned to coincide with a large construction project at Pentrelew, which would greatly enlarge the house. Architect Leonard Buttress Trimen designed a three-storey tower and added round-headed dormer windows in the roof. The renovated house now included eleven bedrooms, two kitchens and pantries, two drawing rooms, water closets, and a large dining room, morning room and study.[231]

Sarah and Henry originally intended to visit friends and sightsee in San Luis Obispo, then visit England via Panama, but it was not to be so. Both were ill and abed for several weeks, then Henry "was confined to his room by a curious attack of something called 'Poison Oak,' wh. It is supposed he must have come in contact with while picking me wild flowers."[232] They returned to Victoria in late August. The *British Colonist* reported:

Sarah Crease in July 1896, at age 69. Eyres, photographer. (BC ARCHIVES A-8924)

Henry Crease with grandchild outside the family home, Pentrelew, 1887.

(BC ARCHIVES A-8943)

Hon. Mr. Justice and Mrs. Crease have returned from a lengthened trip to Southern California. Mrs. Crease's many friends will regret to learn that the change has not benefitted her health as was expected. In the journey from Victoria to San Luis Obispo both Mr. and Mrs. Crease suffered severely from la grippe. Mr. Crease was severely poisoned by poison ivy, and suffered much in consequence....Other than these unpleasant experiences, Mr. Crease stated to a reporter that they saw much that was interesting....Mrs. Crease has somewhat improved in health since her return. It had been the original intention to visit England via Panama, but the serious illness of Mrs. Crease compelled the abandonment of this plan.[233]

Sarah undertook many charitable works. She was involved on committees raising funds for hospitals and other social services. As the wife of a prominent official, her patronage was important, and she took care that her efforts were effective. Her philanthropy was in the form of personal commitment

Tea in the garden at Pentrelew, 1201 Fort Street, Victoria. Four children of
Mary Crease and Frederick George Walker with their aunt, Josephine
Crease, 1897. (BC ARCHIVES F-6877)

The Crease offspring, clockwise from top right: Arthur, Susan,
Mary, Josephine, Lindley, April 1903. (BC ARCHIVES F-6876)

rather than financial contribution. She and Henry were always generous in their support of the church and its various endeavours, contributing money when possible to special projects. It is noteworthy that amid the expense of building additions to Pentrelew in 1890 and the cost of sending Susan and Josephine to England, they made at least one substantial donation to Christ Church. Bishop Hills recorded: "Mr Justice Crease brought me $500 as a contribution from himself & Mrs Crease towards the erection of a new Cathedral of stone. They had a most narrow escape from destruction on a railroad bridge they were crossing on foot when overtaken by a train & they resolved to make a thank offering to God & this was the way they carried out their purpose."[234]

In her latter years Sarah was a founding member and honorary president of the Local Council of Women. Established in 1894, it was an organiza- tion promoting women's rights and the franchise. The Local Council of Women formed the Friendly Help Association to assist families in distress, and it was instrumental in funding a home for aged and infirm women. Sarah also served as a member of the Women's Auxiliary of the Royal Jubilee Hospital and taught Sunday School at Christ Church. Her religious convic- tions remained central to her life and were responsible for guiding and shaping her activities and interests. Both her diaries and correspondence indicate a continual self-examination and evaluation of her beliefs and life- style. In 1878 she recorded: "Self 52 years old today—and what can I say for myself! Alas! Alas! that I should be such a Christian dwarf."[235]

In 1896, after almost 35 years of public service, Henry, then deputy judge in Admiralty of the Exchequer Court of Canada, was recognized with a knighthood. He served his last day in court on 17 January 1896 and re- tired from the bench one week later. He retired to a life of recreational pursuits: of fishing, excursions and grandparenting. Sarah, now Lady Crease, was ready for retirement. As the wife of a leading citizen, it had been incumbent upon her to pay endless social calls and entertain at dinners and parties. The pace was relentless. Both she and Henry were happy to extract themselves from the demands of these many functions, preferring to spend the time with their family in a genteel home atmosphere.

They were grandparents. Mary and the children lived with them at Pen- trelew. The eldest grandchild, Madge, was born in 1886; next were twins

Sarah and Susan having tea on the veranda at Pentrelew. (BC ARCHIVES A-8944)

Freda and Joan, born in 1889, and Harvey, born in 1891. It was a busy household. Sarah was feeling her age. Besides the eye problems, she had rheumatism in her back and increasing deafness. In 1919, at 93, she fell and fractured her hip. After a long and painful recovery, she was confined to Pentrelew for her remaining years.

During the latter half of her life, Sarah channelled her creative energies in a voluminous correspondence with relatives and friends in Britain. These letters included those to friends from the colonies who had returned to Britain, and also to a generation of nieces and nephews and her own children, who were either at school or travelling. As Susan noted, her mother "was a letter writer with a charm and lucidity rarely to be found in these days."[236] She continued to record brief notes in diaries and highlight particular calendar dates in notebooks. These activities required blocks of time, and in some instances created a backlog. She then "denied myself to visitors and wrote letters to England."[237]

In February 1905, Sarah's beloved Henry died at the age of 82. They had been married for almost 52 years and shared many years of both pain and reward. Theirs was a true love story, which survived the trials of separation and hardship to become stronger with each passing year. The affection they retained for each other is remarkable. Sarah's letters to Henry and references to him in her diaries are always "my dearest Hubby" or "my beloved Henry." She refers to herself as "your fondly attached little wifie," while Henry calls her "My sweet Wifie" and refers to himself as "your own Lion." After his death, Sarah stayed at Pentrelew. She continued to be interested in national and local affairs until her death on 11 December 1922, at the age of 96. The Victoria *Colonist* reported: "Lady Crease was revered by all those who know her, being conspicuous during her whole life for her sense of justice and unusual degree of moral as well as physical courage. She was endowed with strong common sense, a deep sense of her duty both to God and her fellow man, [and] an affection for family...."[238] Sarah, Henry and her family are buried in Ross Bay Cemetery, Victoria.

Sarah, Lady Crease, 1911 (detail). (BC ARCHIVES A-8921)

Notes

::::::::::::::::

1 These succinct descriptions are credited to the anonymous Reader "C," who reviewed my manuscript in view of publication funding from the Aid to Scholarly Publications Programme, Ottawa. This reader and others were extremely helpful in their suggestions and criticisms of earlier drafts and for this I would like to acknowledge them.

2 Important and influential men such as James Douglas, Alexander Grant Dallas and others married Indigenous or mixed-descent women.

3 Veronica Strong-Boag and Anita Clair Fellman, Introduction to *Rethinking Canada: the promise of women's history*, 2nd ed. (Toronto, Copp, Clark Pittman Ltd., 1991), 8.

4 Susan Mann Trofimenkoff, "Feminist Biography," *Atlantis* (Spring 1985). This article lists various ideas she views as necessary multiple vantage points for feminist biography.

5 Joy Parr, "Gender History and Historical Practice," *Canadian Historical Review* (September 1995).

6 Peter Baskerville, "'She Has Already Hinted at Board': Enterprising Urban Women in British Columbia, 1863–96," *Histoire sociale/Social History* 26 (1993).

7 Susan Mann Trofimenkoff, "Feminist Biography," *Atlantis* (Spring 1985), 4–5.

8 The post-structuralist premise that identities are made in relationships is an underlying reason for historians' "self-conscious move towards the study of gender, rather than women." Joy Parr, "Gender History and Historical Practice," *Canadian Historical Review* (September 1995), 362.

9 Sarah Crease to Henry Crease, 12 August 1858. Crease Family Fonds, BC Archives. All further manuscript references, unless noted, come from the collections listed in footnote 11.

10 Actual pregnancies not carried to full term are probably reflected in comments made by Henry Crease to James Marigold, 30 March 1871. Henry says, "I have had 6 children buried."

11 The Crease Family Fonds (PR-1344) in the BC Archives was acquired over a number of years, from various family members, notably Arthur Crease. The series MS-2879 is catalogued as three primary groupings, with catalogue numbers AE/C86 representing the bulk of the correspondence and diaries of Sarah, Henry and their children, and most of the letters and diaries quoted in this book. MS-0054 represents Henry's legal papers and MS-0055 includes the documents of Henry and Sarah's parents and grandparents alongside many letters and papers created by all family members. In addition, MS-0056, a smaller grouping, was donated separately by the granddaughter of Mary Maberly Crease. In addition to this manuscript material are approximately 3,000 sketches, many photo albums and photographs, architectural plans and hand-drawn maps.

12 See Gillian Creese and Veronica Strong-Boag, eds., *British Columbia Reconsidered* (Vancouver, Press Gang, 1992).

13 *Rethinking Canada*, introduction p. 8, comments in reference to Margaret Conrad's article in this volume, "Time and Place in Canadian Women's History."

14 Carol Smith-Rosenberg, "The Female World of Love and Ritual: Relations between Women in Nineteenth-Century America, "*Journal of Women in Culture and Society*, 1:1.

15 Barbara Powell, "The Diaries of the Crease Family Women," *BC Studies* (Spring/Summer 1995).

16 *Ibid.*

17 This is a different conclusion than that reached by Barbara Powell in the above article. Powell views the motivation as a self-conscious attempt to preserve "texts intended for the public eye" and to be "self conscious historians of the family." Powell (1995), 57.

18 Evidence in letters written by both Sarah and Henry indicates that they each requested that their earlier correspondences, diaries and personal papers, which had previously been stored for them, be sent out to British Columbia. Likewise, after the deaths of parents, Sarah and Henry also requested that particular records (and also family mementos and small keepsakes) not be sold or disposed of, but instead sent out to them. This is a proactive approach to record-keeping, not merely the result of passive hoarding.

19 Although many other nineteenth century BC family collections include material from England or countries of origin, none contains the depth of documentation over generations seen in the Crease Family Fonds.

20 Joan N. Burstyn, *Victorian Education and the Ideal of Womanhood* (London, Croom Helm Ltd., 1980).

21 Contextualising the immigrant experience is demonstrated in Marion Fowler, *The Embroidered Tent: Five Gentlewomen in Early Canada* (Toronto, Anasi, 1982) and R. Cole Harris and Elizabeth Phillips, eds., *Letters from Windermere* (Vancouver, University of British Columbia Press, 1984).

22 For a complete account of this episode see Mel Rothenburger, *The Wild McLeans* (Victoria, Orca Book Publishers, 1993).

23 For further comparison, see Susannah Moodie, *Roughing It in the Bush or Life in Canada*, first published in 1852, which Sarah read at the time of Henry's first trip to Canada.

24 For further biographical information, see William Gardener, "John Lindley," *Gardeners' Chronicle* 158, issues 23 October to 27 November 1965. A full-length biography has yet to be written.

25 Sir Leslie Stephen and Sir Sidney Lee, *Dictionary of National Biography* (London: Oxford University Press, 1917), 1156–58.

26 Sarah Crease, diary, 1 November 1865.

27 Sarah Crease, notes on family history, 13 March 1912.

28 For biographical information on these men, see *Dictionary of National Biography*.

29 Inscription on reverse of ink portrait of Sarah Drake, BC Archives PDP4780. Augusta Innes Withers (ca. 1793–1860s) was a professional illustrator for floral magazines and "flower painter in ordinary to Queen Adelaide." Ann B. Shtier, *Cultivating Women, Cultivating Science: Flora's daughters and botany in England, 1760–1860* (The Johns Hopkins University Press, Baltimore, 1996), 180.

30 For information on the milieu of Turnham Green and its inhabitants, as well as details on family history, I owe a large debt to Lawrence Duttson, London, who undertook many searches on my behalf and whose forthcoming publication on Acton will include much Lindley detail. Likewise, Robert M. Hamilton of Richmond, BC, compiler of John Lindley correspondence and of historical horticulture, and Sarah Drake chronicler, has been of immense inspiration and great assistance in locating Sarah's published botanical illustrations and in assembling a database and index of Sarah's correspondence with Henry.

31 Advertisement for a Mrs. Taylor's School in Elysium Row, Fulham, quoted in Josephine Kamm, *Hope Deferred: Girls' Education in English History* (London: Methuen and Company, 1965), 136.

32 Inscription on reverse of ink portrait of Emma von Heinrich, BC Archives PDP8141.

33 Susan Crease, Reminiscences, n.d., MS-0055, BC Archives.

34 Charles Fox (1794–1849), line-engraver, was associated with John Burnet, whom Fox assisted with large plates after Sir David Wilkie's pictures. Fox's most important plates were, however, those of his own execution. He also painted in watercolours, mainly portraits of his friends. *Dictionary of National Biography*, 533. The BC Archives has a watercolour portrait of John Lindley by Fox.

35 Sarah Lindley to Henry Crease, 30 April 1850.

36 *Dictionary of National Biography*, 533.

37 This opinion is most clearly explained in Ann B. Shtier, *Cultivating Women, Cultivating Science.*

38 One example of this process is found in the BC Archives collection, which includes the pencil sketch, watercolour painting, engraved copperplate, artist proofs and a small number of signed engravings.

39 This is another historical example of women's work contributing to the hidden household economy, a practice occurring in England and also Canada (and discussed by Canadian historians such as Bettina Bradbury and others).

40 Barbara Lindley to Sarah (Lindley) Crease, 13 March 1860, MS-0055.

41 Mary Smith's parentage is unclear. Baptismal documents list Elizabeth Harriet (née Morehouse, formerly Hunter) and Edward Smith as parents for both Mary and her brother Thomas Edward. Yet family lore and certain public documentation maintain that Penelope Pitt, eldest daughter of George Pitt, the first Lord Rivers, married Edward Smith in 1784. Burke's Peerage and other social registers provide information on Penelope Pitt's siblings, but very little on her. What is confirmed is that she was first married to Edward, Lord Ligonier, and subsequently divorced by act of Parliament. Contemporary publications mention her remarriage to a "Captain Smith," but the information is inconclusive. Henry P.P. Crease, however, maintained that Penelope Pitt was his grandmother and that she was buried in the family vault in Mylor next to his infant brother. However, no burial records for this parish list her name during the appropriate years. Mrs. Edward Smith (whichever one) died in 1831 at Flushing. This is confirmed by independent diary entries. Family lore is strengthened by comments in letters regarding disposition of Pitt jewelry among Henry's sisters, and comments regarding the Pitt physiognomy reflected in certain Crease family members.

42 Charles Blachford Mansfield (1819–1855), chemist and author, was a contemporary of Crease at Clare College, graduating from Cambridge in the same year. Along with Charles Kingsley, another Cambridge graduate, Mansfield and Crease joined others in their efforts at social reform among the workmen of London. See *Dictionary of National Biography*, 975–76.

43 These schools, established among the slum dwellers in London, were inspired by those created decades earlier by socialist reformer Robert Owen (1771–1858). *Dictionary of National Biography*, 1338–46.

44 Lindley Crease, biography of Henry P.P. Crease, 1930, typescript version.

45 In 1845 Henry asked Susan Geach, whom he had known since a child, to marry him. Susan was consumptive, and her health was precarious. She agreed to the engagement, but made it clear to Henry that she would not last long enough to be married. It was, I suppose, a way to publicly acknowledge love and affection with the full understanding that the reality of her health prevented a life together. It was a very romantic and loving gesture. She died when Henry was in Turkey, in 1847.

46 Note accompanying birthday present, Henry Crease to Lindley Crease, 13 March 1901, "when I first encountered him [Nathaniel Lindley] at Lago di Como—and thence forward."

47 Correspondence between Henry Crease and his father, Spring 1848, indicates Henry's intention to come to Cornwall for the summer break and bring a friend.

48 Nathaniel Lindley to Henry Crease, 30 August 1848.

49 Chartism was a movement amongst the working classes that aimed at parliamentary reform. Such reform movements, in the wake of the French Revolution, did little to ease the minds of the franchised population. The movement reached a peak in London on 10 April 1848 at a mass meeting, followed by a parade and petition presented to the House of Commons. Authorities prepared for violent confrontation and sent the Queen to the Isle of Wight for safety. The Duke of Wellington was given military command and some 60,000 to 250,000 special constables, each issued with a special baton, were sworn in to increase the regular police. Many of the special constables had been pressured to sign on, others in romantic enthusiasm to defend their country and government from revolution. For further information, Dorothy Thompson, *The Chartists* (Temple Smith, London, 1984).

50 Lindley Crease, biography of Henry P.P. Crease, 1930, manuscript version.

51 Susan Reynolds Crease, biography of Sarah Crease, 1928.

52 Sarah Crease to Henry Crease, 27 July 1888.

53 "Odds and Ends of Family history—of the Creases...." 1914, Julia Parigiani (née Crease).

54 Henry Crease to A. Benthall, 1848.

55 *Ibid.*

56 Henry Crease to Capt. Henry Crease, 19 December 1848, MDS-0055 v. 10.

57 Capt. Henry Crease to Henry Crease, 8 September 1848.

58 Henry Crease to Benthall, *op. cited.*

59 For further information on this subject, see Arthur Cecil Todd, *The Cornish Miner in America* (Truro, Bradford Barton Ltd., 1970) and T.A. Rickard, *The Copper Mines of Lake Superior* (London, 1905).

60 Capt. Henry Crease to Henry Crease, 1 May 1849.

61 Capt. Henry Crease to Henry Crease, 12 April 1849.

62 Theodosia Crease to Henry Crease, 21 May 1849.

63 Emily Crease to Henry Crease, n.d. [June 1849].

64 Capt. Henry Crease to Henry Crease, 29 June 1849.

65 *Ibid.*

66 Sarah Lindley to Henry Crease, 5 July 1849.

67 Sarah Lindley to Henry Crease, 19 July 1849.

68 Sarah Lindley to Henry Crease, 9 August 1849.

69 Sarah Lindley to Henry Crease, 13 August 1849.

70 Sarah Lindley to Henry Crease, 20 August 1849.

71 Sarah Lindley to Henry Crease, 17 October 1849.

72 Sarah Lindley to Henry Crease, 9 January 1850.

73 Sarah's brother, Nathaniel, met his future wife, Sarah Teale, in 1851. They were engaged several years later, but it was another three years after this "before my income enabled us to marry which we did in August 1858." Like Sarah, Natty had to get John Lindley's permission to marry. Nathaniel Lindley, autobiography, August 1914.

74 Henry Crease, diary, 1849–1850.

75 Sarah Lindley to Henry Crease, 29 December 1850.

76 Sarah Lindley to Henry Crease, 12 February 1851.

77 This would circumvent the economic reality that a husband had all rights over his wife, including her fortune and future inheritances—a situation not changed until the passing of the first *Married Women's Property Act* in 1884.

78 Sarah Lindley to Henry Crease, 21 January 1852.

79 Henry Crease to John Lindley, 7 June 1852.

80 Henry Crease to Capt. Henry Crease, 20 July 1852.

81 Henry Crease to Capt. Henry Crease, 9 June 1852. "Hope deferred maketh the heart sick." Proverbs 13:12.

82 Henry Crease to Capt. Henry Crease, 15 June 1852.

83 Henry Crease to Capt. Henry Crease, 20 July 1852.

84 Henry Crease to Capt. Henry Crease, 23 July 1852.

85 Sarah Lindley to Henry Crease, 11 October 1852.

86 Sarah Lindley to Henry Crease, 30 September 1852.

87 Sarah Lindley to Henry Crease, 20 October 1852.

88 *Ibid.*

89 *Ibid.*

90 Sarah Lindley to Henry Crease, 22 November 1852.

91 Sarah Lindley to Henry Crease, 9 February 1853.

92 Barbara Lindley to Mary (Smith) Crease, 28 April 1853.

93 *Ibid.*

94 Sarah Crease to Henry Crease, 3 September 1852.

95 Sarah Crease to Henry Crease, 6 August 1855.

96 *Ibid.*

97 Sarah Crease to Henry Crease, 27 July 1855.

98 Sarah Crease to Henry Crease, 25 September 1855.

99 Sarah Crease to Henry Crease, 19 October 1855.

100 Sarah Crease to Henry Crease, 7 August 1855.

101 Sarah Crease to Henry Crease, 6 August 1855.

102 Sarah's attitude here, and later in the colonies, towards servants was typical of the nineteenth century middle class. Mistress and servant were only linked by necessity. Social connections or familiarity that might transcend bounds of class and station were not encouraged. See Janet Dunbar, *The Early Victorian Women* (London, George G. Harrop and Co., 1958).

103 "Notting Hill British Day Schools, 4th Annual Report," 21 June 1855, Crease Fonds.

104 "Plan for the Relief of Female Slop-Workers," n.d., Crease Fonds.

105 *Ibid.*

106 By mid-century large numbers of Cornish miners had emigrated overseas to Australia, New Zealand and California, following the various gold rushes. Making the local Cornish work situation more attractive to Cornish miners and families was also intended to discourage such emigration.

107 Henry Crease, diary, 1857.

108 Barbara Lindley to Henry Crease, 17 January 1858.

109 *Ibid.*

110 Barbara Lindley to Henry Crease, 16 February 1858.

111 MS-0055 Box 18, f.19.

112 "Great Wheal Vor United Mines. A letter to the Adventurers by Henry Pering Pellew Crease, Esq. Late Manager," London, 1858.

113 Suit brought by Sir Samuel Spry, n.d. newspaper clipping, MS-0055 box 25 f.5.

114 No correspondence between Sarah and Henry exists for 1856 through to April 1858. Therefore we have no indication of her knowledge of the events or her reaction to the situation in which she found herself. Letters from Barbara to Henry survive. These clearly show a sister's concern for them both and a confidence that eventually the problems would be settled and the family reunited.

115 Barbara Lindley to Henry Crease, 21 January 1858.

116 Barbara Lindley to Henry Crease, 17 January 1858.

117 Barbara Lindley to Henry Crease, 29 January 1858.

118 *Ibid.*

119 Barbara Lindley to Henry Crease, 20 May 1858.

120 Barbara Lindley to Henry Crease, 10 August 1858.

121 Sarah Crease to Henry Crease, 31 March 1856.

122 Sarah Crease to Henry Crease, 1 April 1856.

123 Barbara Powell believes it was a desire to leave only a harmonious record of the family for future readers that is the motivation behind the destruction of Sarah's diaries at a later point in her life. This explanation denies possibilities of accidental destruction or other reasons.

124 Henry Crease, diary, 7 April 1858.

125 *Ibid.*

126 William Gardener, "John Lindley," *Gardeners' Chronicle* 158, issues 23 October to 27 November 1965.

127 Sarah Crease to Henry Crease, 5 August 1858.

128 *Ibid.*

129 P.M. Vankoughnet, born in 1823 at Cornwall, Canada West, was Henry's contemporary in age and profession. Crease met him first in 1849–1850. By 1858, Vankoughnet was an influential politician. See Henry Morgan, *Sketches of Celebrated Canadians and persons connected with Canada* (London, Hunter, Rose & Co., 1860).

130 Copy of letter by John Lindley to Edward Bulwer Lytton, 14 August 1858.

131 P.M. Vankoughnet to Henry Crease, 28 July 1858.

132 Sarah Crease to Henry Crease, 12 August 1858.

133 Copy of letter by John Lindley to Edward Bulwer Lytton, 14 August 1858.

134 Notation in Crease correspondence.

135 Copy of letter by John Lindley to Edward Bulwer Lytton, 14 August 1858.

136 Sarah Crease to Henry Crease, 17 August 1858.

137 Sarah Crease to Henry Crease, 6 September 1858.

138 Henry Crease, letterbook, 1858.

139 Henry Crease to Capt. Henry Crease, 28 July 1858.

140 Crease travelled in company with Thomas Rowlandson, whom he had met in Le Havre. Rowlandson had arrived independently in Toronto, and when Henry's plans took him towards the Pacific coast, Rowlandson, financed by his father, departed with Crease.

141 Henry Crease, diary, 1858.

142 Sarah Crease to Henry Crease, 1 February 1859.

143 Sarah Crease to Henry Crease, 1 April 1859.

144 Henry Crease to Sarah Crease, 12 April 1859.

145 Sarah Crease, diary, 5 September 1859.

146 Sarah Crease to Emily Crease, 7 October 1859.

147 Sarah Crease to Mary Smith Crease, 11 October 1859.

148 Sarah Lindley to Sarah Crease, 14 December 1859.

149 Barbara Lindley to Henry Crease, 29 January 1858.

150 Barbara Lindley to Henry Crease, 10 August 1858.

151 Sarah Lindley to Sarah Crease, 14 December 1859.

152 Susan Reynolds Crease, biography of Sarah Crease, 1928.

153 See *Dictionary of Canadian Biography*, v. 13, 822–23.

154 These two views, presumably along with others sent to relatives in England, gave sufficient information for Sarah's mother-in-law, Mary Smith Crease, to paint a large watercolour, a composite of the views sent by her daughter-in-law. "Fernwood from the Rocks on the S. Side of Cadboro Bay Rd. (Regents Park)" is a remarkably accurate rendition, BC Archives PDP96.

155 Inscription by Sarah Crease on BC Archives PDP4567.

156 For elaboration on this theme, see Myra Rutherdale, "Revisiting Colonization through Gender: Anglican Missionary Women in the Pacific Northwest and the Arctic, 1860–1945," *BC Studies* (Winter 1994).

157 In this respect, she and others of her day were experiencing a general scientific curiosity brought about by the information made available in England about people in other parts of the British Empire, and by scientific collections undertaken on voyages of discovery and exploration. She was also influenced by the great interest in race and racial theories popularized by publications such as Charles Darwin's *On the Origin of Species* (1859).

158 Susan Reynolds Crease, biography of Sarah Crease, 1928.

159 Barbara Lindley to Sarah Crease, 8 August 1863.

160 Henry Crease, diary, 1858.

161 Sarah Freestone Lindley to Sarah Crease, 13 June 1864, Sarah Crease letterbook.

162 Henry Crease, diary, 7 August 1864.

163 Barbara Lindley to Sarah Crease, 15 April 1869.

164 Sarah Crease letterbook, 1863.

165 Sarah Crease to Sally Lindley, letterbook reference, 2 February 1869.

166 Sarah Crease to Emily Crease, 10 August 1869.

167 Sarah Crease to Barbara Lindley, 16 June 1864, Sarah Crease letterbook.

168 Sarah Crease to Barbara Lindley, 5 July 1864, Sarah Crease letterbook.

169 Sarah Crease to Sarah Freestone Lindley, 19 August 1864, letterbook.

170 Notation in letterbook, 1863–1870.

171 Henry Crease, diary, 24 January 1865. Evidently this woman was also the sister of the wife of Henry's brother Charles, thus compounding the situation with ties of family.

172 Sarah Crease to Emily Crease, 14 March 1865, letterbook.

173 Sarah Crease to Barbara Lindley, 19 May 1865, letterbook.

174 Sarah Crease to Barbara Lindley, 14 June 1865.

175 Sarah Crease to Barbara Lindley, 27 June 1865, letterbook.

176 Sarah Crease to Barbara Lindley, n.d. March 1866, letterbook.

177 Sarah Crease to Henry Crease, 14 May 1866.

178 It is probably significant that a Chinese servant was charged with arson in connection with a fire at Pentrelew and another attacked a guest with a knife. Court records may reveal whether these incidents represent a pattern relating to white middle-class households, or whether they are unusual and specific to the Creases.

179 Sarah's calendar notations were written all at one time in yearly diaries.

180 Henry Crease, diary, 1 January 1862, 1 January 1867, 26 October 1865.

181 Henry Crease, diary, 22 October 1862, 29 June 1863, 18 April 1862, 18 and 21 September 1862; Sarah Crease to Ann Hastings, 17 October 1862, letterbook; Sarah Crease to John Lindley, 6 August 1865, letterbook; Sarah Crease to Sarah Teale (Sally) Lindley, 26 June 1866, letterbook.

182 Sarah Crease to John Lindley, 6 August 1865, letterbook.

183 Sarah Crease to Lindley Crease, 25 August 1878.

184 See Smith-Rosenberg, "The Female World of Love and Ritual."

185 As evidenced by Susan Allison, whose attempts to create a friendship with her neighbour Susanne came to naught. See *A Pioneer Gentlewoman in British Columbia*.

186 Mary Smith Crease to Sarah Lindley, n.d. [August 1859].

187 See Sarah Crease, letterbook, various dates, to see the numbers of letters written and received from these women. Also, when Lindley went to England, he stayed with the Moodys, who arranged for his enrollment at school with their own son.

188 J.B. Priestley, *Victoria's Heyday* (Heinemann, London, 1972), 29.

189 Sarah Crease to John Lindley, 1866.

190 Nathaniel Lindley to Sarah Crease, 12 September 1868.

191 Henry Crease, "Rough Sketch of Burrard Inlet, Port Moody and New Westminster," n.d., map.

192 Nathaniel Lindley to Sarah Crease, 17 June 1868.

193 Nathaniel Lindley to Sarah Crease, 12 September 1868.

194 Sarah Crease to Nathaniel Lindley, 29 September 1870.

195 Sarah Crease, "Important Events, 1871." Trust monies were those arising from investments made upon their marriage settlement and also Sarah's one-third share in her mother's estate. She received £2580 after her mother's death in 1869. Nathaniel Lindley to Sarah Crease, 22 August 1869.

196 Sarah Crease to Henry Crease, 28 July 1870.

197 Alexander David Pringle to David Pringle, 31 May 1862, MS-0369.

198 Sarah Crease to Emily Crease, 10 August 1869.

199 Sarah Crease to Nathaniel Lindley, 10 March 1871 and June 1871, letterbook references.

200 Sarah Crease, diary, 3 March 1876.

201 Susan Crease, diary, March 1876. Susan states that Mary's illness is gastritis.

202 See Powell article.

203 Henry Crease to Josephine Crease, 3 June 1890.

204 Sarah Crease letterbook reference, January 1873.

205 *Ibid.*

206 Sarah Crease letterbook reference, May 1873.

207 Sarah Crease letterbook reference, March 1873.

208 Sarah Crease letterbook, 1874.

209 Susan Crease, diary, 10 October 1876.

210 Susan Crease, diary, 18 October 1876.

211 Sarah and Susan Crease, diaries, 1876–1878.

212 Susan Crease, diary, 30 January 1877.

213 Susan Crease, diary, 31 October 1876.

214 Sarah Crease to Josephine Crease, 2 October 1889.

215 Sarah Crease, Daily Bible Readings with annotations, 5 June 1860.

216 Susan Crease, diary, 3 and 4 June 1877.

217 Susan Crease, diary, 19 October 1883.

218 Sarah Crease, diary, 31 October 1883.

219 Susan Crease, diary, 25 November 1883.

220 Mary Maberly Crease to Lindley Crease, 25 November 1883.

221 Susan Crease, diary, 4 February 1877.

222 Susan Crease, diary, 24 November 1883.

223 Much in the same way Henry Crease became engaged to Susan Geach.

224 Susan Crease, diary, 1906.

225 Charges of embezzlement were brought against Walker in 1892. He appeared in police court with Mary at his side. Details are sketchy, but soon after, Walker left the country and his marriage.

226 For further details on the life of Josephine Crease, see Christina Johnson-Dean, "Josephine Crease and the Arts in Victoria" (MA Thesis, University of Victoria, 1980).

227 For further information, see Adele Perry, "'Oh I'm Just Sick of the Faces of Men,' Gender Imbalance, Race, Sexuality and Sociability in Nineteenth Century B.C." *BC Studies* (Spring/Summer 1995).

228 For instance, the Pemberton or Dunsmuir families.

229 Josephine Crease, diary, 1883.

230 Sarah Crease, diary, 1893.

231 The Crease Fonds contains architectural drawings and much correspondence with the architect on the renovation of Pentrelew.

232 Sarah Crease to Lindley Crease, 8 April 1890.

233 *British Colonist*, 20 August 1890.

234 Bishop George Hills, diary, 10 September 1890.

235 Sarah Crease, diary, 20 November 1878.

236 Susan Crease, Reminiscences, n.d.

237 Sarah Crease, diary, 16 February 1880.

238 Victoria *Colonist* newspaper, 12 December 1922.

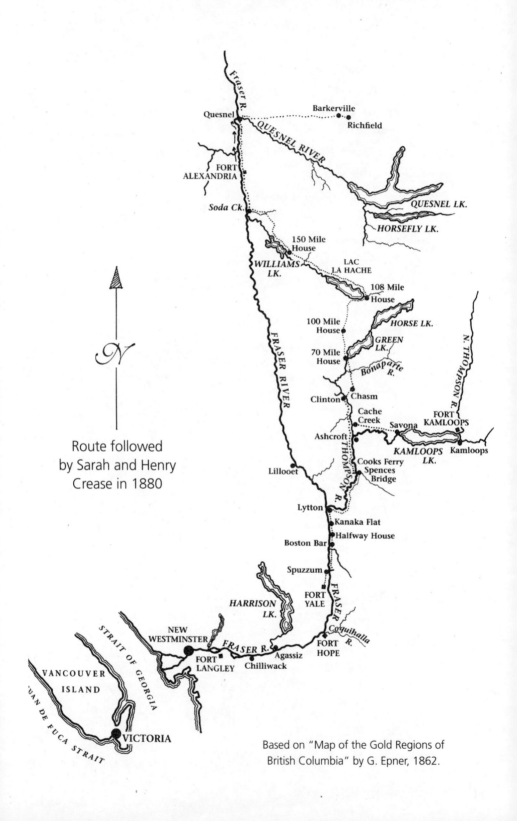

Route followed
by Sarah and Henry
Crease in 1880

Based on "Map of the Gold Regions of
British Columbia" by G. Epner, 1862.

Sarah's 1880 Journal

::::::::::::::::

N OTES of a trip with my dear husband on Circuit to <u>Cariboo—Kam-loops</u> & <u>N. Westr</u> Septr 1st to Decr 7th <u>1880</u>.

::

Sepr 1st Wed.

Henry and I left home (Pentrelew Vic) at 4.30 A.M. in Geo. Winter's hack—Drove to the Hudson Bay Coy's wharf & went on board <u>their</u> steamer for New Westminster—where we found Ben Evans & the Judge's Waggon—In the grey dawn, we hurried on our clothes to go on deck and enjoy the fresh morng air. Dear Henry packed me up in rugs & blankets—being very weary & worn—but now very comfortable. The Rev<u>d</u> M<u>r</u> Mogg was also on deck. Reached N. Westr about 3 P.M. Took rooms at the 'Occiden[tal] Ho [tel]' kept by Howison & wife—very comfortable there. The room clean & spacious—house quiet—& hostess v. kind and attentive. Mrs Mogg and I went to call on the Bishop & M<u>rs</u> Sillitoe at Archdeacon Woods'. Had pleasant chat with them out on the Balcony Henry joined us—he & I strolled through the woods. Mosquitoes found <u>me</u> out! Picked quantities of Partridge Berries (red) in their pretty whorl of green leaves, to send home to trim Susie's eveg dress for the Mason's (Dean) party. M<u>r</u> Mogg dined with us at the hotel—& took leave of him on his return to England with his wife and 3 little children.

Found our bed v. soft & comfortable—was very very tired—but thankful for so many mercies.

::

PENTRELEW, located on Cadboro Bay Road (now Fort Street) in Victoria, the Creases' family home built in 1875, Wright and Saunders, Architects. Original plans and contract specifications are housed in BC Archives. Pentrelew was demolished in 1985. The Victoria Truth Centre was built on the site of Pentrelew, leaving much of the original landscaping and trees intact. As of 2019 a housing development is planned on this site.[1]

GEORGE WINTER'S HACK. Winter ran a carriage business in Victoria for many years. His home off Fairfield Street is a designated municipal heritage site.

HUDSON'S BAY COMPANY WHARF was located at the foot of Fort Street, adjacent to the Finlayson Block, a warehouse structure of stone and brick still standing on Wharf Street. A mooring ring marks the site of the wharf.

BEN EVANS (1821–1899) was Henry Crease's faithful attendant on his circuit trips while judge. Officially Evans was the court usher, serving in this capacity from 1878 until his retirement in 1896. He accompanied many of the judges on their trips into the interior and was a great favourite. Susan Crease recalled: "the Judge generally preferred the cart. So his 'man' had to have all round qualifications. He had to be a judge of horses and a good driver; an able negotiator for lodgings for man and beast; a good provider against emergencies and possessed of unfailing cheerfulness. Such a man was 'Ben' Evans who attended the Judge on many of these occasions. It is told of him that where after much enquiry he failed to obtain two horses of even height, he produced a small one with great glee saying he would do very well for he was a 'sidling' horse to be harnessed on the bank side of the road where the ground was a trifle higher than the edge!"[2]

REVD MR HERBERT H. MOGG arrived in December 1876 and served at St. John's Anglican Church and then St. Paul's, Esquimalt. He was also a popular teacher at the Collegiate School for Boys. He and his wife returned to England on 9 October 1880.

THE OCCIDENTAL HOTEL, run by Justus William Howison and his wife, was on Columbia Street in New Westminster and boasted 40 rooms.

BISHOP AND MRS SILLITOE. The Right Reverend Acton Windeyer Sillitoe (1840/1841–1894) was the first Bishop of New Westminster. He and his wife, Violet, arrived in British Columbia in 1879 and assumed duties in New Westminster on 18 June 1880. He organized an interior mission centred at Kamloops and was most likely engaged in this project during the fall of 1880, when Sarah reports meeting them and, later in the journey, of arriving at Savona's Ferry just after their departure.

PARTRIDGE BERRIES. These berries "red in their pretty whorl of green leaves" are plentiful around Hope, as recorded by Susan Allison, *A Pioneer Gentlewoman in British Columbia*. She describes the plant as small, like a miniature dogwood, bearing small berries.

MASON (DEAN) refers to the Venerable Archdeacon Mason, assistant rector at Christ Church in Victoria.

:::

2d Sepr Thurs.

Kept my room until 4 P.M. repacked our boxes—read little books—slept and rested—House very quiet bed soft—hostess kind & attentive—all an unspeakable comfort—very very thankful for so many tender Mercies. Henry and Evans busy seeing after the horses for the waggon road. After dinner strolled up the hill on my dear husband's arm. Misty effect over the river was very beautiful—noticed several nice new houses. Enjoyed the softness of both air and water. Bishop & Mrs Sillitoe—also Mrs Peele called— did not see anyone.

:::

WAGGON ROAD is the Cariboo Wagon Road, surveyed by the Royal Engineers, who supervised its construction from 1861–1863. The 400-mile road began at Yale, travelling up the Fraser Canyon to Lytton and then along the Thompson to Quesnel. The section through the canyon has been called an engineering feat. Much of the road had to be suspended over the river on piles, wooden bridges and rock cribbing. In many cases, blasting was necessary to widen the flat surface ledges on the walls of the canyon.

:::

3d Sepr Frid.

Up at 8 A.M. greatly refreshed. Did a little shopping and sewing to travelling dress &c &c. Returned Mrs Peele's call—but she was out. Met Mrs Sillitoe and had a talk with her in town. At 4 P.M. Henry, self, Evans waggon & 3 horses went on board the 'Western Slope' for Yale. Young Hammond with his unprepossessing wife & her sister came on board also Florrie

In September 1862, Sarah and Julia Trutch left New Westminster on a week-long trip to Yale. Julia's husband Joseph Trutch at that time was not only involved in building sections of the Cariboo Wagon Road, but was engineer and contractor of the Alexandra Suspension Bridge. These two views of Yale were completed on that trip. (BC ARCHIVES HP62579, D-2126)

Newton—on the way to their respective homes. Maple Ridge, Hammonds farm, not cheerful looking—but they brought lumber—furniture & cooking things to improve matters—every thing landed on the muddy bank. At tea-time Mrs Dewdney appeared en route to visit her mother, <u>Mrs Glenny</u> at Hope.

::

MRS JULIA PEELE (born ca. 1848), wife of Adolphus Peele, chemist and druggist, Columbia St., New Westminster. Peele had been a marksman in the Westminster Volunteer Rifles (formed in 1863) along with Henry Crease.

WESTERN SLOPE, one of two steamers owned by Captain Moore, which travelled twice weekly between New Westminster and Yale.

YOUNG HAMMOND refers to John or William Hammond, original homesteaders in the area now known as Maple Ridge.

This view of the Indian Reserve at Yale, ca. 1880, is taken from the same vantage point as Sarah's 1862 sketch (opposite page). Note Lady Franklin Rock in the centre of both images. The Wagon Road and later the railway wound along the river close to this landmark. (BC ARCHIVES F-5149)

FLORENCE MARY NEWTON (1859–1944) was a daughter of William Henry Newton (1833–1875) and Emmeline Jane, daughter of John Tod. W.H. Newton worked for the HBC in Victoria, and in 1857, took charge of Fort Langley until his retirement in 1864. He later farmed at Port Hammond. Florrie Newton was born at the Royal Engineers' Camp at Sapperton. She lived a long life and remained a popular and entertaining woman who was able to recall much of the early days of Fort Langley and the surrounding area.

MRS. DEWDNEY, née Jane Shaw Moir (1843–1906), sister of Susan Allison, married Edgar Dewdney (1835–1916) in 1864. Dewdney was a civil engineer who entered politics and had a long and varied career, eventually serving as Lieutenant Governor of British Columbia from 1892 to 1897. Jane Dewdney accompanied her husband to Ottawa and later was chatelaine at Government House in Victoria. Before her marriage, Jane lived at New Westminster with her mother and sister, and thus knew the Creases from this time.

MRS. GLENNIE (1816–1906), née Susan Lousia Mildern, later wife of Stratton Moir and later of Thomas Glennie, was the mother of Jane Dewdney and Susan Allison. In 1880, Mrs. Glennie was a resident of Hope, where she taught school in her home.

Engineers' camp alongside the railroad, ca. 1880.
R. Maynard photo. (BC ARCHIVES D-08779)

4th Sepr. Sat.

Did not leave my cabin very early. Scenery about Chiliwack grand & well wooded. At <u>Hope</u> found Mrs John Trutch—walked & talked with her while lumber was being put on board. Dear Hy went with us to see our poor deserted little church—Interior neat, clean & churchlike. Porch out of repair—the whole unused. No Minister—no regular service. In sight of <u>Yale</u> railway houses appear along the left bank of the Frazer. Went to the '<u>California</u>' Hotel kept by Tuttle—house rough, dark & dirty occupants all men, but self. Dined in Saloon, waiter thoughtful & attentive no sitting-room. Went into bedroom as soon as we could get a light. Met Dr. Hanning-ton, John Trutch and Mr Preston neph[ew] to Mrs Joe Trutch. Saw the railroad actually begun.

::

MRS. JOHN TRUTCH, née Sarah (Zoe) Musgrave, married JOHN TRUTCH (1828–1907) in 1870. She met him while acting as chatelaine for her brother Anthony Musgrave, who was then Governor of British Columbia. Later, Zoe Trutch's brother-in-law Joseph Trutch (1826–1904) became Lieutenant-Governor. The Trutch brothers were partners in various road-building contracts constructing sections of the Cariboo Wagon Road. During the construction of the Canadian Pacific Railway (1880–1885), John Trutch was on the staff of Andrew Onderdonk, in charge of some of the most perilous sections of the railway construction.

"POOR DESERTED CHURCH AT HOPE" is Christ Church, designed by Captain J.M. Grant and opened in 1861. When the Creases resided at New Westminster, they often attended services at Christ Church, then officiated by their friend Alex-ander David Pringle.

CALIFORNIA HOTEL was run by Guy Tuttle, age 45, and his wife Ata. It boasted 80 rooms and was the largest in Yale. In 1880 Yale had six hotels plus several boarding houses and restaurants. In August 1881 a fire started in the California and swept through the town, destroying many buildings.

DR. ERNEST BARRON CHANDLER HANINGTON (1851–1916) came to Brit-ish Columbia in 1878 and was the chief medical officer for the CPR labourers on Onderdonk's section of the line, from Boston Bar to Lytton. In 1880 he was appointed chief surgeon at Yale and had charge of medical work from Port Moody to Savon. In 1885, after completion of the railway, Hanington, his wife, Ida Tilly (Peters), and their family moved to Victoria.

SAW THE RAILWAY ACTUALLY BEGUN. This comment is surely a reflection of the long wait British Columbians endured until the federal government finally honoured its 1871 Confederation commitment to link the country by rail. Railway construction in British Columbia did not begin until 1880. In fact, the first symbolic blast of dynamite, thus beginning the railway construction, occurred at Yale on 4 May 1880. The timing of Sarah's journey could not have been better. Construction on the railway had just commenced, and there was little disruption of their travel on the wagon road. The period from 1881 through 1885 saw frequent and dangerous disruptions, because the giant task of building the CPR through the Fraser Canyon caused great damage to the wagon road. Crossings were numerous, and often the cuts for the railway grade jeopardized the road. Detours were many and dangerous.

::

5th Sepr Sund. (20th anniversary of my leaving England)

D[ea]r Henry & self went to our little church saved from the fire. Revd J.B. Good officiated & gave us an admirable sermon, written by the Master of the Temple ch. London. Had little talk with Mr Cambie—much dissatisfied with having no house as promised. At 1.30 oClock Evans started with the horses and our luggage in hired waggon. Black horse bauked badly—could not be made to go—so was changed for another (Buckskin). Henry & self started in own waggon with hired driver & horses—road dreadfully rough for 5 m. through the railway works. Scenery, all along <u>awfully grand</u>. Reached <u>Boston Bar</u> at 8 P.M. <u>Dart's</u> [Tods crossed out] <u>house</u>—rooms very small but clean—had comfortable supper. Thank God for safety & continued mercies.

::

OUR LITTLE CHURCH is Saint John the Divine at Yale, built in 1860 by the Royal Engineers. It was officiated by the Reverend John Booth Good in 1880. Today it is distinguished as being the oldest Protestant church on the mainland of British Columbia, at its original site.

REV. JOHN BOOTH GOOD (1833–1916) came to British Columbia in 1861 and served first in Nanaimo and Comox, then Yale, and in Lytton when he worked under Bishop Sillitoe. In 1882 he was posted again to Nanaimo.

HENRY J. CAMBIE (1836–1928) and HELEN ELIZABETH (FAY) CAMBIE (born ca. 1848) with their four children lived at 12 Mile Flat. Cambie was an engineer employed by the Canadian government and was in charge of construction of the railway from Emory's Bar to Boston Bar. Mrs. Cambie spent April and May 1880 in Victoria and was very friendly with the Creases. Susan Crease stayed with the Cambies for extended vacations in the spring of 1880, the summer of 1881 and the fall of 1882. On this latter occasion she contracted measles and was quarantined.

DART'S HOUSE or hotel at Boston Bar was owned by Henry Braddeck Dart (born ca. 1837). It was originally known as the International Hotel.

::

6th Sepr. Mond.

Travelled 24 miles yesterday.

Had excellent milk porridge for breakfast. Mr Dart has some good fruit—plums—apples pears &c. At 8.30 A.M. Started off very quietly with Evans driving 'Sandy' & 'Buckskin.' Scenery, Grander than ever—feel inclined to hold my breath in awe & admiration. Rocks very deep and narrow at 'Hell's Gate.' Got out to look well at them—road winding high up on mountain side—parts richly wooded—flowers not striking—near Lytton country less beautiful—but the river flats well marked. Drove 35 Miles today and Reached Lytton about 6 oClock. Went to the old house Hautier's—Every thing the picture of misery—& dreary—(Liquor the cause) M de H fine-spoken woman—singer, actress & cook, the poor man O. Emily ran over from the Stevensons to see us. I went there to chat with her till called back to supper. Mrs S. in bed with an infant. Cold wind & dust very disagreeable.

::

HAUTIER'S was also known as the Globe Hotel. It was established in 1862 by Louis Vincent Hautier (1822–1886) and his wife, Josephine, née Vanderbrook (1839–1881). They raised five children on their ranch at Kanaka Bar. The eldest son, Alphonse (1859–1939), took over the hotel in later years. Louis was a Belgian, skilled as a herbalist, and both he and his wife were excellent chefs and pastry cooks. The hotel was famous from Yale to Barkerville for its cuisine. It appears that in 1880, just a year before the death of Mme Hautier, the hotel was a little shabbier than normal. Sarah's attribution that liquor was the cause is not substantiated, although Mme Hautier, overworked and depressed, was very ill. Just after the Creases' stopover, the Hautiers left their son Alphonse in charge of the hotel and retired to their homestead on Kanaka Bar.[3]

Men outside the Globe Hotel, run by the Hautiers, in Lytton, BC. Included is Arthur Stevenson (seated centre with hat on knee). Emily Crease boarded with the Stevensons. (BC ARCHIVES A-3559)

Street scene in Lytton showing the Globe Hotel, ca. 1880s. (BC ARCHIVES D-8778)

EMILY CREASE (1828–1900) was a sister of Henry. She arrived in British Columbia in 1869 to assume duties as headmistress for the Anglican-sponsored Angela College in Victoria. She remained in Victoria until mid-1877, when she moved to Lytton to teach at the mission school. She was killed in an unfortunate accident, run over by a train while on her way to evening services at the church in Lytton. She is buried in Lytton.

STEVENSON'S Emily Crease boarded with Arthur and Agnes (formerly Buie) Stevenson for many years while she taught in Lytton. In the 1881 census, the Stevensons, aged 41 and 31, had seven children. Arthur Stevenson was a road superintendent. In 1887 he was responsible for construction of a swing span bridge over the Thompson River.

::

7th Sepr. Tues.

Wind gone down. Morning pleasanter. Went with Emily to her school—on the side of a hill—clean & decent children, white, halfbreed & Chinese—about 12 in no. Waggon called for me at 11 A.M. Evans had exchanged 'Buckskin' for a better looking little horse the color of 'Sandy' but smaller. We named him 'Jim'—The scenery improving—banks of the Thompson very interesting—mountains grand & simple—with broad pleasing effects. The sage-bush (also wormwood) very abundant & gives soft, pale green color. Had to pass over large, moving mud-slide a mile 1/2 long. Noticed a very recent slide from opposite mountain near Cook's Ferry travelled 23 miles today. Went to Nelson's house. Bed in little Drawingroom. Mrs N. rough, smart & fond of children. Glad to meet Mrs McLeod, her husband's camp 1 1/2 miles further on—She was very kind & attentive. Had good supper in Dining shed—bed soft & clean—room covered with pictures of children—in very low art!

::

COOK'S FERRY was located on the Thompson River about a mile below the mouth of the Nicola. It was established in 1859–1861 by Mortimer Cook in partnership with Charles Kimball. Cook also kept a road house and store at this spot. In 1863 the government gave Thomas Spence a charter to build a bridge across the river near this site, which he did. The first bridge was completed in the spring of 1864, but was swept away by the spring runoff. The second bridge, completed in

March 1865, lasted until 1894. It was a toll bridge until 1872. Over time the place name Spences Bridge replaced that of Cook's Ferry.

MOVING MUD SLIDE/NOTICED A VERY RECENT SLIDE. These observations by Sarah are significant in light of the unusual natural disaster that soon after occurred at this spot. See notes for 23 October for explanation.

NELSON'S HOUSE was a prominent stop for travellers at Cook's Ferry. S. Mard Nelson purchased this roadhouse in 1876.

MRS EMILY MCLEOD, age 40, was the wife of CPR District Engineer H.A.F. McLeod. By 1882 she and her husband lived at Drynoch, seven miles above Nicomen in a house surrounded by fenced and irrigated plots planted with vegetables and grains. This residence was to be the site of a future railway station. At this meeting, the McLeods were temporarily boarding at Cook's Ferry.

::

8th Sepr. Wed.

Scenery much the same as yesterday—fine, bold, and open—small flowers and berries always present—the sage-bush still predominating—reached Cornwall's house about 6.30 directed to Ashcroft. Met at gate by Mr Cornwall & kindly welcomed by him, his wife & Mr & Mrs Henry Corn[wall]. Enlarging their house—gave us a room upstairs—bed, like our own at N. Westr very hard, nice drawingroom & excellent kitchen garden, beautiful little garden—very nice watercolors on walls of drawingroom—and plenty of beautiful photos on the table also bright flowers. Changed my travelling dress for blk silk & velvet. Had tea & cake supper at 9 oClock. Mrs Cornwall has 5 children. No 1 Carrie 8 yrs. Mrs Henry 3 little ones—all seem very happy and healthy. Farm looking very english and orderly—good crop of turnips and red clover—beautiful racing ground. Peacock & hens in stack yard—hound in pen near house.

::

CORNWALL'S HOUSE/ASHCROFT. The estate of Ashcroft was established in 1862–1863 by brothers Clement Francis (1836–1910), who married Charlotte Pemberton (born 1851) in 1870, and Henry Pennant Cornwall (1838–1892). Henry was the Indian agent for the locality, and Clement had a varied career in politics, including appointment to the Canadian Senate and a term as Lieutenant-Governor from 1881 to 1886. The estate included a RACING GROUND for public horse races and imported foxhounds, used for hunting coyotes. By 1880 the occupants at Cornwall's house included five children of Clement and Charlotte and three children of Henry and his wife, Mary.

:::

9th Sepr. Thurs.

Set out again at 8.30. Still lovely weather. Made poor breakfast—Mrs C.' kindly gave us sandwiches and a bottle of milk—Dear children, flowers fr. their gardens. Watered horses at <u>Cache-Creek</u>—road altered by the Boneparte River—saw where dear Henry once nearly escaped drowning while watering his horse. Large School-house—colored children boys & girls tog[ether]. About noon saw a fine grey wolf—near to a farm yard, quickly disappeared before Evans could fire—Scenery becoming more wooded with small lakes lovely drive into <u>Clinton</u> reached <u>Mrs Marshalls</u> at 6 P.M. cold & tired. House very clean & comfortable. Mrs M. formerly Mrs Smith, an honest, talking, rough, kindhearted woman. Food very good—delicious butter & cream—Mr Saunders & his young wife called. Bed soft & comfortable. A young mother (Monroe) travelling down in ill health with her husband & little child.

:::

ONCE NEARLY ESCAPED DROWNING. In 1866 Henry Crease narrowly escaped drowning in the Bonaparte River when his horse slid into the river while leaning forward for a drink. Henry was trapped in the saddle in deep, swiftly moving water.

MRS ELIZA MARSHALL, age 52, was the widow of Tom Marshall. She was formerly the widow of Joseph Smith, who, with Tom Marshall, purchased the hotel in 1868 and greatly enlarged it. The Clinton Hotel, as it was known, was very popular and long-lived until 1958, when it burned to the ground.

MR SANDERS AND HIS YOUNG WIFE must refer to Edward Howard Sanders (1832–1902), former gold commissioner and magistrate of the Lillooet district.

LARGE SCHOOLHOUSE is the Provincial Boarding School at Cache Creek established by the Department of Education in 1874 as a new concept in rural schooling, serving the population of the Thompson-Cariboo. In 1880 the teacher was Thomas Leduc. It operated until 1890, and during this short time it was the subject of mismanagement and scandal, including a very public accounting of the ease in which the girls nightly unlocked the adjoining doors to the boys' quarters.[4]

:::

10th Sepr Frid.

Staid [sic] in bed to rest, read—& repack. Breakfasted on delicious oatmeal porridge and cream. Dear Henry out talking to old acquaintances. Bought Blk coat—& flan[nel] drawers at Foster's store—Mrs Foster nursing Mrs Bell's only child wh. is dangerously ill—its devoted Mother being absent in Victoria. Mrs Marshall brought me a plate of soup at 1 oClock & entertained me with an hours' gossip about herself & neighbours. Arranged to leave two boxes behind—load too great for upper country.

Dressed in black silk & velvet—and after dinner went with dear Hy to return the Saunders' visit. Their house over a fall of water. Comfortable room—pleasant little woman & nice cup of tea—night air cold—but weather clear and fine—Passed a second night at Mrs Marshall's—She has a good son, called Joe Smith—fine young man.

:::

FOSTER'S STORE, run by Dr. F.W. Foster (b. 1832), served as a general mercantile and chemist shop.

MRS BELL, wife of Ewan Bell, an accountant resident at Clinton.

:::

11th Septr Sat.

Drove on again at 10.30 and soon entered the 'Green-timber'—an uninteresting road of 23 miles to day through a Pine forrest [sic]. Sky, deep blue and cloudless. Roads are rough with hard mud ruts. Left the waggon a short distance and went with Henry to get a close view of a tremendous Chasm! Miles long. Reached Sauls' the 70 Mile house at 5 P.M. sun warm & bright. Henry & Evans went after some ducks but returned with nothing but 'a ducking.' Had excellent supper—delicious bread, butter & cream. Mrs Saul quiet, thoughtful woman with young children rooms clean—bed wide, but blankets smelly of cats!!

:::

GREEN TIMBER refers to pine forests on the plateau north of Clinton. This is lodgepole pine, which grows at elevations of 200 to 600 feet. Ponderosa pine is found in drier areas of the Wagon Road.

The CHASM, located a short distance beyond the 59 Mile House, was considered one of the sights on the Wagon Road. Here stages would stop to allow visitors the opportunity to view the 1,000-foot-deep, ¼-mile-wide box canyon. It was referred to as the Painted Chasm because the mineral-filled rocks, exposed to the weather, created a range of coloured surfaces. As one viewer observed, it is "as if a huge slice of the surface had collapsed and sank, leaving perpendicular walls several hundred feet in height—it is V shaped, the apex being at the road end."[5]

SAUL'S at 70 Mile House was one of the most popular stopping places. In 1882 Isaac Saul had made it famous for supplying "a well furnished table and comfortable lodgings."

::

12th Sepr Sund.

(Had no idea it was Sunday until we made the discovery in the evening.)

Set off again at 8.30 and had 30 miles more through the "Green-timber." Had a glympse of the Cariboo Mountains. Roads very rough as before—4 miles down one hill—reached <u>Bridge Creek</u> the 100 mile house, at 5 P.M. Rough dirty house kept by a young bachelor Lindsay. Good Chinaman cook—excellent supper—Bread, cream, butter, jams. Dear Henry & self read some chapters in the Bible and in Thomas à Kempis before going to bed. Heard the Cayotes, at night—27 lbs of butter made daily from 70 cows—Indian campfires in sight of house.

::

100 MILE HOUSE at Bridge Creek, established in 1861 by the Jeffrey brothers, was the resting place for fur brigades coming downriver through the Bridge Creek valley, with their furs en route to Fort Langley. David Lindsay, the young bachelor who kept the place in 1880, was only there for a brief time, filling in for his sister who was on her honeymoon.[6]

::

13th Sepr. Mond.

A little rain before starting. Most lovely drive to day—through most peaceful looking country—rolling Downs—grazing cattle—& smiling lakes. Saw several Prairie chicken. Henry shot one. Scenery very beautiful and often English looking as we neared Lake La Hache. In one of the turns of the road came suddenly upon a fine Bald eagle and two Fish hawks. Henry hit both, but only broke the wing feathers of one, noticed plenty of duck on the lakes. Stopped the night at "Blue-tent" a wretched dirty, delapidated house—and poor miserable-looking young wife—with dirty barefooted children. Swept out our wretched bedroom after our hostess had, as she said 'fixed it up' Removed the blankets & used our own. Henry caught some fish for supper—Bread & butter good—no sugar in house. Dairy only decent Wright the husband young & active looking.

::

BLUE TENT at 127 Mile House, the end of Lac La Hache, was so named because while being built in 1862, Henry Felkner and his family lived in a tent of blue drilling. The establishment was acquired in 1867 by William Wright. The property changed hands several times and at the time of Sarah's visit, had only just been taken over by Wright's son John and his wife, Alice (née Rowebottom), who assumed the roadhouse in a sorry state.[7] Today the site is known as Wright Station.

::

14th Sepr. Tues.

Very pleasant drive again, weather lovely. Beautiful bits of scenery—small flowers and bright berries on either side of the road—also yellow butterflies—& dragonflies.

Reached the 150 mile house at the head of Williams Lake about 5 P.M. This house formerly known as Bates' of good repute, is now kept by a kind good-natured man named Hamilton late of the H.B.C. in the Peace river country. His wife is a halfbreed née Ogden and they have a family of 15 children. Getting in the harvest—rain threatening—our poor host much disheartened by his recent losses of 2500$ by fire & flood. Sawmill burnt & land swept away by overflow of the Creek. Gave us a large comfortable room. I did not go to supper. Wrote letters home.

::

150 MILE HOUSE/BATES. Aschal Sumner Bates and his wife, Margaret (née Ogden) (born ca. 1849), developed a sawmill and grist mill on the ranch site. Both the ranch and stopping house were sold ca. 1878 to Gavin Hamilton (1835–1909), retired chief factor of Fort St. James. The Hamiltons had a run of bad luck beginning with their acquisition. The losses by fire and flood mentioned by Sarah refer

to the sawmill and storehouse, which burned in 1879, and flooding of the land in the spring of 1880. Hamilton was both trader and postmaster when the Creases visited in 1880. The Hamiltons sold the property in 1883. The 150 Mile House was an important junction point for passengers travelling northward, who would transfer from wagon to stages operated by the British Columbia Express Company. In later years the spot was bypassed by a change in the Cariboo Road.

::

15th Sepr. Wed.

Charming drive through the woods first day of indian summer. Colors along road-side very lovely—weather bright & warm—road good. Passed through 'Deep Creek' formerly the supply-house for Cariboo & the Forks of Quesnell. The large houses now all in ruins, and washed away by the floods—country pleasant & open varied with woods & small lakes.

Soda Creek, 266 miles above Yale. Shown here is the sternwheeler *Enterprise*, the Exchange and the Colonial Hotel. This photo was taken in 1867 or 1868 by Frederick Dally, but the scene had changed little by 1880, when Sarah and Henry came to board the steamer *Victoria*. (BC ARCHIVES A-3908)

Went down <u>very steep</u>, winding, sandy road into <u>Soda Creek</u>—light rain. Thank God, arrived safely at 6 P.M. at <u>Dunlevy's house</u>. Mrs D. received us in her nice little parlor—with nurse maid & 2 chil[dre]n.

Dined at the public table. Slept on board the Steamer. Stage came in at midnight—bringing the lawyers Davy and Harrison. Got up steam & left at 4 A.M.

::

DUNLEVYS HOUSE, or the Colonial Hotel, was operated by Peter Curran Dunlevy (1833/1834–1904), one of the first white men to discover gold in the Cariboo. He mined, and he opened stores and trading posts throughout the district, at one time owning nine establishments. Dunlevy married, "according to the custom of the country," a Dene woman by whom he had several children. In 1873 he married Jennie Huston (1856–1925) and had five more children. In 1880 he ran the hotel and store at Soda Creek and was the local express agent.

THE STEAMER was the *Victoria*, built in 1869, and it, along with the *Enterprise*, regularly carried passengers north from Soda Creek up the Fraser to Quesnelmouth, a distance of some 56 miles.

DAVY AND HARRISON refers to Theodore Davie (1852–1898) who was a lawyer, and later a politican and a judge. He served as legal counsel for defendants on Crease's 1880 assize, and notably as counsel for Alex Hare at New Westminster (see 16 November journal entries). Davie later became premier of British Columbia, and it was under his administration that construction on the parliament buildings was undertaken. At the conclusion of his term, he was appointed to the position of chief justice of British Columbia, replacing Sir Matthew Baillie Begbie, despite intense lobbying for the post by Henry Crease. Davie died four years later at the age of 46.[8]

ELI HARRISON JR. (1852–1930), came to British Columbia in 1858 as a young boy. He became Deputy Attorney General and represented the Crown on criminal cases in the assize. He and John Foster McCreight prosecuted in the McLean and Hare trials in 1880 and 1881.

:::

16th Sept. Thurs.

Half stewed in Cabin before I could get dressed & boxes packed. Henry took me into wheel house—goodnatured young American steering. Frazer

Street scene at Quesnel, ca. 1900. (BC ARCHIVES D-447)

looking much quieter than above Hope—weather lovely. Passed the <u>Austra-lian Ranch</u> of 1 mile sq. productive of fruits & vegetables—when a few 100 ft further on a higher bench only grass will grow. Passed curious rocks on right bank (sometimes green)—like organ pipes—and a procession of large figures in long robes. Reached <u>Quesnel Mouth</u> at 5.30 Had a very clean comfortable room at <u>Mrs Browns</u> & a good dinner—joined by Messr[s] Davy & Harrison. Henry & self strolled out afterwards. Moon bright—discussed the clumsy old stage—like those in Eng. hundreds of years ago. Bed narrow & blankets smelled of cats!! Flowers bright & beautiful.

::

AUSTRALIAN RANCH on the Fraser River was established by the Downes brothers and Andrew Olsen in 1863 on pre-empted land. They saw an opportunity to cater to the miners en route to the Cariboo and began selling vegetables, grain, hay and meat. The Australian became renowned for these products, and business flourished. In 1900 ownership changed when a former stage driver by the name of Yorston bought out the remaining Downes brother.

CURIOUS ROCKS. This natural formation, known locally as the Devil's Pallisades, is made of basaltic columns rising from the right bank of the Fraser. It is similar to the Giant's Causeway in Ireland.

MRS. BROWN'S AT QUESNELMOUTH was better known as the Occidental, established in 1864 by Thomas Brown and Hugh Gillis. In 1880 Thomas and Sarah Ann Brown were sole owners. Thomas later died in May 1881. The two-storey hotel with its double-deck verandah on the front catered to the best class of traveller. The common rooms, saloon and restaurant were favoured retreats also for the locals. The name Quesnelmouth, referring to the town's situation at the mouth of the Quesnel River, was shortened in time to simply Quesnel. The HBC established a trading post here in September 1866. It became an important supply headquarters and stopping place. After the disasterous fire at Barkerville in 1868, Quesnel became the social centre of the Cariboo.

::

17th Sepr. Frid.

Very glad to resume our waggon. Road much the same as through the 'Green timber' weather bright & pleasant—rather pretty about 'Sugar-Cane Ranch.' Road bad. Dined at Boyds near Cottonwood. Thriving looking place—Store-house large wood-house and workshop—round dwelling & way-side house. Wife, daughter & little children nice—& respectable—Mrs B. has a sweet thoughtful face. Miss B. a round, rosy, goodnatured one. Had good dinner first taste of Bunch-grass beef—most excellent—wild raspberry & huckleberry jam very good. After dinner strolled round the place with the daughter & children. Bed hard & narrow—room cold, musty & comfortless.

::

GREEN TIMBER refers to the Englemann Spruce, which, unlike the pine forests of further south on the road, has a bluish-green needle.

SUGAR-CANE RANCH was an Indian village and, later, a reserve.

BOYDS NEAR COTTONWOOD refers to Coldspring, one of two establishments run by John Boyd (1834–1909). In 1868 Boyd, who was then a widower, married Janet Fleming of Victoria. Together they raised ten children, the eldest of whom, Mary Ann (daughter by his first wife), was 19 when the Creases visited in 1880. Boyd kept a day ledger, and in it he recorded all the daily transactions, including one at Coldspring on Saturday 18 September 1880: "Judge Crease & Lady. pd. 2 suppers (last Evg) 1.00, Bed this morning .50, 2 horses fed hay 1 night 1.00, 55 lbs. oats fed here and taken away 3.30. Total 5.80"[9]

::

18th Sept. Sat.

Left at 6 A.M. No breakfast—but cup of coffee. Ground covered with hoar frost. Stopped 5 M. at <u>Beaver Pass</u> to speak to Mrs Hyde, a doleful-looking woman. Nice little farm—son helping her—sun now bright & warm—enjoyed walking up the hills. Pushed on to <u>Stanley</u> (Cariboo) fearing snow. Reached at 1 P.M. Had good dinner—rested horses 1h. sent luggage on by empty stage—followed in our own waggon <u>Van Winkle</u> a continuation of Stanley—started well wrapped up. snow ahead. Road very heavy—& getting worse came into snow on the mountain—grey skeleton forest—with dark blue mount[ain] behind. Very striking ravine by Jack-of-Clubs lake— road narow & dark shut in by tall trees & mountain sides—first appear[ance] of small ferns in upper country. Grand view of snow peaks going down into <u>Richfield</u>. Put up at Austin's Hotel. Had 2 airy private rooms. Bed & hangings very clean—floor very dirty. Had small tea. Thanked God for safe journey and unpacked for the night. Mrs Austin formerly Parker—a good looking, tall, fair, lively woman with large family.

::

MRS. HYDE was a widow in 1880, and she operated her farm and rooming house at Beaver Pass with her young son George.

AUSTIN'S HOTEL, operated by Catherine Austin, age 40 (formerly Parker). In the 1881 census, Catherine and John Austin lived with Catherine's four children by her earlier marriage and two children by her marriage to Austin.

::

19th Sept. Sund.

Fine morn[in]g. Bed <u>very hard—narrow</u> & smelling of stale hay! No church open in morn[in]g so dear Henry & self read our ch. service alowd together. Then strolled along the road & got a view of <u>Barkerville</u>—looked like two rows of large, dark old bathing-machines. Scene all around most depressing & degrading looking. Introduced to Mr Thompson the Dominion M.P.!

for Cariboo!! Least said the best. Sun came out hot—& bright—but shed no charm upon any place around. R. C. ch. standing but closed. Had a horrible climb up side of hill & through graveyard. Had pretty good dinner at 4.30 cooking not very grand, a Mr Bowron called to see Henry, a respected old resident—with wife & little children. Henry & self went to the Methodists' meeting in Barkerville (our own ch. being closed) to join in praising God for His many & great mercies. Text "Look unto me & be ye saved all the ends of the earth"—a sound gospel discourse suited in style to the generality of his hearers—Sexsmith the ministers name. Moon bright & clear.

First day of Assize at <u>Richfield Cariboo</u>.

::

MR. JOSHUA SPENCER THOMPSON (1828–1880), an editor of the *Cariboo Sentinel*, was the first M.P. for Cariboo from 1872 until his death in December 1880. By all accounts Thompson was a popular man, being re-elected by acclamation at the general elections in 1874 and 1878. Why did Sarah write such a withering statement, "Least said the best" about him in her journal? The reason is unclear, but perhaps stemmed from rumours, which were confirmed after Thompson's untimely death in Victoria two months later, that despite his appearances as a bachelor, he was really married, but had deserted his wife. A newspaper account reveals: "Twenty-two years ago when Mr. Thomson first came to this province he was regarded as a single man, and it was not until 1871 that it became noised abroad that he was married in California…that shortly after an estrangement took place…relatives who deny that he was ever married, and who are preparing to contest the right of the widow so-called (who is in residence in San Francisco) to share in the estate." And later: "Persons who know all the circumstances inform us that the late Mr. Thompson was really married to the lady who now claims to be his widow, that they lived together at Fort Hope, Fraser River, 21 years ago, and that when he went to Cariboo his wife, dreading the rigorous climate of that region, returned to San Francisco."[10] If the latter is true, Sarah and Henry may have met or known of the Thompsons when resident at New Westminster.

ROMAN CATHOLIC CHURCH STANDING BUT CLOSED (AT BARKERVILLE) was St. Patrick's, built in 1868.

MR. JOHN BOWRON (1837–1906) married Emily Penberthy Edwards in 1869; they had five children. Bowron was one of the overlanders of 1862. He performed various duties in the Cariboo, acting as postmaster, mining recorder, government agent and finally gold commissioner in 1883, and was active in the cultural life of the area, organizing the library and in theatrical productions. He retired in 1905.

OUR OWN CHURCH BEING CLOSED refers to St. Saviour's Church, built in 1868 by the Reverend Reynard. Henry Crease was responsible for soliciting donations from Victoria church-goers to contribute to underwrite the costs of its construction, borne by the small congregation in Barkerville. After Reynard's transfer in 1871, St. Saviour's only had two future resident clergy, in 1881–1884 and 1887–1889. Apart from these times, layreaders from the congregation kept the church going.

WILLIAM SEXSMITH was the minister at the Methodist Church in Barkerville from 1877 to 1880. The following year he was replaced by James Turner (see 17 October journal).

::

20th Sept. Mond.

Morn[in]g bright & fine. At 10.30 Dear Henry went to open Court. Thankful no murder-cases. Cariboo district contains only 500 whites to 1300 Chinese. When alone settled myself to repair our clothes.

Dear Hy returned at 3. P.M. Had a visit from the Sheriff Mr Burns—very dull & irksome. At 6.30 Dined with Capt. Ball. House close by—Snug—comfortable quarters same Chinese cook for 18 years. Mr Brew former master in same house. Capt Ball told us that on Sat. last the Ther[momete] r stood at 20° Fahr—below freezing—& yesterday at 16° Fahr. & that Richfield is 4200 ft above the sea—no wind—& no cooler than when last in Victoria.

::

SHERIFF GEORGE BYRNES (1840–1899) moved from Victoria to the Cariboo, where he was appointed sheriff in 1874, an office that he held until 1883, when he resigned and returned to Victoria to start up an auction house. While resident in Barkerville, Byrnes was also the agent for the BC Express Company.

MR. CHARTRES BREW (1815–1870), an Irishman, was appointed in 1859 as inspector of police. In May 1864, Brew assembled a force of volunteers to chase the murderers responsible for the Bute Inlet massacre. He was later gold commissioner, and he died very suddenly at Barkerville, where he is buried in the cemetery.

CAPT. HENRY MAYNARD BALL (1825–1897) replaced Chartres Brew as gold commissioner. In 1876 he was appointed to the Court of Appeal for Cariboo and retired in 1881.

::

21 Sepr Tues.

Threatened snow fall disappeared. Court opened at 10 A.M. Judge & people walked to a claim two miles off to settle dispute.

Busy all day writing up my notes. Time passed quickly—Hostess kind & attentive.

At 7.30 Had a plate of soup. Court still sitting—At 11 P.M. Dear Henry came in—case finished—and we adjourned to little sittingroom for dinner!

::

22 Sepr. Wed.

No Court today. At 11 A.M. Henry took me down to Barkerville singular looking place. Houses all on stilts—street very narrow. Went into H.B.Co Store & Mr Ross's back room—shewed us 4000$ worth of gold dust. Henry bought some small specimens in quarts [sic]. Also shewed us small bar of gold worth over 8000$—was introduced to Dr Chipp—the medico! Strolled along muddy road—across the stony debris covering up the former town of Cameron & struggled up the opposite rough hillside to reach the Hospital—found col. steward & 3 patients—house clean—remained 1/2 h.

Returned to town met Mr Ferguson waiting to take us to his mine Conklin's Gulch had 1/2 m. rough walking—up the mountain side. Saw 'a wash' taken up—40oz gold = 600$. Went down in the mud bucket to the bottom workings 108 ft. saw a pan washed—offered us the gold. Laughed & refused—saw the gold cleaned weighed & put in leather bag for sale. Went into Miner's Cabin (Ferguson's) Hallam's Hist[ory] of Eng[lan]d on his bed & many others—gave us milk & buns—& very interesting account of himself.

::

HBC STORE AND MR ROSS'S BACK ROOM. In these small centres, the HBC retained a presence in the form of a general mercantile store, which also served as a trading centre. At Barkerville, Hugh Ross (born ca. 1840) was in charge of this store.

DR. JOHN CHIPP (ca. 1832–1893) had been in Barkerville since the 1860s working at the Royal Cariboo Hospital. Chipp arrived in British Columbia in 1862 onboard the *Tynemouth*, the second of the bride ships, where he acted as ship's physician.

MR. GEORGE FERGUSON (born ca. 1833) was one of the partners working a claim in Conklin's Gulch. Ferguson was the local member of the provincial parliament from ca. 1879 to 1886.

::

23 Sepr. Thur.

Very tired—thankful to have a quiet day. Dear Hy—bright and ready for work. Opened Court at 10 A.M. Snow nearly off Bald Mountain—yesterday Old 'Larry' stopped us, to shake hands & give us his blessing! enquired for Bishop & Mrs Hills—was sorry he did not rent their house (years ago) instead of Mr. Ward!!

Wrote to Susie and began one to Lindley. Court sat till 7 P.M. when we dined.

> Richfield Cariboo
> 22d Sepr 1880
> My dearest Lindley
>
> I suppose you will hardly be surprised to receive a letter from me with this date, having doubtless heard from others that Papa was going to take me with him to Cariboo. You will I am sure dear boy, be glad to hear how very well we both are. Your dear father seems just as strong and well as when you started with him for Cassiar three years ago—and for myself—I feel this trip is doing me great good—being such a complete rest of mind from domestic cares—which is what I have wanted for some long time.
>
> 28th Sepr. Quesnel Mouth—When I began this letter dear Lindley I thought I had plenty of time to finish it in Richfield—but the Assize terminated more quickly than I expected—and as the daily expenses there were very heavy—and not much comfort to counterbalance it—your dear father gave the order to start

immediately—so I had to pack up at once—say Good Bye to the two or three people who had expressed kindly intentions towards us. While Evans looked after the waggon and horses and brought them after us as we walked up the high hill leading out of Richfield. It was a lovely morning—and although patches of snow were still to be seen here and there sheltered by rocks or trees yet it was not at all cold—for there was no wind and a bright sun overhead.

When at Richfield we visited the Hospital (where Dr Jones was for some time) found it clean and orderly with only three patients in it. We were also taken into a miner's Cabin, a rough simple looking little hut on the wild side of a mountain. The good-natured owner, named George Ferguson, a member of the Provincial Parliament in Victoria—an honest, simple, selftaught, God-fearing man regaled us with milk & buns—but more especially with an interesting account of his early life—after he left the coalmines of Northumberland. His bed or bunk was covered with books leaving hardly room enough for himself to lie down. One of the books that I turned over was Hallam's His[tor]y of England which he was then studying & which one would hardly expect to find in such a place. Mr Ferguson also took us to see his Gold-mine called Conklins Gulch—where he had arranged that a 'wash up' should be examined for our benefit—that is that we might see the whole process of washing, drying & cleaning gold from first to last, which we did and went 108 ft down into the mine besides to see where the mud & stones came from wh. we had just seen brought up in large iron-bound buckets and washed. Papa & I each had on a miner's waterproof-cap and coat and were lowered down the shaft in the same bucket that brought up the mud and stones. We were much pressed to take away specimens of the gold here as elsewhere, but you know Papa will not allow of such presents—so we risked their displeasure and remained firm. At Quesnel Mouth where we are most comfortably lodged, in the hotel—awaiting the time for the next Assize—viz Oct 1st—there is not much to see or do. No sport for Papa—and no very inviting walk anywhere—but the weather being very lovely we have strolled across the bridge—basked in the sun, watching the industrious Chinamen rocking for gold on the banks of the river Quesnelle which flows past them with a strong, rapid stream. The Frazer also runs past here, and a small steamer takes passengers to and fro from here to Soda Creek once a week. We came up that way—but Papa wishes to drive back—which I also prefer to the water.

When we arrived here on Saturday from Richfield—we found a whole budget of letters awaiting us—from Victoria and from England. Among them were two from you dearest Lindley—and others hearing such a good account of you generally—and of your having gained a prize in your first term at Haileybury, that your dear father and I almost wept with joy over our letters which contained so much to make us thankful and happy. God bless you my dear dear boy—and may you grow in grace, wisdom and knowledge as you grow in years. We are very glad to hear of you having such a happy time with the Moodys—who have been so very kind to you & speak so kindly of you. I cannot write anymore now dear boy as it is time to say Good Night—but I must add, that I am enjoying this trip with your dear father immensely—and never cease admiring the awful grandeur of most of the scenery. With tender love and fond kisses from us both ever dearest Lindley.

Your very affectionate Mother.

::

BISHOP GEORGE HILLS (1816–1895) arrived in British Columbia in January 1860. Hills was the first Bishop of Columbia, appointed in 1859. His diocese, which included almost all of Vancouver Island and the Mainland, was funded by Baroness Angela Burdett-Coutts. In 1880 the diocese was split into two, with Bishop Sillitoe responsible for the Mainland. Hills' wife, Maria Philadelphia Louisa née King (1823–1888), was his constant companion, accompanying him on many journeys. Hills kept diaries thoroughout most of his adult life. Those he kept while in British Columbia are valuable documents of their time.[11]

::

24th Sepr. Friday.

Assizes over. Hotel charges very high $2 50 to Laundress for 1 doz things including only 1 wht shirt—! the rest underclothing including 6 pkts & socks. Packed up our boxes quickly. Called on the Nasons, well to do miner—pretty wife & little children—pressed me to accept some gold dust—refused as before. Went with Henry to say Good Bye to Capt Ball—then we strolled up the long hill—telling Evans to follow us with the horses—at about noon. Morning lovely air soft and balmy—sat on a log to rest & read 38 ch. Isaiah. Horses very fresh down hill nearly all day—road beautifully winding—small flowers bright berries and ferns all along roadside. Grand bit of rock & wood near 'Jack of Clubs' Lake. Passed the first grave in Cariboo Inscription "Sacred to the memory of J. Gronlund a native of Sweden—died June 19th 1864—aged 37 years." Valleys about here very narrow. Trees Pines & Cottonwood very tall & thin dark and light. Road very narrow & heavy. Town of <u>Stanley</u> looked rather better today. Evans stopped to take in our luggage—Henry & self walked up the hill to examine the cemetery—containing 4 graves enclosed in wht rails and well cared for. 'Sandy' cut his foot in a pool of water—bled much—a little lame. Reached <u>Beaver Pass Mrs Hyde's</u> before dark. Poor widow very lonely with her young son George—very glad of company. Sat in kitchen while she cooked the supper—which we all needed. Gave us a soft, clean, bed in a very small room.

::

FIRST GRAVE IN CARIBOO was probably located in the spot later defined as the Stanley cemetery.

::

25 Sepr. Sat.

Coffee & toast at 6 A.M. Morng fine but damp and chilly. Lovely drive along mountain side—deep ravine below with <u>Lightening Creek</u> running in it. Purple spreading mountains in the distance visible now & then over the tops of the trees now in yellow leaf—viz Willow & Cotton.W. Reached the <u>Boyds</u> house at 11.30—he shewed us fine gold dust brought in by Chinamen—offered me a specimen—refused as before. Had a good dinner which refreshed us much. Before reaching Boyd's passed a splendid bit of upheaved rocks partly clothed with vegetation—where the stream had been diverted from its natural bed—by the early gold-miners—soon reached <u>Cottonwood Ranch</u> owned by Boyd—the blue huckleberry with its small red leaves very abundant along the road, also Michaelmas daisies, wht everlasting—& an epilobium in seed. Saw 8 or 9 small lakes at intervals of a few miles. Two of them good for trout near Wallace's farm—here we watered the horses. Wallace a jovial, good natured looking man—very pleased to see Henry. The air still delightfully mild & balmy. The road today through cottonwood & willow brush, in yellow leaf, not interesting, except when relieved by a sight of the distant blue & purple mountains stretching wide over the tops of the trees—which we now & then caught a glympse of as we reached the top of a hill in our very wavy undulating road. Near Wallace's passed an oxteam at rest—with the poor worn animals turned out to graze. Henry shot a grouse (drove 39 miles today). Passed a heavy team with 10 yoke of Oxen moving slowly on. Got into the little town of Quesnelmouth at Sunset—arrived at the 'Occidental'—Mrs Brown's at 7 P.M. Had tea—took posession of 2 comfortable rooms—Read a budget of letters from home, & went to bed.

:::

COTTONWOOD RANCH. Cottonwood House is one of the oldest buildings in British Columbia and is one of the few Cariboo road houses still standing. It was operated continously by the Boyd family until 1951 and is now a provincial historic park. (See 17 September notes.)

ALEX WALLACE'S farm was located 13 miles out of Quesnel. The roadhouse was built in 1864 and run by Wallace from 1866 to 1899.

:::

26th Sepr. Sund.

Rain & wind in morng. I was very, very, tired and poorly. Did not get up until 3 P.M.—No church—school—or anything—but day kept very quiet. In our sittingroom have 2 bouquets of lovely bright flowers—scarlet geraniums—stocks—Phlox—sweet Peas—Chrysanthemums Lupins—wht snapdragons, Mignionette &c &c.

Did not leave the house—reread my letters. Read aloud in eve[nin]g—from the Bible—Thomas a Kempis & Norris on Ch. service. Still very tired—went early to bed. Dr Henry dispatched a heap of letters by the mail at 3 P.M.

:::

27th Sepr. Mond.

Glorious weather again—but still not very well—feeling weak & weary. After breakfast—Henry and self strolled out over sandy ground full of fine smooth white stones. Crossed the bridge over the Quesnel a fine swift river—watched Chinamen rocking for gold—rested on a log overlooking the river & flat country—took out my work while Henry read aloud the Sat[urda]y [?] Review. Sun—very hot. Hy had conversation with a french sportsman. Returned to Hotel at 4 P.M. very tired. Mrs Brown brought me delicious custard. Had early dinner & cosy eveg. Dr Henry complaining of sore throat & cold.

:::

28th Sepr. Tues.

Morng. damp & foggy—at 11 A.M. cleared up bright and warm. We sauntered out along river bank—passed the old ferry-house. Crossed the bridge
& rested up the hill on a log under a tree—sun very hot. Went with Henry
into H.B.C. store for some cloth for gun. Had a chat there with Mr Robt
Skinner over old times at Esquimalt. Also went into Drug Store—saw more
of the Chinamans gold dust from the river—very good. Returned to the
hotel at 3.30 very, very tired—Henry & self did some sewing! until dinner-
time (5 P.M.)

Observed a large Pack-train (about 100 indian horses) across the Frazer—
waiting to cross it.

> Quesnelmouth 28 Sept 1880
> My dearest Boy
> Your two Letters from Conyngham House [School] Aunt Natty's & Uncle
> Natty's Letter with your unexpected report of good progress at Haileybury have
> cheered your old Dad's heart here—just as I was suffering severely from a sud-
> den Cold & sore throat with bronchitus. Whether it was hearing from my dear
> son my boy or the 2 mustard plasters, medicine etc Your mother's nursing I can't
> say but I am getting better again and had need to for the Assize will be on here
> the day after tomorrow & I must be ready to charge the Grand Jury & try the
> Cases.
> I met Hixon at the 150 the man who took you out to walk at the mouth of
> McDaine's [sic] Ck he asked after you. Also I met Louis Blanchard whose horse
> "Bulger" I used to carry me at one end while the Indians steered at the other. If
> you remember I sent Dan Emory a splendid travelling pocketknife. Blanchard
> says he went about to everybody at Telegraph Creek—boasting about it & giv-
> ing "drinks" all round. We are on our way down Country. Leave by "Victoria"
> Str. for Soda Cr. on Sunday (no choice). Thence down to Clinton & Kamloops
> thence to Yale on 30 Oct & NW on 10 Nov., yr loving Dad.
> I did not at first see that Mama had left me this side so I jump at it (as Sir
> Walter Scott says "like a Cock at a grossart" & continue my tale.
> Mama herself has been poorly & only just got well in time to nurse me. I
> think the cold arose from change of climate bet[wee]n Cariboo & Quesnelle.
> There was snow on 'the Divide.'… the height of land (5200 ft. above the sea)
> going into Richfield. The Assize this year is a month late so my Circuit is a race

with the Cold frost & snow & the roads have been (except one day) eyecrable—ruts 1ft to 3 ft. deep for miles long at a time.

So the Great Trunk Road which we took so much pains to build and perfect under Sir James Douglas, the <u>one man Govt</u>—so much abused for its arbitrariness—is now almost entirely neglected by the much reunited <u>Responsible</u> Govt who have not executed one single Great national at work. However it was a great piece of engineering in its day & Mr Bray the foreman of the Canadian Pacific Railway now <u>under construction</u> from Yale to Savonas Ferry places which I hope to travel over with my own dear boy, one day together, told me he had never heard of such determined pluck & skill in any young Colony in his life before. God bless you Dear boy, ever . . . loving Dad

::

ROBERT JAMES SKINNER, age 36, was the chief trader of the HBC at Quesnel. He was the son of Thomas Skinner, an early settler in Esquimalt. Robert Skinner grew up at Constance Cove farm on Esquimalt Harbour.

PACK TRAIN (about 100 Indian horses) crossing Fraser. Could refer to Cataline and his business.

::

29th Sepr. Wed.

Heavy damp fog in morn[in]g. Dr Hy had very bad night. Applied mustard plaisters [sic]. Took Sweet Sp. Nitre—Bromide of Potash—Proposed sending for Dr Chipp—Nurse advised to wait—& take usual medicine. Patient assented—& stopped in bed until 3 P.M. Neither of us went out of doors. Self also suffering aches & pains & <u>great</u> lassitude. Had our little meals in private room. Did a <u>little</u> sewing, reading and writing.

Weather in mid-day very bright & warm—Ind[ian] summer. Slept in sittingroom (very snug) to attend to fire & dr Hy. Hypophosphite of Lime a great comfort to him. The pill draught—& Bro. of Pot also did him much good.

::

30th Sepr. Thurs.

Thank God—dear Henry is much better. Morn[in]g still damp & foggy. Hy did not get up until 1 P.M. We then strolled out for a little fresh air.

Went to see Mrs Hutchinson's flowers. Pretty, tidy, little house—with green-house opening into sitting room. Large Oleander in bud—Fine scarlet geraniums—Large Petunias Fuschias—Asters—Verbenas &c &c &c

We sauntered on the sands at the mouth of Quesnel. Sun very hot—both feeling great lassitude. Glad to get back to Hotel. At 6 P.M. Steamer came in from Soda Creek, 3 passengers. Got letters from home.

Retired early to our separate couches. After reading dear Lindley's Chap. (5. II Kings) for his class in Sund. Sch. at Clipston—the first time.

::

October 1st Friday.

<u>Assizes begin</u> at 11 A.M. in Bar-room of the Occidental—at <u>Quesnel Mouth</u>

Lovely weather—but did not go out all day. Henry came in to lunch I wrote letters to England—Natty—Lindley—Aunt Hastings—Capt Machell & Mr Findlay. In evening read 'Our Times' aloud—Dined at 7 P.M.

1 Oct. Quesnelle Mouth

Just a line more dearest Lindley to thank you for your little note from Clipston—Recd Last night. It must have seemed strange to you taking a class in the S[unday] S[chool] but I am glad the first time is now over. You made a very nice selection in yr. chapter—5 of II Kings which I read aloud to Papa before going to bed—indeed I read parts of the Bible aloud to him mong. & eveg. first a P[aragraph] or two—then some chapters in Isiah or the Acts—as I have those in thin covers for the convenience of travelling & try to read them through as if I had never heard <u>or read</u> them before. We are also reading tog. Norris on the Prayer Book. An excellent book of instruction wh. I should much like you to read dear boy. Papa is reading it especially with a view to teaching it to his class at S. School Dr. Tanner I think is more <u>wicked</u> than foolish in trying such experiments. I have no patience with him.

Your father is holding Court in the adjoining room. I <u>could</u> hear all that goes on if I listened—but I prefer spending my time answering letters. It does seem so funny being here—Papa often comes in while the Jury is sent out to consider some matter.

Good Bye—God bless you my darling boy. I have not time for more. Mr Findlay has been very ill—he sent us a Newspaper the other day from London.

October 1st Friday -

Assizes begin at 11. A. M. in
Bar-room at Quesnel Mouth
of the occidental)

Lovely weather - but did not go out
all day - Henry came in to lunch
I wrote letters to England - Natty -
Lindley - Aunt Hastings - Capt Machell
& Mr Findlay - In evening read
'Our Times' aloud - Dined at 7. P. M.

2d Oct. Saturday - Court sat again

weather still beautiful -
Wrote to Mary - Susie - Zeffie -
Funny & Mr Richards -
Assize over - Dined at 5 P.M.
Afterwards Henry & myself took
a few turns on the Bridge -
Twilight very short -
eveg. damp & chilly -

Quesnelle Bridge built 1877

A page from Sarah's 1880 journal. (BC ARCHIVES)

::

2d Oct. Saturday.

Court sat again weather still beautiful.

Wrote to Mary—Susie—Zeffie—Dunny & Mrs Richards. Assize over. Dined at 5 P.M. Afterwards Henry and self took a few turns on the Bridge. Twilight very short—eveg. damp & chilly.

> Quesnelle Mouth
> 2d Oct. 1880
> Cariboo
> My dearest Mary
>
> Papa no doubt has told you how we rejoiced to get such a budget of letters from home—as we found here on our arrival a week ago. We had not heard from any of you since leaving Yale? I think—at all events but once since we left home, so of course they had accumulated on the way. I was very unwell on Sunday when the mail went out & so obliged to let Papa's letters go without a line from myself but I am thankful to say I am all right again now—and Papa also who was very poorly indeed for a couple of days with cold & sore throat. I leave you to imagine how the druggist's store has been ransacked to get means of relief—and wonderful to relate it contained all that was required but Keatings Lozenges—but as it <u>had Brown's</u> I don't think there was much to complain of. I fancy we must both have had a touch of Mountain fever. I escaped the cold & sore throat but otherwise our complaints were very similar—both suffering from such unusual lassitude and pains in the limbs. It has been a mercy that it came in here, where we are not only in the <u>most</u> comfortable quarters on the road, but have had the time to lay up and nurse ourselves, and thank God, we are now in travelling condition again for our time is up tomorrow when the Steamer leaves here for Soda Creek.
>
> I wrote Susie a long letter from Richfield, the contents of which she doubtless made common property, as was intended. There is not much to say of this place, for there is no striking feature to recommend it. The town looks much like others in Cariboo—without so strong a Chinese appearance—& without being propped up on logs. The Frazer is running past our window with scrub willow & cottonwood which is in varied stages of faded green & yellow. Almost at right angles to the Frazer is the Quesnel a swift river,

though now very low, leaving a wide sandy beach on wh. you can walk until tired. There is a wooden bridge over Quesnel not very picturesque but something like this. You must fancy Chinamen rocking for gold along its banks & a hot mid-day sun pouring down upon everything—& it will then be much as we have experienced it. The morn[in]gs here, have been very damp and foggy—such a contrast to Richfield where the air was so very dry. Which sudden change—may be, we have been feeling—together with the <u>Shaking up of an unusually long drive</u>. Private. I am sorry Mrs Jackson should have shewn any coolness towards you—& can see no occasion for it, but I think you will all be quite right to keep away for a while. I am glad you have been to Mrs Stirlings—for there it is quite different. I suppose there are a great many red eyes and aching hearts in Victoria to day!! But am very glad my own dear girls have no cause for either on the departure of the "Triumph" for unless it were indeed a triumph it had better be nothing at all. We are very curious to know the real state of things at Armadale! If a disappointment. I have no sympathy with it. If a conquest I shall not believe until it becomes un fait accompli. Please remember me particularly to Sir Matthew when you see him—also to Capt Layton & Mr Jones and Mr Pearse.

I am sorry to hear such an acct of poor Mrs Burns—but hope she is doing well. Have you seen anything of the Duponts. I fancy not. Give my love to poor Mrs Gray & the girls. I suppose Mabel keeps up the Lawntennis practise. I have had a nice letter from Ernest he has safely reached Winnipeg as doubtless you know—after a very narrow escape of <u>losing his leg</u> from the neglected bite of a sand-fly. Poor fellow, he <u>must</u> have suffered Agonies but I hope he will be wiser for the future. I have nothing more to say dearest Mary, but trust that you are also <u>wise</u> in taking care of <u>your own</u> little self—for although small it is very precious to me and I fully hope and trust, it will some day, be <u>still more precious</u> to one who will know how to value it—so don't waste a good thing, or spoil your looks over a mid night lamp.

Papa who is holding Court in the adjoining room, seems now to be bringing things to a close—wh. reminds me that I must do the same, for it is my last chance of writing for sometime, until we reach another good resting place. So Good Bye my darling girl—don't sew your fingers to the bone—or <u>worry</u> yourself about any of these sublimary things! I hope Paul has found you a good successor & that Sing behaves well. In our budget was a letter from Mrs Richards, which I will try to answer by this Mail. I also owe one to Dear Babs and Zeffie. I shall only write to the latter this time—as Babs <u>may not</u> yet have returned home & I shall not have time for all. Papa has just come in and sends you all his

<u>Love</u> which I am to write with a great L! he says he was intending to write Artie but has not the time now—but hopes he is a good boy, and at least does what he is <u>told</u> to do. Give the dear little man my love also & tell him I miss his kisses very much and hope he will save up plenty for me. We were glad to hear he has become punctual at meals & hope he will keep up the good habit—also that he will not forget to look after his bootlaces. Did you ever get the black lining I sent from N. Westr? Remember me very kindly to the Bishop and Mrs Hills—a queer old man called 'Larry' asked especialy after them at Richfield, he is a R.C. but has a very kindly remembrance of them.

Remember me also very kindly to the Wards. I sincerely hope she is getting strong and well. My love also to Mrs Mason & the Archdeacon also to the Moggs if still in Victoria. What news of the Missing Mr Grogan?

God bless and protect you all my dear children—and with heaps of love all round—and a <u>good, good hug</u> to dear <u>Babs</u> if really at home. Ever dearest Mary Your loving Mother

:::

3d Oct. Sund.

Lovely morng. Packed up everything—& breakfasted at 11 A.M. Mail came down at 12 oClock & we left Quesnel Mouth on board the Steamer at 1 P.M. for Soda Creek. Sat out on the deck with Henry. Mr Hamilton amused us with stories of Bears and Indians. Passed Fort Alexandra an important H.B. Fort in early days, now all in ruins—Observed hundreds of geese & ducks on the river beach—arrived at Soda Creek at 6 P.M. Mr & Mrs Dunlevy received us at their private house before dinner. Had a good dinner in the public room—returned to the private house & Mrs Dunlevy gave us some music on her fine Piano (a Steiner from N. York). Would play well with more practise.

Retired early to our own room in the wayside house—a wretchedly dark and dirty place—Bed-room very small and open at the top, with other rooms. Doublebed with very short clothes. Towel—a kitchen runner! Chairs in sittingroom—3 out of 4 without seats. Our host & hostess were however personnally [sic] kind & attentive. Their Two small children & their nurse were always at the table!—

:::

Plate 16. *Yates Street*, October 1860. This watercolour was also used as a basis for an engraved illustration in R.C. Mayne's book and later reproduced in various illustrated journals. Sarah sketched it from a balcony overlooking the street. (BC ARCHIVES PDP2894)

Plate 17. *Tsartlip Indian Huts outside the Governor's Garden*, October 1860.
(BC ARCHIVES PDP2899)

Plate 18. *Government Street*, 8 October 1860. Notes on the reverse identify the major building on the right as Smith's grocers, and farther up the street is the post office. The large brick houses include the private residence of Harris, the butcher; Col. Moody's first residence; and the Attorney General Cary's chambers. The old bastion of the Fort was pulled down by 1861. Henry's chambers were just beyond the Colonial French Hotel Restaurant [on the left]. (BC ARCHIVES PDP2895)

Plate 19. *S.W. Bastion of the old Fort with 12 nine-pounder guns*, 8 September 1860. (BC ARCHIVES PDP2893)

Plate 20. View of Pentrelew, young Arthur Crease on tricycle, 1878.

Plate 21. Panoramic view of Yale, ca. 1880. Note the sternwheeler docked alongside the bank of the Fraser and the long walkway down from Front Street to the river's edge. The California Hotel is visible on Front Street next to the "Branch." St. John's Church with its distinctive fencing is on the rise. Richard Maynard photo. (BC ARCHIVES A-316, A-3585)

Plate 22. This scene is three miles above Yale, looking down the valley. Above is the new CPR line at Fountain Bluff. Below is the Cariboo Wagon Road, clearly the worse for wear, ca. 1880. R. Maynard photo. (BC ARCHIVES A-5938)

Plate 23. Sternwheeler *Western Slope* docked at Yale, BC, the head of navigation on the Fraser River. (BC ARCHIVES A-153)

Plate 24. Yale during construction of the Canadian Pacific Railway, which was built right through the town. This photo shows the tracks nearing completion, just down river from the townsite. The Cariboo Wagon Road is visible running parallel to the track. (BC ARCHIVES D-0728)

Plate 25. 17 Mile Bluff on the Cariboo Wagon Road, 1867–1868. Note the cribbing and bridgework necessary to support the road as it clung to the walls of the Fraser Canyon. F. Dally photo. (BC ARCHIVES A-3872)

Plate 26. The Cariboo Wagon Road meets the CPR at tunnel #14. Here we can clearly see the interface between old and new. Note fish-drying racks on left and salmon cache in tree above. (BC ARCHIVES D-8622)

Plate 27. The Cariboo Wagon Road one mile above Yale, ca. 1870s. Today's modern highway is built high above the old road away from the river. (BC ARCHIVES A-3931)

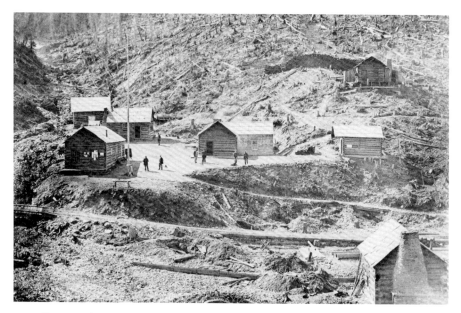

Plate 28. The government buildings at Richfield, BC, 1884. The courthouse where Henry conducted the assize is indicated by the large flagpole. (BC ARCHIVES A-4286)

Plate 29. Lytton, BC, ca. 1885. It was here that Henry's sister Emily Crease taught school and was later buried, following a dreadful train accident. (BC ARCHIVES F-7901)

FORT ALEXANDRIA, built in 1821, was the last post established by the North-west Company west of the Rocky Mountains, and it operated until 1867. It was the transhipment point for furs bound for the coast, but also marks Sir Alexander Mackenzie's farthest part of his descent of the Fraser River in 1773. By 1880 the fort was abandoned and in ruins.

::

4th Oct. Mond.

Beautiful weather still. Henry and self walked up the high hill on leaving Soda Creek. Indian chief ran after us to shake hands with the Judge's wife! River-benches very well marked here & beautifully covered with trees. View of the little town & Creek <u>very pretty</u> from 1/2 way up the hill. Watermill & Bridge also very picturesque—Indian Ranch beautifully situated in a wide grassy valley. Pretty picture of Colts drinking at a clear stream. Road winding round mountainsides with deep valley & tall Pines—very fine—called <u>Deep Creek</u>—the old farm-house & buildings all in ruins, swept away—much inequity here in early days. Country round about in beautiful hill & vale—with fine grass—for cattle—also ligh[t]ly wooded—& lovely small lakes—the same extending to <u>Carpenter's Ranch</u> & <u>Mountain</u> on rather a larger & more open scale. Passed 7 ox-team on the road all together. Very lovely scenery about 1 mile from <u>the 150 Mile house or Bates!</u>—now <u>Hamilton's</u>—a nephew of Lord Macauley's!! <u>Looks little</u> like a <u>gentleman</u>—but has bright intelligent features—small person—thick blk hair.

::

CARPENTER'S RANCH AND MOUNTAIN were named for Captain Carpenter, who was employed by G.B. Wright on road construction. In 1865 he bought land and established a roadhouse and ranch.

::

5th Oct. Tues.

Messrs Hamilton & Boyd drove Henry and self to <u>Charlie Eagle's</u> farm, a very hard-working dutch American with an indian wife, family, and tilli-cums! <u>Very fond of flowers</u>—allowed a bouquet to be gathered for me—& ordered milk to be brought to us. Farm looked well—but house &

surroundings as dirty as might be expected!—saw 'Sugar-cane Ranch' in distance at head of Williams' Lake—very fine undulating grazing ground—with thickets of trees. Sap from the Blk Pine—very excellent eating in the Spring—Inner lining of Birch-bark very excellent cure for burns. Visited R.C. Mission houses at Williams Lake. At the girls' school saw 3 Sisters & the 2 girls of 'Pat Gannon's'—& The private chapel all very clean & orderly. The Mission church a separate building—spacious & very prettily finished inside with light wood. At the boys' sch. saw only the master—being holidays. William's Lake very beautiful with acres of level ground. Birch-trees like gold & silver—small lakes plentiful. Mr Hamilton entertained us with a number of murder stories among indians. Carried 2 guns with us—only 1 duck shot.

::

CHARLIE EAGLE'S FARM was near 150 Mile. Eagle (b. ca. 1840) was of Dutch-American extraction. He and his six children are listed in the 1881 census.

RC MISSION HOUSES AT WILLIAM'S LAKE refers to St Joseph's Mission at 150 Mile House, run by Father Grandidier and others.

PAT GANNON had a ranch at Lac La Hache; his daughters attended St. Ann's Convent and Mission School at 150 Mile House.

::

6th Oct. Wed.

Left 150 mile house in the rain—soon met 4 Indians on horseback—stopped the carriage & Henry had a long talk with 'William' the Chief through an interpreter. He wished to shake hands with me! Saw a Cayoti [sic]—Evans had a shot at him. Poor 'Sandy' very lame—'Jim' the same. Passed Falker's (bad man) nice looking clean house—still improving. A small lake near Murphy's covered with about 1000 Ducks & Geese!

'San Juan' or La Hache River, small & deep like a canal—from William's Lake to Lake La Hache. Rain clearing up. Rather open country—constant hill & dale. Much cattle grazing on the hills. Acres of hay waiting to be stacked. Met the Stage. Swan Lake 1½ miles long. Sun came out bright at 4 P.M. Road very heavy today—Stopped at 'The Blue Tent'—127 Mile house. Found a great improvement in the appearance of things. Poor little

Mrs Wright had done her best, to make herself, the children, and the place, clean & comfortable. Henry caught a dish of Trout in the creek before the house. Evan shot 2 large musk rats. Had a good supper—and fire in bed-room—wh. was quite respectable this time.

::

WILLIAM, THE CHIEF of the Sugar Cane band. According to one source, Wil-liams Lake takes its name from this man.[12]

GEORGE FALKER was a native of Germany. In 1880 he was 52 years of age, and lived with his wife, Antoinette, and his widowed mother, Mary, age 80, on a farm at 144 Mile House.

::

7th Oct. Thurs.

Henry caught fine trout before breakfast.

Morning cloudy but fine. Made a false start from the 'Blue tent'—horses broke a w[h]ippletree. Met a mule team. Lake La Hache a beautiful sheet of water 13 miles long.

Still harvesting at Roper's farm, that was. This country of a 1000 hills looked lovely in its autumn colors. Passed hundreds of cattle grazing in separate 'Bands.' Mr Theodore Davy passed us here on horse-back. Beauti-ful field of barley & oats waving in the sunshine along the banks of the Lake. Pat Gannons Ranch (that was) splendidly situated—to my mind the best of any I have seen.

McKinley's Ranch looks well also—plenty of turkeys & white goats. Drove over much Alkali ground. Henry shot a brace of Prairie chicken. Passed 3 ox-teams above Manson's—111 m. house. Watered at the Creek by Man-son's farm. Team of Pack-mules passed us. Another beautiful Lake at the 108—& 105 mile—farm house near. Country the same beautiful rolling grassland with small thickets of trees—to within 3 miles of The 100 Mile house. Bridge Creek which we reached at dusk 6 P.M. The last 3 miles of the road very heavy with deep mud. Had a good dinner—rooms clean & fresh this time—Mr Davy here also.

::

108 Mile House, once owned by Thomas Roper, 1867–1868. This is a typical roadhouse, similar to many Sarah stayed in on her 1880 trip. F. Dally photo. (BC ARCHIVES E-2793)

ARCHIBALD MCKINLAY'S RANCH, at 115 Mile House. McKinlay (1811–1891), a former HBC employee, lived here with his wife, Sarah Julia (née Ogden), age 45. McKinlay, like Gavin Hamilton and many other fur traders, married women of mixed descent. Sarah Julia, whom he married in 1840, was a daughter of Peter Skene Ogden and Julia Rivet of the Nez Perce.[13]

ALKALI GROUND. This local phenomenon also creates Alkali Lakes which form in areas of low rainfall when salts, leached out from the surrounding hills, are left by evaporating water.

MANSON'S FARM at 111 Mile was owned by Donald, age 24, and William Manson, stock raisers and sons of former HBC trader Donald Manson and his wife, Adelaide Ogden, sister to Sarah Julia McKinlay.

::

8th Oct. Frid.

Had excellent breakfast—Cook Ah Fou. Morning cloudy but fine. Had 2 extra horses & a native driver—to help us <u>over the bad road—up the long</u>

hill. Passed a train of Pack-mules—preparing for their day's work—each animal went in front of his own Apparaho. Small lakes—& little openings of grass on each side of the road through the Green Timber to day. Road very rough & heavy—Light fall of snow & hail—snow on the ground & distant mountains. Met 2 ox-team—yoke each. Little further on met 3 large trains of Pack-Mules (Spanish) Sandy broke one of traces. Met 3 more ox-team, 1 with 10 yoke. Passed close to Mt Begbie—Here we got a beautiful view of the Lillooet Mountains covered with snow. Met 4 more ox-teams at the 83 mile house—2 more ox-team 8 yoke each—also 2 others at rest for the night. Lovely mountain view near Loch Lomand at 5 P.M. sun bright—no snow. Reached Saul's 70 mile house at 6 P.M. with our 4 horses & excellent indian driver, after the roughest & muddiest drive we have yet had—feeling very tired & as if off a long voyage.

::

AH FOU, COOK AT 100 MILE. Apart from his name, at the time of writing nothing is known of this individual. This is true of most of the Chinese men who came to the province to find employment, whose names are often recorded only on employee lists. Likewise, Indigenous people with whom Sarah and other travellers came in contact did not generate written records. Identifying individuals for the purposes of historical enquiry remains difficult and frustrating.

APPARAHO (APAREJO) is Spanish for harness, or the gear that separated the mules in a pack train.

::

9th October Sat.

Bright morn[in]g—hard frost. Sent the Indian & 2 horses back to Bridge Creek—Ground lightly covered with snow. Met a heavy mule-team with 2 waggons. Road not so heavy as yesterday. Henry and self left the waggon to have another look at the awful Chasm. Still travelling through the Green-timber Lovely peep of the Lillooet Mountains above the tree tops at the end of our vista. Met an Indian leading two horses from the Races at Ashcroft to those at 150 M. house. Met 2 heavy ox-team of 8 & 9 yoke. Approaching Clinton (or the Junction of the Douglas & Lillooet route with the Yale & Lytton route to Cariboo) the wood became more parklike and the big blue mountains looked very grand through the trees. The last 5 miles of the road winding round the skirt of the hills presented a succession of very beautiful views of wood—water—pasture—hill & dale backed by the snowy topped mountains. The town lies in the valley and looks its best from this side viz <u>coming down</u> country. Reached Mrs Marshall's hotel at 4 P.M. in bright sunshine—shook hands at the door with Mr Robertson Q.C. & Mr Davy. Houseful of people for the Assizes on Monday.

::

ALEXANDER ROCKE ROBERTSON, Q.C. (1841–1881) came to British Columbia in 1864 and was a lawyer and editor of Victoria's *Daily Chronicle*. He established a reputation as an outstanding advocate and acted both for the Crown and as defence attorney at assize court at Barkerville. He had a very distinguished political career.[14] In 1880 he represented the Crown (with McCreight and Walkem) at the first trial of the McLeans. In November 1880 he was appointed to the Supreme Court of British Columbia and took up residence in Kamloops.

::

10th Oct. Sund.

Very hard frost. Ice 1/4 in. thick at noon. Sun bright—No church here— Rested & read in bed all day. Dr Henry sat with me & wrote letters.

::

11th Oct. Mond.

Bright clear morn[in]g. Walked with Henry to the Sheriff's (Connor) house—at the back of the Court-house found Mrs Connor busy in domestic matters—her rooms got up with great care—& walls hung with photos—neatness to perfection even through the kitchen—no children—returned to little room and wrote letters.

::

12th Oct. Tues.

Henry in Court all day. I amused myself in the little room with writing— and sewing—much the same as yesterday. At 5 P.M. I joined Henry—Mr Robertson & Mr Davy at dinner—afterward they all returned to Court & I to my little room. At 9 oClock Henry came back & said the Assize was over.

::

13th Oct. Wed.

Fine morn[in]g—but dusty. Said Good Bye to kind Mrs Marshall.

Very beautiful scenery out of Clinton—Lakes—Woods—Mountains and a good road winding among the hills. Met a band of mounted indians—men & <u>women </u>who ride like men & carry their children both before and behind them.

Near the 8 mile house saw a fine field of hay in cocks. Several small farms along the road. About noon the sun was warm and pleasant.

Harvesting was still going on at Allen's farm—we stopped to shake hands with the two Mrs Allens at 'Grave Creek.' Russet browns and Greens in the trees along the valley of the Boneparte were very beautiful backed by the blues & greys of the mountains.* More bands of mounted Indians men, women, children & dogs returning from the races at Ashcroft. A <u>very black</u> stormy sky—but we caught only a few drops of rain—met 2 oxteam & one horse-team to day. Reached <u>Cache Creek </u>at 4 P.M. The public school-house is a large plain building chiefly used by halfbreed children & is quite near the hotel where we stopped for the night. Cache-Creek house kept by Mr & Mrs Newland about 6 P.M. the rain began to pour down.

* In the valley of the Boneparte close to 'Hat Creek' house stands the cottage of old McLean whose 3 sons are now in prison at N. Westr for murder & horse stealing.

Passed a large Indian Rancherie deserted for winter Kekelee houses—the road hedged in by wild rose bushes 6 ft high—and covered with hips.

::

ALLEN'S FARM AT "GRAVE CREEK," on the Bonaparte River south of Clinton, probably refers to the preemption of John Allen.

CACHE CREEK HOUSE was kept by Mary (née Pringle) and James A. Newland (d. 1898). The Newlands married in 1875 but had no children at the time of Sarah's visit. They were soon to leave (see 23 October journal entry), moving to Kamloops.

Savona, BC, ca. 1880s. x #1 shows James Uren's Hotel, x #2 is J. B. Leighton's house and telegraph offices. (BC ARCHIVES NA-41834)

OLD McLEAN was Donald McLean (1805–1864), a former HBC employee who was killed in the Chilcotin uprising. Three of his sons were to be tried in the New Westminster assize in 1880 for murder. The small log cabin mentioned by Sarah is still situated on the present Hat Creek Ranch, a provincial heritage site.

KEKELEE or Kekuli holes were dug into the earth to create a belowground winter house used by the Indigenous peoples of the Interior region. Rafters above ground supported a roughly conical-shaped roof of split wood. Entry was gained through a notched log acting as a ladder.

RETURNING FROM THE RACES AT ASHCROFT refers to horse racing, established in 1865. These "Ashcroft Derbys" were very popular social occasions, drawing participants and spectators from miles around.

::

14th Oct. Thurs.

Started about 9 A.M. fine grey morn[in]g. Hills in Cache Creek valley curiously furrowed—no trees on them but the blues and green greys very beautiful. Small farms along the road—fine haystacks. Acres of fine sun-flowers on each side of the road sage plants very abundant still on the hills. Cactus (small) also by roadside. Splendid views of the serpentine Thompson from the top of the hills—fine—open level country for miles—backed in by rugged mountains. Herds of cattle and bands of horses feeding on the slopes. Delightful walk along the hill sides of the Thompson—sun bright and warm. Magnificient view. Trees chiefly along the <u>tops</u> of the mountains— River terraces very fine. A long hill winding down to the little bridge over '<u>Dead Mans river</u>' the red & yellow colors of the Shumack [sic] and Cottonwood very beautiful.

Most charming drive the whole morning—weather glorious—reached <u>Savonnas Ferry</u> at 3 P.M. where the Thompson runs into Kamloops Lake 15 miles long. Warmly welcomed by Mrs Urens, a kind portly Cornish woman—gave us 3 beautiful rooms. House & furniture chiefly made by her husband. Shewed me 4 more comfortable bedrooms upstairs with one room 20 X 40 ft with Piano and violins.

The Bishop & Mrs Sillitoe left here only yesterday. Sat on the rocky beach of the lake & saw numbers of large fish (salmon & trout) jumping. Had excellent dinner of Beef—Yorkshire pudding and fresh vegetables. (Charges high)

::

SAVONA'S FERRY. There was no bridge crossing at the foot of Kamloops Lake so a ferry service was maintained, which crossed the lake to where the sternwheelers docked. One then travelled by steamer to Kamloops. The ferry was established in 1859, and the first bridge built in 1884. As an interesting note, at the October Assize in Kamloops, Francis Savona was tried and acquitted of horse theft.

MRS. URENS was really Malvina Jane Toy (1831–1884), the common-law wife of James Uren (ca. 1832–1886). Together they operated a number of businesses. Uren came to British Columbia in 1859, worked as a freighter, then moved to Savona and became the ferry man, then operated the hotel. Besides overseeing the hotel, Jane Toy was also the postmistress at Savona's Ferry.

::

15th Oct. Friday.

Fine morn[in]g crossed the end of the Lake on the little Steamer & drove along the other side—walking now and then up the hills. Pretty little lakes among the hills. Came out upon a magnificient view of Kamloops Lake and the distant mountains. The large Pine grows here as above with reddish Bark streaked with black. Stopped a few m. at <u>Cherry Creek</u> Mr Roper's farm (formerly Hare's, father to one of the outlaws now in prison—) Did not leave the carriage but had some bread, butter & apples brought to us. Country hereabout wonderfully hilly & mountainous with some beautiful slopes & benches—with grazing cattle. More Alkaline lakes—and open downs—with cattle everywhere. Have seen the skin and bones of numbers of the poor cattle that perished last winter, when the snow was so unusually deep. <u>More</u> small lakes as we approach Kamloops—one long one with rocks beautifully reflected in it with a red and rosy margin from the weeds growing there. From the top of the hills before descending into Kamloops valley we came upon a magnificient panoramic view of the South and North forks of the Thompson fringed with Cottonwood trees in all shades of green & orange and as we kept on descending the Lake also came into view. Saw a Cayote on the mountain—very shy. The little town lay under the brow of the hill so that it was hidden from sight until we were close upon it. We stopped at Mr Tait's house (of the H.B.C.) where we had been told we were expected—very kindly received by the father & daughters—in a clean comfortable house. Fine moonlight eveg—went to the Hotel in town for dinner—Mr & Miss Tait with us. Mr Fred Bennett brother to Preston Bennett was at house assisting to entertain us! Felt as if we had made a mistake & wished myself at the Hotel.

::

STEAMER TAKEN CROSS THE END OF KAMLOOPS LAKE refers to the *Lady Dufferin* built in 1878 by William Fortune.

CHERRY CREEK, MR ROPER'S FARM (FORMERLY HARE'S). This pioneer cattle ranch was owned by William James Roper (b. 1841) who had previously worked for the HBC as a teamster, operated a roadhouse, and then in 1872 preempted land at Cherry Creek. Roper added to his holdings in 1877 by purchasing land from

The SS *Lady Dufferin* at Eagle Pass Landing. This is the steamer Sarah and Henry boarded at Savona bound for Kamloops. (BC ARCHIVES I-30815)

Nicholas Hare (father of Alex Hare, who would be tried for murder in November 1880).

MR. JOHN TAIT (1831?–1911) was for many years HBC factor at Kamloops. He was a widower who lived with his four daughters; the eldest two, Emma and Mary (Minnie), were 18 and 17 years old. He, too, married an Indigenous woman. Sarah's comments about the Taits remain guarded, despite Tait's social standing, because of her inability to accept as full social peers those of mixed descent.

FRED BENNETT (b. ca. 1846) and PRESTON BENNETT (ca. 1841–1882) were ranchers. Preston Bennett came to the Cariboo in 1862, became an HBC clerk in Kamloops and was elected the local M.P.P. in 1878. He was to die at the age of 41 of tuberculosis. The Bennett brothers were business partners on their farm with Moses Lumby, after whom the town of Lumby, near Vernon, was named.

::

16th October 1880 Sat.

<u>Kamloops</u>—glorious morng. Breakfasted with the Tait family. Read in the warm bright sittingroom with little 'Lilly'—& wrote my Diary. Took a short walk with little Lilly—sun hot—so faint & tired could hardly keep up. <u>Very</u> thankful for a cup of tea at 4 oClock brought into my room by Minnie.

Mrs Arthur Pemberton arrived by the 6 oClock boat. Mr Tait dined at home & remained the evening. Had pleasant chattings. Was reconciled to our imagined mistake.

Poor Mrs Thos Roper called—& enjoyed a chat with Henry.

::

MRS. ARTHUR PEMBERTON was Sarah (née Cochrane), age 35. Her husband, Arthur Gore Pemberton (1842–1907), a nephew of colonial surveyor Joseph Despard Pemberton, arrived in British Columbia in 1859 and started at the Kamloops HBC post in 1862. In 1866 he pre-empted land on the north shore of Kamloops Lake, gradually expanding his holdings alongside the hill known today as Pemberton Range.

MRS. THOMAS ROPER, married to a farmer and stock raiser at Kamloops. No information on why she was "poor," although Sarah undoubtedly meant her personal situation or circumstance.

::

17th Oct. Sund. (Kamloops)

No church anywhere—this morng. Talked with Mrs Arthur Pemberton in the warm sunny sittingroom. In afternoon took a little walk met Mr Preston Bennett & his stout partner Mr Lumby* In eveg—we all attended the Methodist Meeting in the Court house, with prisoners cells looking into it. Mr Turner (a Ranting radical) addressed the Meeting—painfully unedifying. Hope never to be in such a place again—or obliged to listen to anything so illogical and irreverential. Lovely moonlight walk home—to light little supper.

*Mr Sheldon (the medical missionary]) arrived to attend the poor Mr Herman whose arm was smashed by a threshing machine at Spellimacheen—he pushed on at once.

Kamloops, BC, ca. 1881, before the CPR tracks were laid. (BC ARCHIVES A-3630)

::

MR. TURNER, RADICAL METHODIST, was none other than the Reverend James Turner, nicknamed the "saddlebags parson." Turner was an itinerant preacher responsible for the whole interior of the province. In 1881, after five years in the saddle, Turner took over the Methodist Church in Barkerville for a short while.

::

18th Oct. Mond. (Kamloops)

First day of Assizes, heavy Callender [sic]. Father Grandidier called—very pleasant & great favorite with <u>all</u>.

Some of the Nicola <u>ladies</u>! called—Mrs & Miss Scott & her lover—Mrs Edwards (née Scott) & her baby. Lovely weather—but I did not go from the house until 5 P.M. when Emma Tait & Mrs Pemberton accompanied me to dine at the Hotel in Town (Spelman's) with Henry. Mr Arthur Pemberton also came in—and escorted us back afterwards—we looked into the Court House from the road & saw the Judge in his wig sitting in his place opposite the open door. Ladies express much interest in the cases—especially in young Hare and Hector McLean who they hope will be hanged.

::

FATHER GRANDIDIER was the Rev. Joseph Charles Grandidier (1832–1884) OMI. He was ordained as a priest in 1858 and was on the west coast two years later. He served in the Okanagan from 1872 to 1880, opening the Mission of St. Louis in Kamloops in 1876.

SOME OF THE NICOLA LADIES refers to the native wives and mixed-descent daughters of settlers in the Nicola Valley some 60 miles from Kamloops. Sarah's use of the phrase "Nicola Ladies" is slightly derogatory, suggesting their desire to be socially acceptable, but in Sarah's world, the need for them to be separately categorized. Mrs. Scott and her daughters must have been the family of Robert Scott.

SPELMAN'S HOTEL refers to the hotel kept by Thomas Spelman (d. 1884) known as the Cosmopolitan Hotel.

::

19th Oct. Tues. (Kamloops)

Grand & Petit Jurors constantly in and out of house viz—Mrssrs Pemberton—Bennett—Lumby—Roper. Mr Sheldon returned with bad news of poor Herman but complimented the amateur surgeons.

After lunch Emma Tait took me to see the new Mission houses & call on the Sisters—had a pleasant walk—& returned quite tired. The young Pearses came in—much struck with Donald the younger one's appearance.

At 5 P.M. Minnie Tait & Mrs Pemberton accompanied me to dinner again at the hotel with Henry.

::

GRAND AND PETIT JURORS, MSSRS. PEMBERTON, BENNETT, LUMBY AND ROPER. Jurors had to be property owners, and attended each trial at more than one location on the circuit.

MISSION HOUSES of the Sisters of St. Ann were completed in 1879, with the Sisters arriving the following year. By the end of 1880 there were 10 boarders at this residential school.

YOUNG PEARSES, DONALD THE YOUNGER ONE refers to two young brothers: Donald, 18, and Ernest, 21. They were the nephews of Benjamin William Pearse, whose first wife was a Pemberton. B.W. Pearse was a close friend of Sarah and Henry, and he acted as a trustee, overseeing investments made with their marriage settlement monies. These Pearse nephews resided with the Pemberton and Fortune families at Tranquille.

:::

20th Oct. Wed. (Kamloops)

Called by myself on poor little Mrs Ussher—Nice pretty house. She went with me to poor Mrs Will[ia]m Roper's house—sad destitution of comfort—saw her 3 little girls & her bad husband returning home on the waggon—All the respectable people delighted with the Bishop & Mrs Sillitoe's first visit—& a hope of school &c &c

Did not leave the house for dinner today. Had a very pleasant music eveg. Mrs Pemberton played her best—several pieces—Mr P. sang, Mr Bennett sang well—Mr Walkem sang comic songs very quietly & well—and Henry did the same. Mr Tait not present.

:::

MRS. ANNIE CLARA USSHER (b. ca. 1853) was the widow of John Ussher, government agent at Kamloops, who was murdered by the McLean brothers and Alex Hare in 1879. These men were tried in New Westminster by Henry Crease in November 1880.[15]

MR. WALKEM (1834–1908) must be the then-premier of British Columbia, George Anthony Walkem. Walkem represented the Cariboo in the legislature, and was thus in his riding when the Creases met him. He was a lawyer trained in Canada West. After entering politics, Walkem served two terms as premier, from 1874 to 1876 and 1878 to 1882. As a lawyer, he was not favoured by Crease and others on the Supreme Court. This situation festered and was partially the cause of a mistrial of the McLeans and Alex Hare, necessitating a retrial in 1881.

:::

21st Oct. Thurs. (Kamloops)

People in & out of the house all day as before. A Mr Martin (son of an Admiral) sat down to the lunch table with us—looking little better than a dirty low Indian!!—Spent Afternoon in repacking our boxes until very tired. Changed my dress for dinner as usual. Great interest expressed in Hector McLean's trial—and terror and amazement at hearing of his being found 'not guilty'—and consequently liberated.

:::

MR. GEORGE BOHUN MARTIN (1841–1933) was a stock raiser and farmer at Kamloops. He and his Indigenous wife, Annie St. Paul, had five children in 1880. Martin first served in the British Navy, then became a clerk for the HBC. In 1882 he was elected as the local member of the provincial parliament. He later became minister of public works.

HECTOR MCLEAN'S TRIAL occurred in the Kamloops Assize. Hector, the brother of the three McLeans charged in the death of John Ussher, was accused of conspiracy in the murder. Evidence brought forth in the trial proved he had no such involvement, and thus he was acquitted.

:::

22nd Oct. Friday. (Kamloops)

Left our kind friends Emma & Minnie Tait—Mr & Mrs Pemberton (Arthur) the Mr Bennetts. Mr Lumby & Mr Roper came down & saw us on board the little Steamer for Savonna's Ferry.

The Counsel Robertson, Davy—& Harrison (alias 'young Putty') also on board—also Mr Tait & other witnesses in cases coming on. The little boat very crowded—with waggons or buggies, horses and passengers. Made myself very comfortable in my own seat on our waggon & had a beautiful view from the bows of the boat of the lovely lake.

Saw a tribe of indian women & children on the outside of Hector McLean's hut waving to the boat as it went by. Passed Tranquille on our right, a place belonging to one Will Fortune owner of the boat. A few miles lower down on the opposite side, passed 'Cherry Creek' with a pretty waterfall.

At 3 P.M. reached Urens—Savonna Ferry. Had hot lunch in haste. Mrs U. delighted with Hector's release. Met Mr & Mrs Onderdonk there with 2 child[re]n. The American millionaires Mills and Perrott of the Railway Syndicate also there.

Our horses had a bad start on the stony beach & broke a wippletree—engaged others to take us up the hill & then put in our own & pushed on to <u>Cache Creek</u>.

At dusk a waggonful of men passed us, where teams of oxen were at rest for the night and the teamsters were cooking their supper over a bright fire. At a place for watering horses we overtook the men driving a 'span' of horses & as it was dark & Evans unused to the road—we thankfully followed in their rear—especially round the short turns in the road overlooking the river. Thank God we all got safely to J. Newland's at <u>Cache Creek</u> by 9 P.M. Found a bright warm room for our reception and a more comfortable bedroom than before—which we took possession of after a good supper.

<u>Note</u>

In the morng on my clothes I found a horrible the first met with on our journey hitherto.

::

WILLIAM FORTUNE (1835/1839–1914) was a miller and farmer at Tranquille, married to Jane McWha (b. ca. 1842). Fortune built the *Lady Dufferin*, the steamer that carried the Creases to Kamloops. His mill at Tranquille was famous for its extensive orchards.

ANDREW ONDERDONK (1848/1849–1905) and his family lived at Yale in a large house he had constructed. By 1880 he and wife Sarah Delia had four children, although only two appear to have made this trip to Savona. Onderdonk was a young U.S. engineer who supervised construction of the CPR from Port Moody to Savona's Ferry, and then on to Craigellachie. He was funded by a U.S. syndicate of millionaires, Darius Ogden Mills, Levi Parsons and Morton Perrott. Onderdonk incurred great costs in constructing the railway. The roughest section of the entire CPR construction was the 127 miles between Emory Creek and Savona's Ferry. To lower expenses he imported some 7,000 Chinese labourers, who were willing to work for lower wages than his white labourers. This policy was controversial primarily because of racial intolerance and also because of the exploitation of the Chinese, many of whom were killed while they were performing their duties. The section from Yale to Spuzzum in the Fraser Canyon required blasting to remove or penetrate rock outcroppings. Chinese people were considered expendible, so they were used in these jobs.

::

23rd Oct. Sat.

Made acquaintance with Mrs Uriah Nelson & child. Her husband was so very kind to Henry at the time of his accident at Cassiar. Lively morng at Cache Creek with Buggies, oxteam and Mail-coach. (J. Newlands giving up hotel & bar-keeping for employment at Kamloops as Storekeeper for Mr Onderdonk.)

Arriving at Cornwall's left our waggon & horses & Henry & self walked up to Ashcroft at 10 A.M., a lovely morng. Found the 2 Mrs Cornwall & Carrie (the gentlemen were out hunting) Chatted for an hour—& returned to our waggon. A great excitement a few days ago—in consequence of great mountain slide a few miles above 'Oregon Jacks' which dammed back the Thompson river & flooded the adjacent ground. All right again when we passed, but, the color of the water wh. was muddy to its very mouth into the Frazer at Lytton 40 miles fr. the slide. Valley of the Thompson very sombre and grand—Trees scattered over the tops of Mts—lower ones bare—road good—but dust thick. Road alongside the Thompson very like that on the Frazer—cut into the mountain side—up and down hill—turning in and out as the rocks may be. Scene about "Jump off Bluff" very grand—Mountain terraces very fine—General character bare, bold—& more open than on the Frazer. Observed 5 neat long log houses belonging to the Railway on a lower flat nearly opposite to Barnard's Stables. Railway works generally going on in various places along the opposite bank, at present disconnected. Trees on sandbanks in the river looked very pretty in their rich autumn colors. The same about the little bridge at the mouth of Nicola. Stopped a minute at Murray's to speak to Mrs McLeod (boarding there) before crossing Spences Bridge to Nelson's house Cook's Ferry where we stopped the night. Mr Sheldon kindly welcomed us. After dinner, Henry got a lantern & we went to see the McLeods in their bright warm comfortable little room at Murrays—gave me fine Pansies.

::

MRS URIAH NELSON was the wife of a prominent Spences Bridge merchant. Her husband helped Henry when he had an accident in 1877 on circuit in the Cassiar district. This accident was later recalled by Lindley Crease who accompanied his father on this trip. "On the trail near McDames Creek [father] was injured by fall of his horse. Borne out to Sylvesters Landing on a rough stretcher. With great fortitude completed the Assize before would consent to being conveyed back by canoe and stretcher some 100 miles to Glenora on the Stickeen [sic] River."[16] Henry sustained internal damage when the pommel of his saddle was driven into his abdomen. He was severely incapacitated for several years after the accident.

GREAT MOUNTAIN SLIDE refers to a natural event ocurring on 14 October 1880 at about 9 p.m. A huge landslide of earth and gravel slid down the mountainside across the Thompson River three miles south of Ashcroft. For over 40 hours no water passed over this barrier, which backed up the waters of the Thompson, flooding upriver. Between Spences Bridge and Cache Creek the Thompson dwindled to a stream. Above the mouth of the Nicola River, feeding into the Thompson, it was practically dry, with small pools and dead fish. Finally, fearing further damage from upriver flooding and the potential deluge when the river finally burst over the slide, men were put to work cutting a channel through the debris, which successfully eased the pressure and eventually allowed the river passage once more.

OREGON JACKS was a stopping house northeast of Cook's Ferry operated by Jack Dowling.

"JUMP OFF BLUFF" ON THE THOMPSON was somewhere between Ashcroft and Spences Bridge.

BARNARD'S STABLES OPPOSITE THE RAILWAY WORKS also between Ashcroft and Spences Bridge.

::

24th Oct. Sund. (Cook's Ferry)

Henry stopped a gang of Gamblers from breaking the law at least in the face of the Court—Fine morng. Left at 10 A.M. very sorry we could not stop for Mr Sheldon's morng. service. [He is] the medical miss[ionar]y who came out with the Bishop & Mrs Sillitoe.

Passed a heavy mule-team on the Mt. side overhanging the river—only just room. Passed Chinese Camps—dressing, shaving, washing & gambling. Observed small ind[ia]n burial ground with figure in a woman's white dress—very like a child's playground. Also saw ind. women wading in a mud pool feeling for salmon!—

For some miles about here we were driving over a moving mud slide—not so perceptible now that the ground is dry & hard. (This requires clever engineering for the Railway & is in Mr McLeod's division.) On the opposite side are perpendicular violet tinted rocks—bleak, bare & rugged. General scene very bold & wild. Road smooth & hard—very winding—& up and down the whole way to Lytton. Delayed mending our drag. Left my flowers to put around poor old Thomson just dead—found so by a neighbour in his cottage—met his old horse carrying a man to Cook's Ferry with the news. Passed the engineers camp among the trees down by the waterside—the white tents with the Engl[ish] flag flying looked very pretty. Mr McLeod's house being put up close by. A very large pack-train of about 60 mules with tents, boxes &c &c passed us. Met an oxteam in a very narrow part of the road. Henry & self got out of the waggon—& Evans drove by scraping their wheels. The road alive with teams, Chinamen & indians. Watered our horses at Nicomen Mills. Had cup of tea & bit of B. & Butter without leaving the carriage. Admired the Waterfall from the high rock—& the bold creek running beside the house. Another packtrain passed while stopping. Further on came upon a magnificent view of snowy mountain range seen through the tall Pine trees along the roadside. Rocky banks of the Thompson seen deep down below. Just light enough to see <u>Lytton</u> Bridge over the mouth of the T. as it joins the Frazer before we entered the town. Emily met us at Hautiers hotel.

::

CHINESE CAMPS SOUTH OF COOKS·FERRY were filled with the imported railway labourers.

NICOMEN MILLS on the Nicomen River was a campsite for CPR workers, boasting a good hotel.

::

25th Oct. Mond. (Lytton)

Strong wind & rain during the night. Dear Henry opened the <u>Assize</u> at 11 A.M. in the School house & ended it at 7 P.M.

Wrote my Diary & letters to Mary and Susie. Emily came in & chatted over the Bishop's proposal of Kamloops. I returned with her to see Mrs Stevenson (Buey [sic—Buie] that was) very good looking young woman.

Emily dined with us at the hotel (Hautiers) & returned to pack up for an early start in the morng.

Air soft & full—with drops of rain.

Note Found the rooms more clean & comfortable than before—but the cooking not so good.

Note A wonderful trial here of a deaf & dumb Indian—case of stealing—sentenced to Penetentiary for 4 years.

::

BISHOP'S PROPOSAL OF KAMLOOPS was the decision by newly appointed Bishop Sillitoe to establish a mission at Kamloops.

::

26th Oct, Tues. (Lytton)

Left without breakfast. Damp morng. Emily joined us to go down to Victoria.

Passed several teams and indians. Stopped on Ciskoe Flat (formerly a rich mining place) at the old Frenchman and asked for a water-melon. This is a pretty, half cultivated little place. Clouds breaking a little. Several small indian burial grounds with images about here. Pretty effect of a rainbow among the mountaintops. Beautiful moss & lovely small ferns begin to appear about here. Mountains closer and more wooded than on the Thompson. At Kanacker's Bar—found Mme Hautier very ill on a wretched bed. Did our best to help her. Evans managed to get a little breakfast for us—a very rough dirty place. Procured eggs from Barnard's Stables close by. A long pull up Jackass Mountain—very fine view from the bridge at the top 1000 ft above the Frazer which here is a muddy narrow stream between precipitous mts on either side covered with Fir-trees.

A lovely little waterfall 1/2 way down Jackass Mt. Passed nice little indian houses with small patches of 1/2 cultivated ground. Splendid cabbages.

Passed a waggon team at Salters old wayside house—a picturesque scene with Mts & tall trees. Another tidy Indian rancherie with a 'kikelee' (or underground) house near Boothroyd's Flat. Old rich mining ground all

"Boothroyd's Hostelry," 36 miles above Yale, one of the largest establishments along the Cariboo Road, 1867–1868. F. Dally photo. (BC ARCHIVES A-3875)

along the river about here. A noble brook or Creek at the 8 mile house— Nice small grass enclosures as we approach Boston Bar. Noticed many Bush fires nearly opposite the Hotel (Dart's) which we thankfully reached at 5.30 oClock after a wet drive all the afternoon. After a nice warm supper went to a very comfortable <u>soft</u> bed—recd a letter from home—dr. Babs.

Victoria
Pentrelew
Oct. 11th 1880
My dearest Mama

Many Many thanks for your kind messages to your too undeserving daughter—Who is once more safe at our beautiful home—where everything looks so nice & fresh & green—I suppose you & dear Papa are on your downward trip now. I hope the fever that you spoke of has quite left you now. How very horrid it must be to have anything the matter with one when so completely out of the way of everybody. Haven't you made any sketches yet? I should think there must be such lovely views from the road up there—that it might be tempting well to your most <u>disinclined</u> self to try some. I have been home now for some weeks—& have of late been paying several visits to Dr Cool—about a horrid back tooth which does ache sometimes most apparently—after about six more he promises that the tooth will be "fixed" so as to last for 4 or 5 years more.

Of course you will have heard from the others all about the Moggs leaving us. Mary, Zeffie, Artie, Lidy Richards & I drove down to Esquimalt to see them off. The wharf was crow[d]ed with people for the same purpose at least & their respective friends of whom there was no small number on board. Mrs Dewdney left to join Mr D. in "Manitoba" the O'Reillys—& Mrs Joe Trutch being there to see her off (I suppose) also the Wards, Masons, McDonalds & what looked very nice indeed—were a number of the Collegiate boys & their teachers—assembled there to say a last goodbye to Mr & Mrs Mogg at the last "three cheers"—from the boys the former was not visible again & the steamer immediately weighed anchor & was off—we then drove round to the little beach near "Fishers Folly" & tied up the horses we sat down on the rocks & had some sandwiches & lime juice which we had brought with us—by way of lunch before returning home, It was a lovely day for their start—the water as smooth as glass. Mrs & Miss Harvey honoured us with a call the other day though I [think it] really was to say goodbye to Mrs Mogg who had not then left us for Govt House. Miss Harvey said that she had heard of your existance somewhere about Clinton. I think she had been staying with Mrs Foster & had just returned.

We have just got a new chinaman—he is one that Hem got for us—& we hope he will be able to remain—he seems at all events Clean & willing—which are rather important traits—but I am afraid rather slow—Sing is still invaluable as ever for outdoor work. Now the Moggs have left I believe we are to have the Bishop at the Cathedral both morning & evening as Mr Mason has of course undertaken the Esquimalt district entirely now.

Tomorrow Susy is to go out whiting fishing with the Wakes & then Aliss Wake is to return for a short stay here of two or three days—with her.

There have [been] some most exciting paper chases for the last few Saturdays—starting from "Stadacona" at which Jose'did her rides & herself credit—especially at the high jumps—I think they are over now for this season at anyrate—being got up very much for the benefit of the Fleet consisting of the Triumph & Rocket.

I see by yesterday's paper that Mrs Jackson has returned. No I do not know if the Miss Woods have accompanied her as their names did not appear—I saw Miss Musgrave yesterday & she asked particuliarly after you & Papa also if Aunt

Emily was likely to be coming back with you—which last I did not know what to tell her—except that we did not know anything for certain—about her present movements.

Will Papa have to go all through that Poole Murder Case again—or will any of the other Judges do so instead of him.

Please excuse this untidy Scrawl—but I am rather in a hurry & My pen is not of the finest. I hear the whole family of Grays are talking about leaving the island altog[ether] for a change as soon as Mr Gray can get leave of absence which I believe he has not got yet. Zeffie is waiting for me to hem a flounce for her—so I must now leave off. With fond fond love to you darling Mama & Same to Papa.

Believe me

Your Loving Child

Barbara

P.S. I am glad you are really enjoying the change & at least hope it may make our home at Pentrelew not the less desirable when you return.

::

CISKOE FLAT is undoubtedly Siska Flat, a grassy bench along the Fraser River six miles south of Lytton on which the 50 Mile House was established in the 1860s. The old Frenchman is not identified, but like other farmers in the region surrounding Lytton, he grew melons. The long hot summer temperatures in this valley were perfect for melons of many varieties. The area was renowned for this crop.

JACKASS MOUNTAIN, a treacherous climb in the early wagon days, was the highest point on the old road. It marks the division between the coastal wet climate, dominated by Douglas-fir, and the dry interior climate where a scantier forest of ponderosa pine prevails alongside cottonwood and aspen.

SALTER'S WAYSIDE at 42 Mile House, near the foot of Jackass Mountain, was built by George Salter (d. 1876) in 1861 and was a popular stopover for freighters who maneuvered their loaded wagons up the steep slope of Jackass Mountain.

BOOTHROYD'S FLAT, largely deserted in 1880, had been one of the largest roadhouses and ranches on the wagon road. It was established in the 1860s by brothers George Washington and William Harrison Boothroyd and was alternately known as Forest House or 36 Mile Post.

::

27th Oct. Wed. (Boston Bar)

Fine morng. A resting day (Reading & writing). At 2 P.M. strolled out—just down the road with Henry & Emily. Air fresh & cold. Had quiet dinner alone at 5 P.M. In eveg a carriage & 4 drove up to the door with the Onderdonk party & Mrs McLeod—all managed to squeeze into the little parlour with ourselves—& had a pleasant chat while waiting for their dinner.

::

28th Oct. Thurs.

Morng fine. Onderdonk party left at 7 A.M. We at 9.30 Self feeling very poorly could touch no breakfast. Crossed the longest bridge on the Mainland at <u>Boston Bar</u>. Close by passed a number of Indian houses on an upper ledge of the Frazer also Ind. men & women packing their horses ready for work. Ind. burial grounds not as grotesquely ornamented as formerly. A †now appears in most of them with a few dolls. Drove over rich old mining ground—All got down and walked up '<u>China Bluff</u>,' beautiful fresh morng.

Indigenous burial ground along the Fraser River near Boston Bar. (BC ARCHIVES H-534)

Fine spring of delicious water—Rocks very grand—River—narrow, seething, muddy & dangerous. Mountains close and precipitous at 'Hells Gate' of somewhat Basaltic nature and awfully grand. River tremendously swift and deep. Had another little walk over 'China Bluff' wonderful pieces of cribbing—road cut right through the rock in 3 places. Numerous little wooden bridges over the ravines with narrow mountain streams running below—near 'Rambro's Flat' which is a pretty green enclosure with fruit trees & a wayside house backed by wild rocky mountains & old Pine trees—are splendid groups of fine rocks more or less mossy. Stopped to watch the Railway works at the Ferry 1 mile above "Alexandra Bridge," on the upper end of the long tunnel. Passed two waggon teams at 'Chapman Bar.' Road dry & good with here & there nice green little enclosures. Chinamen working at intervals all along R.W. line to Yale. Beautiful view from the Alexandra Bridge.

Stopped at the Chinaman's Wayside house at Spuzzum & bought a bottle of beer for lunch in carriage. Self still feeling very poorly & had a little hot brandy & water with small bit of B. [&] Butter. A grand brook at 8 mile flat. Splendid island rock in sight of town from here it began to rain steadily and could see little more until we stopped at the 'California' kept by Tuttle—in Yale. Hotel full—but gave us a good bedroom. Kind invitation to the John Trutches house. Emily accepted it in my place for that night. Mr Robertson & Rocky dined with us in the public room—very good dinner & comfortable bed at night—very thankful to feel better.

::

INDIAN BURIAL GROUNDS can still be seen alongside the highway north of Boston Bar.

CHINA BLUFF was one of the most treacherous sections of the original Cariboo Wagon Road, which clung to the steep canyonside on cribbing high above the rushing river. When the modern highway was built, this was replaced by the China Bar Tunnel and a mile or so of roadway (reputedly the most expensive section of two-lane highway ever constructed in the province, costing some $5 million for the one mile section).

ALEXANDRA BRIDGE, opened in 1863; Henry and Sarah travelled from New Westminster for the occasion. It was the first suspension bridge in British Columbia

The Alexandra Suspension Bridge over the Fraser River opened in 1863 at a public
ceremony attended by Sarah and Henry. This bridge was still in use in 1880.
(BC ARCHIVES A-3928)

crossing the Fraser River between Spuzzum and Chapman's Bar; the bridge was
considered a feat of engineering. A replacement bridge was built on the site in
1926. Today's bridge is slightly downriver.

SPLENDID ISLAND ROCK IN SIGHT OF TOWN must be the Lady Franklin
Rock situated in the middle of the Fraser upriver from Yale. It was named for the
widow of Arctic explorer Sir John Franklin, who visited British Columbia in 1861.

:::

29th Oct. Friday—Yale Assize

Fine day. Met Mr Drake in Breakfast room. Mrs John Trutch called with
Arthur & Minnie Agassey to take me to her house—one of Teague's—a
pretty Cottage—beautifully situated—near Mrs Onderdonk's.

Henry joined us at dinner also Mr Robertson & Rocky. They 3 returned to
the hotel to sleep.

St. John's Church, Yale, BC, in foreground. L to R: Henry Ridley, who in 1883 was engaged to Barbara Crease; an unidentified woman; and Reverend Mr. Horlock.
(BC ARCHIVES A-3603)

::

LEWIS ARTHUR AND MINNIE AGASSEY (AGASSIZ) lived in a cottage designed by John Teague on land adjacent to Ferny Coombe, the home of Capt. Lewis Nunn Agassiz, located 20 miles below Hope.

::::::::::::::::::::::::::::::::::::::

30th Oct. Sat.

Lovely day. Called on Mrs Onderdonk, Mrs McLeod & Mrs Croasdaile at Mrs Hanington's where we were invited to meet them at Luncheon but did not go. Quiet eveg—at the Trutches. Court sat until midnight.

::::::::::::::::::::::::::::::::::::::

MRS. CROASDAILE, Ella Teresa (1855–1913), wife of Henry Edward Croasdaile (1846–1915).

::::::::::::::::::::::::::::::::::::::

31st Oct. Sund.

Very wet morng. Could not go to church. Mr J. Trutch read church prayers at home. Mr Tait & Alice called—on their return to Kamloops.

Henry & self dined at the Onderdonks at 5 oClock. Met Mrs McLeod— Mr Cambie and other of the R.W. Engineers. Had Sacred Music. Returned with Henry to the Hotel & packed up our boxes for an <u>early</u> start in the morng.

::

1st November Mond.

Went on board the 'Cassiar' Opposition boat to New Westminster. Little Purser (Bishop) very obliging & gave us his cabin. Breakfast & Lunch table <u>very</u> clean and well served. <u>At Hope took farewell of the Mountains</u> sorry to leave them—now beautifully sprinkled with snow. Soon came on to rain— and could see no more—!!

Reached <u>New Westminster</u> at Dusk. Went to the 'Occidental' Mrs Howison had prepared snug rooms for us—looked so warm & comfortable. Dined by ourselves within green curtains in the public room. Mrs Croasdaile arrived by the 'Irvine' 2 hours after the 'Cassiar.' Engaged a room for her next our own. She was very poorly from the voyage.

::

THE CASSIAR plyed the Fraser between Yale and New Westminster, working a twice weekly schedule.

HENRY F. BISHOP was the purser on the *Cassiar*.

::

2nd Novr. Tues.

Writing letters & looking after dear Mrs Croasdaile who is <u>much better</u> today. Weather fine & bright—Henry decided to send Evans home with the waggon & horses. Funds becoming very low. In eveg. Sir Matt[hew] Begbie called on his way to Langley for a little shooting. Mr Smith Deputy Minister of Marine & Fisheries at Ottawa called late in eveg. & had a long & interesting talk with Henry.

Pentrelew, Victoria
Nov 1st 1880
Dearest Mamma—

Many thanks for yrs recd on Saturday. I am sorry to hear from Aunt Emily—
that you are not feeling so well. I suppose you have been doing a little too much
lately—I think you find when you <u>return</u> that Zeffie is a good deal improved in
many ways. She practises very perserveringly at her music & seems to be getting
on. I feel we were right about Miss Bagnall for her she seems to take great pains
with her. She is also improving in her sketching. She has a geography lesson with
me once a week, a german lesson the same that with two music lessons two
drawing ditto & reading French history & Modern prevents her from wasting
her time, besides as you said she might have french lessons, I have arranged with
Mrs Richards for her to have them with Lidy & Mary Langley at Govt House
from Miss Perceval. Lidy & Mary are both going to leave Mrs Henderson as
they did not get on with her. I still teach at the Collegiate as Mr Jenns said I had
better end up the Term. I hope dear Mamma you won't come down suddenly
without giving us a few days notice for of course there are several things that we
do not try to put in order till just before you come—all things are put away in
your room just as they were when the Moggs left for they would only get dusty
if put out too soon. I think we have two nice Chinamen at last. The House man
"Chu" was brought by "Hem" who comes sometimes to see how he is getting
on. "Chu" has the same quiet way of speaking as "Hem" & is being teachable,
clean & pleasant & makes <u>excellent</u> bread. We have been trying to live eco-
nomically but it seems as if we eat a frightful amount. I feel quite horrified when
I think of it. I will send you your Brown dress etc etc if you will let me know
where & what address would make it <u>certain</u> to reach you. I don't like to venture
it till I know exactly. Also I want to know if you would like me to get you anything in the way of a winter dress. You did say something about a black material before you left & they have such nice things in town now. If you do have a
dress, one made like Mrs Trutch's would suit you I think. We are having very
uncertain weather just now—sudden storms of rain & just as sudden sunshine.
Would you like me to get you any Xmas & New Years cards to send home—if
you would I could do so & forward them with your dress. Zeffie has asked me
to give a little money for some as she wants to send one to Annie Lindley &
Clare so I have given her half a dollar, she said you sometimes gave it when she
asked. Zeffie Moody sent me a very pretty little black apron worked in silk also
some crewel pat[tern]s & wool. Now dearest Mother goodbye. I have plenty of

things I wanted to tell you but am so hurried that I can't now remember one of them. With fondest love.

Believe me

Your loving daughter

Mary M. Crease

::

3rd Novr. Wed. N. Westr—

Fine calm morng. Henry saw Mrs Croasdaile on board the 'Enterprise.' We did a little shopping. Henry & self strolled up to Sapperton to call on the Bishop & Mrs Sillitoe—Found the Bishop <u>very busy</u>, not wanting visitors. Their house still full of workmen. On our return met Mrs Sillitoe & Revd Mr Basket. Called to see Mrs Hyde and Mrs Hitchcock also to deliver the small nuggets to the Boyds eldest son, at school with Mrs Hitchcock. The scenery up the river is certainly pretty—sometimes <u>beautiful</u>—but so <u>tame</u> after the upper country. Reached the hotel for dinner, very, very tired. In eveg. read "The Bertram's" (Trollope) aloud to Henry.

::

MRS. ALICIA F. HYDE, a widow.

ELIZABETH (ELIZA) EUNICE HITCHCOCK (1855–1891) was 24 years old and the widow of William Hitchcock (1825–1877), formerly of Barkerville.

::

4th Novr. Thurs.

Calm fine day. Henry and self went to see poor old Mrs Ferris with her broken leg. Visited the Hospital also. Called to enquire for Archdeacon Woods—Had a nice talk with Fanny. Went over Air Isaac Fisher's new house—(Showy, but not well arranged) Returned to our 5 oClock dinner tired, but having greatly enjoyed the walk & weather.

::

MRS. FERRIS was Isabella Jane (1861–1930), the wife of William Douglas Ferris, a real estate agent and former mayor of New Westminster.

ARCHDEACON CHARLES THOMAS WOODS (1826–1895) was formerly the rector of St Mary's Church, Sapperton and of Holy Trinity in New Westminster.

His daughter Fanny was to be married on 27 November to Captain Jemmett. Woods was Episcopalian, a "Ritualist" in the eyes of Sarah.

ISAAC BIRCH FISHER (1847–1905) came to British Columbia with his parents in 1863. He entered the employ of the Bank of British Columbia and became manager of the Branch in the Cariboo from 1872–1876, and after that, of the New Westminster branch.

::

5th Novr. Friday.

Wet day. Neither Henry nor self very well—taken cold. Had callers. Henry had an eveg sitting in Court until midnight. Preston Bennett called in to see me—also Sir Matt. Begbie on his way down. Very poor sport at Langley.

::

6th Novr. Sat.

Rearranged the pictures in our sittingroom to our landlady's (Howison) great satisfaction. Did not go out today—feeling sick and tired. Received Box with clothes & letters. Henry read "The Bertrams" aloud while I sewed. Delightful.

::

7th Novr. Sund.

Fine day. Morng Prayers in Cathedral at 10 A.M. Ordination of Mr Blanchard (as Deacon) at 11 A.M. Archdeacon Woods just well enough to preach the sermon. Mr Ditcham (deacon) read lesson. In eveg. Mr Blanchard preached his 1st sermon. Excellent ideas on our love to God. Henry & self took some flowers to poor old Mrs Ferris.

::

MR. C. BLANCHARD was earlier at Christ Church in Victoria and later became the clergyman at St. Saviour's, Barkerville in 1881.

::

8th Novr. Mond.

Got up to Luncheon. Went out with dear Henry & bought presents for the Tait girls at Kamloops—& a clock for Mary. Wrote letters home in

Victoria—Henry very busy with lawcases. P. Bennett called in eveg—very weary. Went over the saw & planing Mills with Mr Ebenezer Brown.

::

EBENEZER BROWN (b. ca. 1823) was a former New Westminster city councillor. He was a liquor importer with offices on Columbia Street.

::

9th Novr. Tues.

Prince of Wales! birthday. Dear Henry & self went to Morng. Prayers in the Cathed[ra]l—No mention of Royal Family!! In the eveg—we had a good spell at 'The Bertrams.'

::

10th Novr. Wed. New Westminster Assize*

Not feeling at all well—but went with dear Henry to the Court House & heard his address to the Grand Jury—weather lovely—sat a little with old Mrs Ferris. Court out early. Strolled about with Henry in the sunshine—found out our lots in the swamp.

*Very heavy Crim. Calendar. (The McLean & Hare case over again) Trial of the Pool murder of Pool family.

::

THE MURDER OF POOL FAMILY occured in the spring of 1879. Thomas Pool and the charred bodies of his two children were found murdered and their house burned down around them. There were several arrests in the case, but no hard evidence surfaced. One man was tried and acquitted, and then an earlier suspect was re-arrested and eventually tried at the 1880 assize in New Westminster. See 3 December journal entry.

::

11th Novr. Thurs. New Westr.

Fine day. Dressed for calling and found out Mrs McInnes—Mrs Trew—Armstrong—Pittendrigh Andrew Fisher—Corbould & Mrs (Archdeacon) Woods all at home. In eveg. finished 'The Bertrams'—enjoyed it very much.

::

JANE McINNES, age 49, was married in 1865 to Loftus R. McInnes, a medical doctor who later in 1882 was mayor of New Westminster.

HARRIET TREW, aged 35, was the wife of Dr. Charles Newland Trew, aged 43. They had three children in 1880 and lived on Mary Street in New Westminster.

HONOR CHENHALLS ARMSTRONG née Ladner (1832–1925) married William James Armstrong (1826–1915) in 1861. Armstrong was the first merchant in New Westminster, and he built and operated the first flour mill in the province. During the Creases' days in the city, the Armstrongs ran a general store on Royal Avenue, living upstairs. Armstrong served as a justice of the peace, member of provincial parliament, and provincial secretary. In 1880 they lived on Mary Street.

MARIA PITTENDRIGH (1842–1892) was married to Captain George Pittendrigh (b. 1831), agent for Dominion Savings Bank. Their residence was on Pelham Street.

ANDREW FISHER had a farm on the Fraser River near Ladner.

GORDON EDWARD CORBOULD (b. 1847), a barrister, and his wife, Arabella Almond (Down), lived on Columbia Street with their two children.

::

12th Novr. Frid.

Lovely day—read & sewed until Lunch with Henry. Dressed for calling— on Mrs Homer & Mrs Sillitoe. Met the Bishop & Mrs S. not far from their lodging—walked back into town with them. Saw Miss Kendal the new school teacher.

::

SOPHIA HOMER, aged 40, was married to Joshua Atwood Reynolds Homer, an early resident of Queensboro and later New Westminster. Homer was the local Member of Parliament. He also owned a sawmill and was a commission merchant.

MISS KENDALL, according to the census of 1881, was really Rosa Rendall, then aged 25 and the principal at Columbia College. She lived with the Woods family.

::

13th Novr. Sat.

Very lovely day. Read & sewed until dear H. came to lunch. Mrs Woods and Mrs Agassey called & had a chat. Put on Cap & Ulster & went to see old Mrs Ferris—then took a quiet walk by myself along the Royal Avenue & meditated on the changes & improvements in the place during the last 15 years. Greatly enjoyed the lovely view of the river, mountains, trees & houses. Poor Ince Cottage <u>very</u> dilapidated.

::

INCE COTTAGE was built in 1862 for the Creases in New Westminster. After the Creases moved to Victoria in 1868, Ince Cottage was rented to a succession of tenants and finally sold.

::

14th Novr. Sund.

Weather perfect. Henry & self attended morng. church. Archdeacon Woods took the whole service—good congregation. Lunched at the Archdeacons. Afterwards dear Henry & self strolled into the backwoods—& found out our old lots—not much to be <u>seen</u> from them the one nearest the water the best lookout—returned to the hotel very tired—dined—rested—& church in eveg. The Bishop preached a clever, excellent sermon on the Powers of Darkness Ephesians VI. 12—delivery slow & impressive—articulation—good.

::

15th Novr. Mond.

Foggy morng. Went alone to the opening of Columbia College 9 A.M. service in the schoolroom—the Bishop & Archn officiated. Beautiful short address from the Bishop. In afternoon went to see Mrs Ferris & Mrs Mc-Coll that was.

::

16th Novr. Tues.

Glorious weather. Still in New Westminster. Took a turn up the hill with dear Henry. He has the painful duty this morng. of pronouncing sentence of death on the 3 McLeans & Hare (the Kamloops outlaws) for a double murder—Ussher and Kelly. In afternoon called on Mrs Haynes—looking ill—but Mr Haynes so much improved—had not seen him for many years. Returned to Hotel and wrote letters. Mrs Sillitoe called & the Bishop came in later. Mr Preston Bennett dined with us.

Pentrelew
Nov. 14th 1880
My darling Mama

I will <u>never</u> trouble you again about sending me away and am more than contented with your decision about it because I feel from my very heart that you know best. Do not mind anything I said in my letter. It was written very hastily and probably very clumsily expressed but <u>indeed</u> dearest Mama I did not mean you to draw <u>any</u> inferences—and am <u>very</u> sorry to have pained you. I do not remember exactly what I said and have since been trying to recall it—please do not trouble about it, or say anything more about loving me as I "<u>deserve</u>." You do that already & more—& may God bless you always for doing so.

Between Barbara and me, I fear you have been anxious & troubled—& I am so sorry. We are all <u>quite well</u>—Arthur is growing fat & fills out his clothes in a most satisfactory way. He is very good and tries to help occasionally in the garden. He enjoys Sir Matthew's visits immensely, for he tosses him about & teases till he (Arthur) is exhausted from laughing. We have had several visitors today, Mr Major, Mr Elkington, Mr William Drake & Captain Layton & Mr A. Jones. I did not see the two first, but the others were here when I came in. We went to see the races yesterday and were much interested in "Davie" who lost the first race by balking one of the hurdles & after going back & taking it properly, got in in pretty good time. Mr Dupont rode him then, & some people said he was really too heavy. In the last (a flat race) Mr Drake rode him & he won.

People ask us so often, "When is your Father coming home." "Is your Mother back yet"—that it is an Exercise for the imagination trying to vary the words in which to express the same meaning. We say "next week I think" till we are tired & then change to "a few days more I think" or "Soon I hope" etc etc. It feels an age since you left, though really not three months.

Mary sends her fondest love to dear Papa & you & says she is Emily's fellow traveller as far as Yale. Miss Musgrave says she does not think she will go so soon but wait to hear again fr. her sister.

There is really nothing to tell you. With fondest love from us all to you and dear Papa.

Your loving daughter
Susan R. Crease

P.S. Aunt Emily was photographed to-day—with tolerable success she thinks.

Please excuse the blots—they are partly the effects of haste & partly of bad blotting paper.

GEORGE W. HAYNES (1833–1897) worked at the Moodyville sawmill. In 1869 he married S. Adelaide Hart.

17th Novr. Wed.

In afternoon called to see Mrs Ferris & Mrs Edwards—went to afternoon service at the cathedral. Called on Miss Kendall at Columbia College. Much pleased with her quiet staied [sic] manner. House but slightly furnished—8 pupils to begin with.

18th Novr. Thurs.

Susie's birthday. Cold frosty morng. Henry & self got up early & went to church at Sapperton, at 7.30 Holy Communion. The Bishop officiated. The service very impressive. The <u>first</u> time of our attending an early communion.

Wrote to dear Lindley—Mrs McColl called to see me—also Miss Kendall.

New Westminster
18th Novr 1880
Dearest Lindley,

I have been intending to write to you, day after day—but something has happened continually to put it off, so at last I have determined that <u>other</u> things shall <u>now</u> be put off until I have written to my darling boy so far away—which is how I always think of you.

Your dear father the other day received two such very nicely written letters from you, with a paper and little red book containing the names of the Haileybury Masters and boys. We are <u>very glad</u> to have the latter & I shall take care of it for future reference. I see by it that your friend Rashdall is 2 yrs or nearly so, older than yourself & comes from a Rectory in Cambridgeshire all of which we like to know and more besides, about anyone you care for. It must be very pleasant for you boys to go to such a nice place as Mrs Culling Hanburys must be—and you are very fortunate dear Lindley to be amongst the favored ones. I suspect, thanks are due to dear Mrs Moody for that. I hope George Moody is getting on at his school, and when he goes to Haileybury, that you will have opportunities of being kind to him.

I have not heard from Aunty Bar or Aunt Natty for a long time—but then, I am such a poor correspondent myself that I cannot complain—but I am sorry to hear that neither of them have been well. I must write to both when i have finished this to you, dear boy. I must also write to Mrs Moody to whom I owe a letter.

But now for ourselves—and on that subject I <u>could</u> say so much that I know not <u>where</u> to begin—and so must work backwards and tell you that your dear father is still in the midst of a heavy Assize here. The day before yesterday he had to pronounce the awful sentence of death <u>once again</u> (because of some error in the Judge's Commission of the Last Assize) on the 4 Kamloops Outlaws (3 McLeans and Hare) and this time for a <u>double</u> murder a second one having been proved against each. It is a very sad case—the 4 prisoners all being very young and strong halfbreed men—but they are so wild and reckless and connected with so many others of the same sort, that for the safety of other people living in the wild country districts it is not desired that they should even be recommended to mercy excepting of course the mercy of Almighty God. There is another dreadful case coming on of a whole family being murdered, (wh. was only accidentally? discovered) So with all this terrible work on hand—I try to take him for a little walk, when he is out of Court for an hour—for the weather is so glorious—it must do him good to be in the open air and bright sunshine—and then we have an amusing book for the evenings—which diverts his mind from the sad and tedious work of the day, so that with a pleasant cup of tea and a bright fire in the room we make ourselves very comfortable even in the "Occident" which this time we have preferred to the "Colonial"—our rooms being more snug and quiet. Aunt Emily is coming up tomorrow on her return to Lytton but I think we shall be here for another week. I am not sure dear Lindley, if I have ever thanked you by letter for yours to me of 20th Sepr which followed me up country on my travels with Papa.

Before this reaches you will have discovered your mistake in fancying it has been the Cassiar Circuit instead of the Cariboo. I have so very much enjoyed this long trip with your dear father—that I think I shall never refuse another offer to go anywhere with him—not even to Cassiar—if he should be required to go again. The change and long rest have also done me great good and I have become so stout that I can hardly get into the dresses I wore last year. Your dear father also has been complimented, all along the road upon his healthy appearance—and I am thankful to know there is good reason for it.

I have a gold nugget for you dear Lindley, from Cariboo. I will send it to you by the first opportunity—and when you get it—you may either keep it yourself or make a present of it to one of your cousins, or to anyone who has been kind to you and who would value it as a curiosity. Papa bought a small one for each of your sisters & Artie—but this one was given to me by a stranger and my greatest pleasure in it will be to send it to you, my darling boy.

I have also kept a diary of our trip—which I have had some thoughts of copying out for your amusement but as nearly all the places and people are strange to you, I am not sure that you would care for it—and it would take me several days to write it. There are no nice stories or adventures in it so I think you would find it very dull and I have not taken a single sketch to add to it.

I can hardly understand how it is, I have been so throughly disinclined to take a pencil or brush into my hand, when such splendid views and simple, grand effects have been so frequently before me, but so it is. I have <u>nothing</u> of the kind to take back with me.

On our way down we were four days or rather <u>nights</u> at Yale. You can hardly now see where the fire was. So many new houses have been built up—<u>and out of</u> the town there are two or three very pretty ones. Mr Onderdonk the great contractor for the railway works has a beautiful house there. He is a very nice quiet man, with a goodnatured fat little wife and some pretty children. They are all Americans but Mr O. has none of their unpleasant peculiarities. We dined there one eveg with a number of the engineers when Papa and Mr Onderdonk took quite a fancy to each other. I have been interrupted here by a visit from Mrs McColl, <u>now</u> Mrs Turner who nursed you, as an infant. I have hunted in vain for your photograph to shew her—but I think Papa <u>must</u> have it with him. Old Mrs Ferris has asked for you & spoke of a night that you spent with Papa and Mr Pearse on their farm—the poor old woman has been laid up for six weeks with a broken leg, but it is getting on very well & she hopes to be about by Xmas. Mrs James Hall, who always asks affectionately after you—is now at Yale with her husband who is doing much better there. Yale is such a <u>busy</u> place. They are tunnelling through the great bluffs and rocks working night and day— they have a special doctor for the workmen—and a very good one too. Then they are grading the side of the Mountains, making bridges & all sorts of things connected with the railway and now dearest Lindley I have written over two sheets of paper and have hardly told you anything. I daresay you remember that this is Susie's birthday. Your letter which came in one of Papas by the last mail will be just in time for it. This morng Papa & I (for the first time) walked to an early service at Sapperton. The church in which you were Xtened. The new Bishop (Sillitoe) is a very earnest clever man and reads the services very impressively. So that it really <u>helps</u> one to think & feel more as Xtian worshippers ought to do. I found out in conversation with Mrs Sillitoe the Bishop's wife that she knows two of the masters at Haileybury, The Revds Couchman & Butler and that Mr Couchman is a cousin of her. It is very funny, how often one makes such little discoveries. There is no Master yet for the Collegiate School in Victoria to take Mr Mogg's place when you see him, I think you will understand how he came to be so great a favorite with the boys, and what a loss he is to them.

While I think of it, dear Lindley, I want you please to send me a <u>penny Almanack for the new year</u> with a <u>blank side opposite</u> to the Calendar of each month, for the purpose of making housekeeper's little notes opposite to the days of the weeks. I have tried year after year to get one of this kind, but they are not sent to Victoria, most useful as they would generally be. I have often meant to ask Auntie Bar to send me one of the little 1d books we used to have years ago—but now dear Lindley I must <u>really</u> say Good Bye. Papa has come in and wants dinner at <u>once</u> while the jurymen are coming to a decision, so—<u>God bless you</u> My dear little son and with heaps of tender love & kisses from Papa & myself believe me ever

Your loving Mother

P.S. We saw <u>beautiful</u> icicles this mor[nin]g on the road to the old Govt House hanging 8 & 10 inches long under the bank in which there is a small spring of water.

I have put in St Paul's Epistle to the Romans for yr. pocket dear boy. It is good at times to read the separated parts of the Bible steadily through by themselves and for that purpose these little numbers are very convenient. I have not been without one all through our journey to read at odd times—when our Bible was packed away.

God <u>bless</u> & bless you my dear little son.

19th Novr. Frid.

Dull & cloudy but fine. Took a short turn with dear Henry—wrote to Sally—Mr Isaac Fisher called.

Emily, Miss Musgrave, Mrs Pinder & 2 child[re]n came up on 'Enterprise' from Victoria. Emily & Miss Musgrave dined with us, & returned to the Steamer for the night.

ANNIE PINDER, aged 26, and her small children Josephine, 3, and William, 2, were on their way to Victoria. Husband George Pinder was a civil engineer.

20th Novr. Sat. <u>New Westminster Assize</u>

Dull heavy morng. Emily, Miss Musgrave Mrs Pinder and children lunched with me—saw them on board the Irvine for Yale. Went to see Mrs Peele.

::::::::::::::::::::::::::::::::::::::

21st Nov. Sund.

Lunched at the Archdeacons again—afterwards Henry & I walked out through the woods to the Butts. Bishop Sillitoe preached two very excellent sermons for the hospitals.

::::::::::::::::::::::::::::::::::::::

THE BUTTS was a rifle shooting area established by Adolphus Peele in 1870. It was located in Alice Gardens on Royal Avenue, one of the many gardens designed by Richard Moody of the Royal Engineers.

::::::::::::::::::::::::::::::::::::::

22nd Novr. Mond.

Splendid weather—walked with dear Henry after lunch as usual & discussed church matters.

::::::::::::::::::::::::::::::::::::::

23rd Novr. Tues.

Dear Babs's birthday—went to church in morng to pray & return thanks for her. Mrs Woods called and chatted. Mrs Robertson came up to consider the offer of Judgeship for her hus[band].

::::::::::::::::::::::::::::::::::::::

24th Novr. Wed.

After lunch walk as usual—weather glorious. Walked out to Mr Baskett's house beyond Sapperton church to enquire for Mrs Sillitoe—returned very warm & tired.

::::::::::::::::::::::::::::::::::::::

25th Novr. Thurd.

Took a lovely turn up the hill with dear Henry after lunch. Returned to write letters. Mrs Andrew Fisher called, also Archdeacon Woods. In eveg we finished "The Quaker Cousins" by Miss McDonnell—very good.

Haileybury College

Nov. 7 Sunday 1880

My dear Father & Mother

Thank you <u>very</u> much indeed for your letters. I was <u>very</u> glad to hear from you, I was rather surprised to when I saw Cariboo at the heading. Aunt Natty told me you were going up to Cassiar, that is what I wondered at so much, that you were going on such a rough journey. I am so sorry you were unwell.

A little more has been going on in regard to myself than usual. Nothing much happened at the beginning of the week, for three day[s] we had some pretty sharp frosts on the heath & Goose green the ponds were frozen but not enough to bear, since then the weather has been mild.

I have heard both from Aunt Natty & Aunty Bar. Aunt Natty had not much news, she was very busy. Annie, Frank & Connie were very poorley & the weather very bad. Aunty Bar was very busy & the village library or something like that was going to be opened, the choir treat [?] was going to take place very soon, so she was also very busy.

On Thursday I played for my house for the first time, we played against Trevelyan & have beaten them as yet, but the match is not yet finished, I hope I will not be turned out.

It has been settled that the end of the term is on the 18th of December or rather that the holidays begin then, so we have already past the half term. We had our half terms [?]der given us yesterday, my place was 10th unless I get up 2 or 3 places I shall not get my remove. I expect I shall be lower than I have been this term.

On Friday I went to tea with one of the masters, Mr Johnstone, he takes the arithmetic set that I am in, he is a new master as he came last term. Last night there was an entertainment given in "honour" I suppose of the "Old Boys" who came down to play the school we were beaten as usual by 1 goal and a try to nothing.

Today is rather dull & cold, there is no sun, & there is a cold wind, so I do not know if I shall go for my usual walk. Last night there were some fireworks at Benges, a preparatory school near here. Here it is against rules to have any, because some years there was a regular rebellion, bonfires were made in the quad. & when the prefects went to one side of the quad to stop the fireworks there, they began on the other, & so on so after that they were not allowed.

With heaps of love & kisses to you & all at home. I try to do what I know Ever, dear Father to <u>be right</u>.

your loving son

Lindley Crease

26th Novr. Frid.

Wrote letters in morng. Walked out with Henry as usual after lunch—& went on alone to see Mrs Sillitoe. Helped her and the Bishop to unpack their furniture from Germany. Much of all kinds broken! Returning to town met Mr Trutch and Mr O'Reilly—just up from Victoria. Afterwards hunted through the town by lamplight for a wedding present for F. Woods took a cake-basket. After dinner—Capt Jemmett called—Mrs Robertson—& Jack Gray.

PETER O'REILLY (1828–1905) arrived in the colony in 1859 and was appointed stipendiary magistrate. He subsequently served as magistrate and Gold Commissioner in the Cariboo and other areas. In 1881 he became Indian Reserve Commissioner for the province. O'Reilly's wife, Caroline Agnes, was a sister to John and Joseph Trutch. Their daughter Kathleen was a contemporary of the Crease daughters. O'Reilly and his family lived at Point Ellice in Victoria.

CAPT. JEMMETT, a land surveyor.

JACK GRAY was a civil engineer near Boston Bar.

27th Novr. Sat.

Light fall of snow—no sunshine. Fanny Woods married to Capt. Jemmett at 8 A.M. Henry, self, Mr O'Reilly & many more present in the church. Mr Trutch called on me and talked over church matters—no sympathy with these ritualist[s]. Went on board the 'Irvine' with dear Henry & found out Mrs Cambie & her children. Mrs Corbould & children called—also Mrs Trew—discussed church matters again, will have no high ritual.

28th Novr. Sund.

Dear Henry & self rather late for the early Communion walked afterwards up the hill—down to the waters' edge & back by the lower road—hard white frost—very beautiful. After Morng. Church walked over to the Cemetery—and to our girl's lots—the sun bright & warm—the view lovely—returned to hotel very tired—but went to church in eveg.

::

29th Novr. Mond.

Bright frost—very tired did not get dressed until 2 P.M. My dear brother 52 years old to day—remembered him especially in my prayers to day. Callers in afternoon Late with Mrs Trew, who invited me to a cup of tea.

::

30th Novr. Tues.

My own birthday—2 yrs older than my dear brother. Dear Henry went with me to the Holy Comn. in Cathedral at 7.30 light snow. Went to afternoon prayers alone. Met Mr Croasdaile in the street just come up from Victoria. Reed, a budget of dear letters from home.

> Pentrelew
> Victoria
> Nov 28/80
> My dearest Mamma
>
> As Tuesday will be the 30th I hope you will get a good budget of letters from home. I hope you will have a very happy birthday & many many returns of it. I send you my fondest love & a good kiss. I trust your English letters progress better than mine do, after all your wanderings this summer you will have no lack of news as for me, my mind seems a perfect blank. I have written so many letters that all my ideas seem to have Vanished. I hope Papa recd the Newspapers alright with the <u>Letters</u> enclosed? Jack Gray said he would deliver them. By the Bye we all seem agreed in suggesting him for Xmas? He is liked by all. If not him, I suppose Capt. Layton?
>
> Mrs Spalding seems to have appreciated your letters to her <u>very much</u> thinks you are a wonderful letter writer—poor woman, it is quite pitiful to see her—she does try so hard to be cheerful & take interest in other people's affairs—but her face shows what she has gone through. Mrs Hett has a little daughter. I have not heard how she is this morning. She has had the nurse in the house for some time. Poor Mrs Dobbin is dead, they had moved to their own house I believe when it happened. Barbara & I went to St John's last night, but I shall not go again for a long time. I do not like it at all. It hardly seems to me like church, people all stare at one so & then one can't kneel down with anything like ease. Barbara, who is not <u>very</u> slim! had the greatest difficulty in getting up when once down & I began to feel sick with the seat pressing against my back. I can't imagine how you can manage. We walked home with Mr Richards who thought

I did not enjoy the service as I ought because of a difficiency of intellect. Now goodbye & with fondest love to you & Papa.

Believe me dearest Mamma

Yr loving daughter

Mary M. Crease

Pentrelew 28th November 1880

My dear Mama

I wish you many happy returns of your birthday. Mr Ward has got a new cow & he has sent both his horses out to Cedar hill for the winter. The horses which were in the cart that came for them looked so handsome, they arched their necks so prettily. Yesterday I went to play with the Wards, we made fires & burned up all the rubbish & leaves round their place. We made a new rabbit hutch & put 10 young rabbits in it. They have 17 rabbits now, but 3 belong to Hugo Beaven 1 of them weighing 10 lbs. One of the Wards nurses is *very* ill. There has been some thick ice & it has been freezing ev[e]ry night & it is freezing now. Tomorrow if I am a good boy Mary is going to drive me out to the "Royal Oak" with Susy. Now I must say goodbye.

I remain

your loving son

A.D. Crease.

Please give my love to papa

here is yours xxx oooo

oooooooo

xxxx xx xxxx x

here is Papas ooo xxx

oooooo oooooo

xxxx xx xxxx x

N. B. Please let me know next time you write if I may take a bit from my purse to spend on Christmas cards.

[Sarah's note says] Recd, at New Westr. on my birthday—1880. Written by Artie quite alone at 8 yrs 8 m. Old.

Pentrelew

Victoria

1880

My dearest Mama

I must try and write you a little better letter than the last one. We are having the most glorious weather, cold but bright. Mr Elkington is better & is sitting up. I hope that next Tuesday will be a nice day and that you will have many

Happy Returns of it. I have nothing to send you but my very best love & kisses. Please give some of both to Papa. It is getting almost too cold for tennis, but we generally have a game of it up at Government House on Wednesdays between painting & French, as a sort of rest from work. We had the Ancient & Modern Hymn books this morning in church. We have not seen anything of the Wakes lately. I suppose you heard that Mrs Dobbin is dead. Mary Langley has joined Mr Mason's lectures. He is trying to get all the first class girls to come to it which is very nice. I have only done one or two pictures since you have been away & they are of Government House. I like it much better than copying them. Mary has given us a moonlight scene to do from whatever we choose. My subject is the "Arched Rock" in the Isle of White [sic], with the moon just peeping through the arch & smuggler[s] landing their goods on the beach. It is a pretty picture if I can only do it. I do not know what Mary & Lidy have chosen for theirs. My room is looking much cosier than it used to do, but I shan't tell you what has been done to it although you are sure to guess. Mrs Spalding is down here staying with Mrs Trutch. Yesterday morning it tried hard to snow, but was unable so to do & had to turn into sleet which lasted for about an hour. I sent some cards to England…of cards cross bound with blue ribbon (…Barbara's) to Annie Lindley. I must now say Good Bye dear Mama & I remain your affectionate daughter Zeffie.

Pentrelew
Nov. 28th 1880
Dearest Mama

There are a number of little things I want to tell you about this time, if I can only remember what they are—but first however I send you my best and fondest wishes for many happy returns of your Birthday when I hope this will reach you.

What a tremendous Assize this is. We look at the short notices in the papers of such a case coming on & wonder when the last will be. I really shall not be much surprised if we only see you a week or two before Xmas.

I saw Mrs Hett the other day and she said she hoped to have a little daughter to show you when you came back, and now she has one, born today.

Mrs Spalding is here now, staying with Ms Trutch. She does not look well and is more wraith-like than ever. She stopped to speak to us this morning and asked very kindly for you & told us to send her love when we wrote. She said also that you were such a good correspondent! I said I should tell you this for I thought you often reproached yourself with being a very bad one. Then, she said you had been very good to her in that respect. She seems very sad and lonely & I cannot think how Vernon could leave her for so long.

Mrs Holmes (of Cowichan) wrote to me the other day asking me to be God-mother to her little 5 months daughter. She wanted an answer immediately as the baby was to be christened very soon, so I have accepted the honour, but do not quite see in what way "Susan Holmes" jr. will be benefitted. Arthur is very busy writing to you—if he puts half the ideas on paper with which his brain seems turning, if one may judge by the incessant chatter he keeps up—your letter will not be wanting in quantity. It will at all events have the charm of originality for it is entirely his own production.

The new hymn books, used for the first time today, are a great success, though Sir Matthew likes them as little as Papa used to. I am sure you will be pleased with the print of one we have, it is so nearly as plain as that of the large printed "St John" you have.

Sir Matthew is a sort of pro: tem paterfamilias to us—he generally comes in once a week to see how we are getting on. We do not attempt to entertain him, for Backgammon he does not like at all, nor Draughts nor Go bang—and round games we are all tired of—so sometimes we have a game of whist, but oftener we hunt up something we want done in the musical way and the other night he read some of Bon Gautier's parodies to us—which he certainly can do very well. But it is getting late and I must make haste and see about tea—so with heaps and heaps of love to you & dearest Papa

Ever your loving daughter

Susy.

Don't trouble about answering my letters. I know you are busy and only write because I want to tell you the news and I like to—a woman's reason is it not.

Pentrelew

November 28th

My dearest Mama

Thank you & dear Papa so very much for your most kind birthday wishes and for the pretty card sent to your (too undeserving daughter) who can only send you "very very best" wishes for many Happy returns of your Birthday—on which day I hope these will reach you with fondest love & if possible a few homemade biscuits or something to commemorate it beyond this I am afraid you must not look for anything more. Is there any book of lightish literature that we could send down to you? (or rather "up") I confess I am almost afraid to look among my muslin & fancy work in case—another stray <u>unfinished</u> night cap!!! should turn up as it not infrequently has done about the 30th of Nov. I do somehow think there really is still a part of one put away somewhere.

The Gray's Sale took place last Thursday as announced tho' with what results we have not heard except that Mrs Gray did say I believe that they lost on the large but gained on the smaller things. How are you getting on with your English letters? You can hardly be at a loss for writing "matter" this year I sh. think after your most unusual proceedings travelling adventure. I don't know why I am asking any questions—for <u>please don't</u> bother about answering this or you will <u>not</u> progress very much in your English correspondence which for Xmas is far more important I am quite sure. We all went to St Johns, this Evening & I could not help rather wondering if Mr Jenns when speaking referring to Advent of the final <u>(Great Assize)</u> the thought of this late & long tedious one now in progress, ever entered his mind—(especially perhaps as Papa was one of his congregation) of course I may be quite wrong as is not all unlikely, only the idea just struck me.

Now Goodbye darling Mama with best Love from all for your Birthday. Believe me

Ever Your loving child

Barbara

P.S. I can almost see I <u>shan't</u> be able to send "Anything"—<u>this time.</u>

George Elkington is I hear getting much better & well over his accident.

::

December.

Real winter weather began—cold winds snow—ice—pouring rains.

::

3d Decr. Frid.

The 'Poole case' over at last. Verdict for 'Scotty' <u>not</u> guilty!!!

5th … 6th … snow & ice—7th … Rain—packing up for '<u>home again.</u>'

::

VERDICT FOR SCOTTY NOT GUILTY refers to the outcome of the Pool murder trial. The defendent James "Scotty" Halliday was aquitted and the murder never solved.

::

During Nov. 1880—

Read with intense interest nos of 'Our Work'—lent me by Archdeacon Woods

also Read of an eveg. with dear Henry

'The Bertrams' Anty Trollope

Quaker Cousins Agnes Macdonell

Kingsdene Hon Mrs Fetherstonhaugh

An Eye for an Eye Amty Trollope

all very good

::

NOTES

1 Information for these notes comes from many sources, most consistently the Crease Family Fonds, but also the Canada Census, 1881; Henderson's British Columbia Directory, 1882; the newspaper clipping and "Vertical Files" at the BC Archives; and other sources regarding the Cariboo Road and the Cariboo, as noted in the bibliography.

2 Susan Reynolds Crease, biography/reminiscences of Sarah Crease, September 6, 1928.

3 I have relied quite heavily on Branwen Patenaude, *Trails to Gold* (Victoria: Horsdal & Schubart, 1995) and *Trails to Gold, Volume Two, Roadhouses of the Cariboo* (Surrey: Heritage House, 1996) for much of the information on the stopping houses and their proprietors.

4 For further information read Wayne Norton, "The Provincial Boarding School 1874–1890," in *Reflections, Thompson Valley Histories* (Kamloops: Plateau Press, 1994).

5 Mark Wade, *The Cariboo Road*, 152.

6 Patenaude, *Trails to Gold, Volume Two*, 34.

7 *Ibid.*, 73.

8 See *Dictionary of Canadian Biography*, Volume XII.

9 Coldspring House Daybook, 18 September 1880.

10 *British Colonist*, October 1880.

11 For further information on Hills and a transcript of his 1860 diary, see Roberta L. Bagshaw, *No Better Land. The 1860 Diaries of the Anglican Colonial Bishop George Hills* (Victoria: Sono Nis Press, 1996).

12 Akrigg, G.P.V., and Helen Akrigg, *1001 British Columbia Place Names*.

13 Sylvia Van Kirk, *Many Tender Ties* (Winnipeg: Watson & Dwyer, 1980), 30.

14 For further information see the *Dictionary of Canadian Biography*, Volume XI.

15 See Mel Rothenberger, *The Wild McLeans*, for details regarding the trial and its aftermath.

16 Lindley Crease, Biography of Henry P.P. Crease, 1930.

Bibliography

::::::::::::::::

PRIMARY SOURCES, PUBLISHED

British Colonist. Victoria, BC: 1858–1865.

New Westminster Times. New Westminster, BC: 1858–1865.

Gazette. Victoria, BC: 1858–1866.

Daily Chronicle. Victoria, BC: 1862–1866.

Guide to the Province of British Columbia, 1977–1878. Victoria: T.N. Hibben & Co., 1877.

The British Columbia Directory 1882–1883. Victoria: R.T. Williams, 1882.

Crease, Henry Pering Pellew. *Great Wheal Vor United Mines. A Letter to the Adventurers*. London: 1858.

Fawcett, Edgar. *Some Reminiscences of Old Victoria*. Toronto: W. Briggs, 1912.

Knowles, James, ed. *The Nineteenth Century*. London: Kegan, Paul, Trenen and Co., 1886.

Macfie, Matthew. *Vancouver Island and British Columbia*. London: Longman, Green, 1865.

Mallandaine, Edward. *First Victoria Directory*. Victoria: Edward Mallandaine and Co., 1860.

Mayne, Richard Charles. *Four Years in British Columbia and Vancouver Island*. London: J. Murray, 1862.

Moodie, Susanna Strickland. *Roughing It in the Bush*. London: R. Bentley, 1852.

Morgan, Henry J. *Sketches of Celebrated Canadians and Persons Connected with Canada*. London: Hunter, Rose & Co., 1960.

Wakefield, Edward Gibbon. *England and America*. New York: Harper, 1833, reprinted 1967.

———. *A View of the Art of Colonization*. New York: A. M. Kelly, 1849, reprinted 1969.

MANUSCRIPT SOURCES

Alston, Edward Graham. Diary, 1859–1860. BC Archives.

Anderson, James Robert. Memoirs, BC Archives.

Bishop, John S. Diary, BC Archives.

Boyd, John C. Daybooks, Cold Spring House, May 1866–May 1886. BC Archives microfilm.

———. Daybooks, Cottonwood House, 1874–1901, BC Archives microfilm.

Cheney, Martha Ella. Diary, BC Archives.

Crease and Lindley families. Crease Family Fonds PR-1344, correspondence, diaries, notebooks, artworks, photographs and maps created and maintained by various family members, notably Sarah, Henry, Susan, Josephine and Mary Crease. Includes correspondence and documents from pre–British Columbia times, principally relating to the business and private papers of Henry P.P. Crease and his father Henry Crease, and antecedents; also Sarah Lindley and her parents, John and Sarah Lindley. ca. 1801–1968, BC Archives. MS-0054, MS-0055, MS-0056 and AE/C86/C86 series (now MS-2879), manuscripts.

Cridge, Edward. Correspondence and diaries, BC Archives.

Fawcett Family. Family Collection: diaries, correspondence and memoirs, 1850s–1900. BC Archives.

Hills, George. Diary, 1861–1890. BC Archives microfilm.

Lindley, Nathaniel, "Autobiography," August 1914, Private Collection.

O'Reilly Family. O'Reilly Family Fonds: diaries, correspondence, notebooks and other materials created and maintained by Peter, Caroline and Charlotte Kathleen O'Reilly, 1850S–1900. BC Archives.

Pringle, Alexander David. Correspondence, 1860s. BC Archives manuscript.

Vertical files, various subjects (newspaper clippings), BC Archives microfilm.

Women's Auxiliary Royal Jubilee Hospital. Membership and minutes 1899–1901, BC Archives.

SECONDARY SOURCES, PUBLISHED AND THESES

Adburgham, Alison. *A Punch History of Manners and Modes, 1841–1940*. London: Hutchinson, 1961.

Altick, Richard D. *Victorian People and Ideas*. New York: W.W. Norton and Company, 1973.

Bagshaw, Roberta L. *No Better Land: The 1860 Diaries of the Anglican Colonial Bishop George Hills*. Victoria: Sono Nis Press, 1996.

Barman, Jean. *The West Beyond the West*. Toronto: University of Toronto Press, 1991.

Baskerville, Peter. "'She Has Already Hinted at Board': Enterprising Urban Women in British Columbia, 1863–96." *Histoire sociale/Social History* 26, 1993.

Bentley, Nicholas. *The Victorian Scene*. London: George Weidenfeld and Nicholson Ltd., 1968.

Best, Geoffrey. *Mid Victorian Britain 1851–70*. Suffolk: Richard Clay Ltd., 1971.

Blom, Margaret Howard, and Thomas E. Blom. *Canada Home: Juliana Horatia Ewing's Frederickton Letters*. Vancouver: University of British Columbia Press, 1983.

Brandt, Gail Cuthbert. "Postmodern Patchwork: Some Recent Trends in the Writing of Women's History in Canada." *Canadian Historical Review* LXXII (1991): 441.

Bridge, Kathryn Anne. "Two Victorian Gentlewomen in the colonies of Vancouver Island and British Columbia: Eleanor Hill Fellows and Sarah Lindley Crease." MA Thesis, University of Victoria, 1984.

Briggs, Asa. *Victorian People*. Chicago: University of Chicago Press, 1972.

Burstyn, Joan N. *Victorian Education and the Ideal of Womanhood*. London: Croom Helm Ltd., 1980.

Creese, Gillian, and Veronica Strong-Boag, ed. *British Columbia Reconsidered*. Vancouver: Press Gang, 1992.

Dodge, Dorothy. "Hot Spot of the Interior." In *Reflections: Thompson Valley Histories*, ed. Wayne Norton and Wilf Schmidt. Kamloops: Plateau Press, 1994.

Downs, Art. *Paddlewheels on the Frontier, the Story of B.C. Sternwheel Steamers*. Surrey: Heritage House, 1967.

———, ed. *Victoria-Kamloops Through Historic Fraser and Thompson River Canyons*. Surrey: Heritage House, 1986.

Dunbar, Janet. *The Early Victorian Women*. London: George G. Harrop & Co., 1958.

Forbes, Elizabeth. *Wild Roses at their Feet: Pioneer Women of Vancouver Island*. Vancouver: Evergreen Press Ltd., 1971.

Fowler, Marion. *The Embroidered Tent: Five Gentlewomen in Early Canada*. Toronto: Anansi, 1982.

Gresko, Jacqueline. "'Roughing it in the Bush' in British Columbia: Mary Moody's Pioneer Life in New Westminster, 1859–1863." In *British Columbia Reconsidered*, ed. Gillian Creese and Veronica Strong-Boag. Vancouver: Press Gang, 1992.

Hammerton, A. James. *Emigrant Gentlewomen, Genteel Poverty and Female Emigration, 1880–1914*. London: Croom Helm Ltd., 1979.

Harris, R. Cole, and Elizabeth Phillips, ed. *Letters from Windermere*. Vancouver: University of British Columbia Press, 1984.

Harrison, J.F.C. *The Early Victorians*. London: Panther Books, 1973.

Hendrickson, James Emil, ed. *Journals of the colonial legislatures of the colonies of Vancouver Island and British Columbia, 1851–1871*. Victoria: Provincial Archives of British Columbia, 1980.

Higgins, Stella. "Colonial Vancouver Island and British Columbia as seen through British eyes, 1849–1871." MA Thesis, University of Victoria, 1972.

Jackel, Susan, ed. *A Flannel Shirt and Liberty: British Emigrant Gentlewomen in the Canadian West, 1880–1914*. Vancouver: University of British Columbia Press, 1982.

Jeffrey, Julie Roy. *Frontier Women, the Trans Mississippi Experience, 1840–1880*. New York: Hill and Wang, 1979.

Jelinek, Estelle C. *The Tradition of Women's Autobiography: From Antiquity to the Present.* Boston: Twayn Publishers, 1986.

Johnson-Dean, Christina B. *The Crease Family Archives: A Record of Settlement and Service in British Columbia.* Victoria: Provincial Archives of British Columbia, 1981.

———. "Josephine Crease and the Arts in Victoria, British Columbia." MA Thesis, University of Victoria, 1980.

Kamm, Josephine. *Hope Deferred, Girls' Education in English History.* London: Methuen and Company, 1965.

Latham, Barbara and Roberta J. Pazdro, ed. *Not Just Pin Money.* Victoria: Camosun College, 1984.

Light, Beth, and Alison Prentice, ed. *Pioneer Gentlewomen of British North America.* Toronto: New Hogtown Press, 1980.

Lindley, Alice, and William Gardener. "John Lindley (6 part series)." *The Gardeners' Chronicle* (October–November 1965).

Loo, Tina. "Henry Pering Pellew Crease." In *Dictionary of Canadian Biography,* ed. Ramsay Cook. XIII (1901–1910). Toronto: University of Toronto Press, 1994.

———. *Making Law, Order, and Authority in British Columbia, 1821–1871.* Toronto: University of Toronto Press, 1994.

Lugrin, Nora de Bertrand. *The Pioneer Women of Vancouver Island, 1845–1866.* Victoria: The Women's Canadian Club, 1928.

Lyons, C. P. *Milestones on the Mighty Fraser.* Vancouver: 1956.

Norton, Wayne. "The Provincial Boarding School 1874–1890." In *Reflections: Thompson Valley Histories,* 1994.

Ormsby, Margaret A. *British Columbia: A History.* Toronto: McClelland and Stewart, 1958.

———. *A Pioneer Gentlewoman in British Columbia: The Recollections of Susan Allison.* Vancouver: University of British Columbia Press, 1976.

Parr, Joy. "Nature and Hierarchy: Reflections on Writing the History of Women and Children." *Atlantis* II (Fall 1985).

———. *The Gender of Breadwinners: Women, Men and Change in Two Industrial Towns, 1880–1950.* Toronto: University of Toronto Press, 1990.

———. "Gender History and Historical Practice." *Canadian Historical Review* 76 (3, September 1995).

Patenaude, Branwen C. *Trails to Gold.* Victoria: Horsdal and Schubart, 1995.

———. *Trails to Gold.* Volume Two. Surrey: Heritage House, 1996.

Perkin, Joan. *Women and Marriage in Nineteenth Century England.* Chicago: Lyceum, 1989.

Perry, Adele. "'I'm So Sick of the Faces of Men, Gender Imbalance, Race, Sexuality and Sociability in Nineteenth Century B.C." *BC Studies,* Spring/Summer 1995.

Peters, Helen Bergen. *Painting in the Colonial Period in B.C., 1858–1871.* Victoria: Sono Nis Press, 1979.

Petrie, Sir Charles. *The Victorians.* London: Eyre and Spottiswoode, 1960.

Powell, Barbara. "The Diaries of the Crease Family Women." *BC Studies*, Summer 1995.

Priestley, J.B. *Victoria's Heyday.* London: Heinemann, 1912.

Rice, Steve. "Crossing the Thompson." In *Reflections: Thompson Valley Histories*, 1994.

Rickard, T. A. *The Copper Mines of Lake Superior.* London: 1905.

Rose, Phyllis. *Parallel Lives: Five Victorian Marriages.* New York: Vintage Books, 1983.

Rothenburger, Mel. *The Wild McLeans.* Victoria: Orca Book Publishers, 1993.

Rutherford, Myra. "Revisiting Colonization Through Gender. Anglican Missionary Women in the Pacific Northwest and the Arctic, 1860–1945." *BC Studies*, Winter 1995.

Shewchuk, Murphy. *Thompson-Cariboo.* Vol. 1. Backroads Explorer, Vancouver: Maclean Hunter, 1985.

Shtier, Ann B. *Cultivating Women, Cultivating Science: Flora's daughters and botany in England, 1760–1860.* Baltimore: The Johns Hopkins University Press, 1996.

Silverman, Elaine Leslau. "Writing Canadian Women's History, 1970–1982: An Historiographical Analysis." *Canadian Historical Review* LXIII (1982): 513.

Smith-Rosenberg, Carol. "The Female World of Love and Ritual: Relations Between Women in Nineteenth Century America," *Journal of Women in Culture and Society*, v. 1 no. 1. Chicago: University of Chicago, 1975.

Steegman, John. *Victorian Taste.* London: Century Hutchison Ltd, 1987.

Stephen, Sir Leslie, and Sir Sidney Lee, ed. *Dictionary of National Biography.* London: Oxford University Press, 1917.

Strong-Boag, Veronica. "Raising Clio's Consciousness: Women's History and Archives in Canada." *Archivaria* 6 (Summer 1978).

———. "Writing about Women." In *Writing about Canada: A Handbook for Canadian Modern History*, ed. John Schultz. Scarborough: Prentice-Hall Canada, 1990.

Strong-Boag, Veronica, and Anita Clair Fellman, ed. *Rethinking Canada. The promise of women's history.* Second edition, Toronto: Copp Clark Pitman, 1991.

Thompson, Dorothy. *The Chartists.* London: Temple Smith, 1984.

Todd, Arthur Cecil. *The Cornish Miner in America.* Truro, Bradfore, Barton Ltd., 1970.

Trofimenkoff, Susan Mann. "Feminist Biography," *Atlantis*, Spring, 1985.

Van Kirk, Sylvia. *Many Tender Ties.* Winnipeg: Watson and Dwyer Publishing Ltd., 1991.

———. "A Vital Presence: Women in the Cariboo Gold Rush, 1862–1875." In *British Columbia Reconsidered*, ed. Gillian Creese and Veronica Strong-Boag. Vancouver: Press Gang, 1992.

Wade, Mark S. *The Cariboo Road.* Victoria: The Haunted Bookshop, 1979.

Walden, Frederick E. "Social History of Victoria, British Columbia, 1858–1871." Essay for bachelor's degree in history, University of British Columbia, 1951.

ACKNOWLEDGEMENTS

::::::::::::::::

In 1996 this book could not have been written without the contributions of a number of people who provided inspiration, direction, experience, factual knowledge and above all, friendship. Catherine Henderson typed my masters thesis in 1984 and has travelled with me, retracing Sarah's footsteps (and listening to me ramble), over the years since then. Richard Mackie said "It's a great idea!" opened publishing doors for me, and read and reviewed several proposals and first drafts. Jean Wilson and Jean Barman provided valuable editorial comment. Robert M. Hamilton has, without reservation, unstintingly shared his database, his botanical expertise and his knowledge of John Lindley. Lawrence Duttson has scoured public record offices in England, contacted Lindley descendants and stood on the ruins of the Wheal Vor mines. Lindley Roff, great great granddaughter of Sarah Crease, has been extremely helpful over the years in sharing her family research and endorsing this project. Ann West at Sono Nis Press and Jim Bennett at Morriss Printing both understood the need to have "lots of illustrations" and were supportive of my requests. Kevin, Emma and Brendan have been endlessly patient.

This 2019 printing by the Royal British Columbia Museum preserves the intentions of the 1996 book while presenting a new look with an updated cover, design and typeface. At the same time we have been able to undertake minor edits in the text to ensure accuracy and currency.

ILLUSTRATIONS

::::::::::::::::::

All drawings and paintings are by Sarah Crease unless otherwise stated.

COLOUR INSERTS

INDEX

::::::::::::::::::

Illustrations are indicated by boldface.
Plates appear in the galleries following page 72 and page 168.